Working on the Quinlan project has been a privilege and a pleasure and I am grateful to everyone who has helped, inspired and encouraged me along the way. My sincere thanks go to Mark Fitzpatrick, Janis Lee and the IISS publications team, Josh Freedman, Mary and Tony Quinlan, William Walker, Lawrence Freedman, Richard Mottram, Brian Wicker, Frank Winters, Jeremy Greenstock, Brian Burnell, and most of all to my husband Alastair Percival, and my family.

Thank you also to all those who provided financial support for the project: the Stanton Foundation, the International Institute for Strategic Studies, John Brademas, Nicholas Goodison, Barbara Judge, John Kemp-Welch, Anthony Loehnis, John Major, Glen Moreno, Jeremy Morse, Christopher Tugendhat and Robert Worcester.

Tanya Ogilvie-White, July 2011

One of the intellectually most brilliant and influential civil servants of his generation ... The philosopher of defence ... The leading civilian thinker within the British Government on defence policy ... admired for his powers of analysis, respected for his integrity and liked for his infinite courtesy, his kindness and his generosity. There indeed is the Michael so many of us, to different extents and in many different contexts, had the privilege of knowing.

Fr Michael Holman SJ,
Sir Michael Quinlan Thanksgiving Mass,
Westminster Cathedral, 18 June 2009

Editorial Note

I have sought the consent of all of the living correspondents whose private letters are discussed in this book, and in many cases, was able to enrich the text through the anecdotes and feedback that some of them provided. Biographical information for Quinlan's correspondents that I have cited (both living and dead) is included, along with notes about key people who are mentioned in the letters.

The format I have adopted for this book is quite unusual for a book of correspondence, in that I have presented extracts from Quinlan's letters, linked by passages of analysis. I have also provided brief histories where necessary and have drawn on numerous relevant publications (including Quinlan's own published work). I decided on this approach because it suits the nature of the material. Quinlan's letters typically contain long and detailed critiques of draft texts sent to him by his correspondents. While the first part of his letters can be captivating, the same is not true of all the detailed, point-by-point critiques. For that reason I included very few of the latter, relying mainly on extracts from the opening paragraphs. I took the liberty of leaving out the letter endings, because (with very few exceptions), Quinlan signed off his letters using the same words: 'yours sincerely' (to people he did not know well) and 'yours ever' (to friends and colleagues). I omitted all of these to avoid repetition. I also deleted the numbers from Quinlan's numbered paragraphs, because this bureaucratic style (widely used in the civil service worldwide) doesn't lend itself to a book of correspondence.

The letters (of which there are thousands) were filed alphabetically and often without contextual material, and it quickly became obvious that they needed to be presented thematically and framed using a variety of different sources to make them more accessible. With this in mind, I decided to organise the correspondence around three themes, to show how Quinlan's thinking on nuclear weapons developed. These topics are: the logic and morality of nuclear deterrence; key strategic decisions in which he was closely involved; and arms control and disarmament. Nearly all of the correspondence fits within these themes. I did not deliberately miss out any major topics that are covered in the files that I collected from the Quinlans' home. There was nothing at all, for example, on the topic that Richard Mottram mentions in his foreword – the issue of reshaping the British Armed Forces for a post-Cold War world. It is possible, however, that additional subjects are addressed in the letters that were removed before the start of the project (this is explained in the introduction). I might also have missed interesting points in some of Quinlan's handwritten letters, as many of these had faded with time. Thankfully, the vast majority of the correspondence was typed.

As a final note, it is worth pointing out that the volume of Quinlan's letters became thinner and then petered out altogether by the mid-1990s, and as a result there is far less material covering Quinlan's post-retirement thinking about nuclear weapons. Part of the reason for this is the advent of e-mail, which became the dominant means of communication as the 1990s progressed, and which, due to its instant nature, is often less valued than a letter by both writer and recipient, and therefore less consciously collected and stored for posterity. This is a great loss to historians and scholars, because nothing can replace the 'sense of person' that a collection of letters can provide. We know how Quinlan's ideas changed thanks to his post-retirement speeches and publications, many of which continued to focus on the topics of deterrence logic and morality, and others that covered new ground on regional proliferation, global terrorism and, finally, disarmament. But speeches and formal publications lack the appeal of personal correspondence: they are honed by the author and the editor into a polished finished product. Because of this, they hide the scribblings and the inner workings of the mind that expose individual motivations and illuminate personality. As this book reveals, Quinlan left behind a gold mine of correspondence that offers unique and deep insight into his thinking and that of the Western defence experts and moral philosophers in the 1980s.

Foreword by Sir Richard Mottram

Given his formidable intellect, fascination with testing and weighing propositions, and energy and commitment, it should not perhaps come as a surprise that Michael Quinlan found time – even as a busy official – to write many private letters on defence-related issues, which he carefully preserved. We might in a 'Quinlanesque' spirit of inquiry ask 'why publish extracts from this correspondence now?' Four reasons come to mind.

Firstly, from the 1970s until his death in 2009 Michael Quinlan played key roles in formulating and communicating British defence policy. His influence continued long after his retirement from the civil service in 1992 both through those civil servants who – like me – had learned and continued to learn much from him, and from a wider circle of admirers amongst politicians, journalists and academics.

Secondly, from his spells serving in NATO in the early 1970s, and above all in the key Ministry of Defence (MoD) post responsible for strategy and policy from 1977–81, he greatly influenced NATO policy and built a wide circle of international contacts and friendships which he also kept up for the rest of his life.

Alongside these official dimensions to his life there was a third personal strand. Michael Quinlan was a Catholic with a strong interest in ethical issues. He came to the top of the civil service at a time when defence was a big political issue. The possibility of nuclear war and its consequences became an issue of wider public interest, in which religious voices mattered. He had the credibility to influence this debate if only, while he was a serving official, discreetly in the background. Later his interest in 'just war' led him to cogent and uncomfortable questioning of the justification for the invasion of Iraq.

Finally, while much of this correspondence is of historical interest, it also has contemporary relevance to, for example, the debate around the future of the British nuclear deterrent, on which it will be seen he had a more nuanced view than is often assumed.

Quinlan spent much of his official and subsequent life thinking about nuclear weapons – summarised in his book of that title published shortly after his death. As he himself commented, the nuclear issue was intellectually congenial to him because of its complexity and abstract nature. The correspondence shows to the full his interest in logic and rationality and there are many examples in what follows of their profitable application to the analysis of complex problems. At the same time we need perhaps to pose the question – as he accepted – of how far such finely graded argument drove motivation and action, amongst both our friends and prospective enemies.

His underlying interest was not in nuclear weapons. It was more fundamental: how to prevent war of any kind between the major powers. The contribution of effective deterrence to this task was a crucial element in his thinking particularly in the Cold War years. But as the world changed so he looked at issues from a fresh perspective, as this book illuminates.

What follows is inevitably a selection of material from within a broader collection that was itself constrained by what could be written about and shared on an unclassified basis. It is fascinating and rewarding, but perhaps risks giving a false impression of the focus of his official life. I had the great good fortune to work for him on the future of the deterrent in the late 1970s and later as the deputy secretary for policy (a post he had earlier held) when he was the permanent undersecretary (PUS) of the MoD. We did not spend too much of our time on philosophical and ethical pursuits. Nor as PUS of the MoD did he interfere in the more esoteric aspects of defence policy, tempting though this might have been. Instead, for example, we spent much of our time working with ministers and military colleagues on the reshaping of our armed forces for a post-Cold War world, a subject hardly touched on in the correspondence included here.

Michael Quinlan was a remarkable man and his correspondence reflects this, though it may not quite capture his breadth of interests and sense of fun. Editing Quinlan must rank as one of life's more daunting tasks and I congratulate Tanya Ogilvie-White on how she has brought to life and so skilfully placed in context all of this material. And on behalf of all who now get the chance to read what otherwise would have been available only in an archive, I want to thank IISS for making this publication possible.

Richard Mottram

Correspondents and key people

Sydney Bailey (d.1995), eminent Quaker, human-rights activist and internationally respected political scientist. He served on the Church of England working party that wrote *The Church and the Bomb: Nuclear Weapons and the Christian Conscience* (Hodder and Stoughton, 1982).

Frank Barnaby, nuclear physicist and defence analyst. He has written widely on nuclear issues and is a long-time sceptic of nuclear deterrence.

John Barry, award-winning British journalist who writes for *Newsweek* and the *Times*. From 1981–85, he worked on a book trying to unravel US/NATO nuclear policies (actual as well as declaratory) since 1967, the INF negotiations, and the British decision to procure *Trident*. Although he did not complete the book, much of his research found its way into newspaper articles and TV programmes, and it was during this time that he met Quinlan.

Hugh Beach, retired British Army general and leading British disarmament advocate. He was deputy commander-in-chief of United Kingdom Land Forces from 1976–77 and master-general of the ordnance from 1977–81. After his retirement from the armed forces in 1981, he served as warden of St George's House from 1981–86 and director of the Council for Arms Control from 1986–89. He writes on arms control and disarmament issues, and in 2009 published a joint letter in the *Times* arguing that the UK should not replace *Trident* but instead invest in more useful, usable weaponry that is more appropriate to contemporary British defence needs. See Field Master Lord Bramall, General Lord Ramsbotham and General Sir Hugh Beach, 'UK Does Not Need a Nuclear Deterrent', *Times*, 16 January 2009.

Margaret Beckett, Labour Party MP and advocate of multilateral nuclear disarmament. She served in a number of positions in the cabinet of Tony Blair, and was appointed foreign secretary for a brief period from 2006–07 (the first woman to serve as foreign secretary in the British government, and only the second woman to hold one of the great offices of state). She is currently a member of the Top Level Group of UK Parliamentarians for Multilateral Nuclear Disarmament and Non-Proliferation, which was launched in 2009.

Robert (Bob) Beresford, secretary of the Bishops' Conference Committee for International Justice and Peace, 1975–98. Originally a Methodist minister, he converted to Catholicism and was ordained deacon in the Southwark diocese at St Matthew's, West Norwood, in 1982.

John Boyd, retired British diplomat. During the 1980s, he served as deputy undersecretary for defence policy at the FCO and as chief clerk, the DUS responsible for Diplomatic Service administration.

Harold Brown, US secretary of defense from 1977–81 in the Carter administration.

Basil Christopher Butler (d.1986), convert from the Church of England to Catholicism, a Roman Catholic priest, the 7th abbot of Downside Abbey, one-time abbot president of the English Benedictine Congregation, a bishop and an internationally respected scripture scholar. In the early 1980s, he became preoccupied by moral debates about the Falklands War and nuclear deterrence ethics.

Jimmy Carter, president of the United States 1977–81, negotiated the terms of the original *Trident* deal (the *Trident* I missiles) with the Thatcher government in 1980.

Michael Carver (d.2001), commander in chief Far East of the British Army (1967–69); chief of general staff (1971–72); chief of defence staff (1973–76), and outspoken critic of UK and NATO nuclear policy. Author of *A Policy for Peace* (London: Faber and Faber, 1983) on nuclear policy, and of numerous works on military history. He served on the 1995 Canberra Commission on the Elimination of Nuclear Weapons. For more details of Carver's life, see Dan Van der Vat, 'Field Marshal Lord Carver', *Guardian*, 12 December 2001.

Alun Chalfont, retired British Conservative Party politician and author of a number of books on military history and defence issues. Among his many publications, he wrote *Star Wars: Suicide or Survival?* (London: Weidenfeld and Nicolson, 1985).

Leonard Cheshire (d.1992), British Royal Air Force pilot who served in the Second World War, during which he received the

Victoria Cross for gallantry in the face of the enemy. He was the official British observer of the nuclear bombing of Nagasaki. After the war, he set up Leonard Cheshire Disability, which provides support for disabled people around the world. When Quinlan learned of Cheshire's death in 1992, he wrote to his wife, the well-known philanthropist, Sue Ryder, describing Cheshire as 'the most admirable person I have ever met; his blend of courage, clear sight, integrity, generosity, humour and faith will be vivid always in my mind'.

John Chick, head of corporate services in the UK Foreign and Commonwealth Office, where he has worked all his life (mainly promoting UK trade and industry).

John Coles, retired British diplomat and former head of the Diplomatic Service. He served as private secretary to Prime Minister Margaret Thatcher from 1981–84.

Jon Connell, former defence editor, *Sunday Times*, author on defence issues and a fierce critic of the Reagan administration.

Lynn Davis, former US deputy assistant secretary of defense for policy plans, 1977–81 and undersecretary of state for arms control and international security affairs, 1993–97. In between, she worked as a professor at the US National Defense University and editor of *Survival* at IISS. She is currently Director of the Washington office of RAND.

Scilla Elworthy, founder of Oxford Research Group in 1982 (an organisation set up to develop effective dialogue between nuclear weapons policymakers and their critics). She was awarded the Niwano Peace Prize in 2003 and has been nominated three times for the Nobel Peace Prize.

David Gilmore (d.1999), British diplomat, appointed head of the defence department in the Foreign and Commonwealth Office in 1979 and assistant undersecretary of state in 1981.

David Goodall, retired British diplomat, Deputy Secretary in the Cabinet Office from 1982–84 and former chairman of the Leonard Cheshire Foundation.

Oleg Antonovich Gordievsky, former KGB colonel and KGB bureau chief in London who passed Soviet secrets to MI6 from 1974 to 1985. Author of a number of publications on the KGB.

Beatrice Heuser, professor of international relations at the University of Reading. Prior to her current appointment, she was a lecturer and then professor of strategic studies at King's College, London and research fellow at the Royal Institute of International Affairs. Her publications include *Nuclear Mentalities? Strategies and Belief Systems in Britain, France and the FRG* (London: Macmillan, and New York: St Martin's Press, 1998).

Arthur Hockaday (d.2004), NATO assistant secretary general for defence planning and policy 1967–69; assistant under-secretary of state at the MoD 1969–72; deputy undersecretary of state 1973–76; second permanent undersecretary of state 1976–82; director general of the Commonwealth War Graves Commission 1982–89; and chairman of the Council on Christian Approaches to Defence and Disarmament (CCADD) 1989–99. Like Quinlan, he was deeply religious and was known for his interest in and knowledge of ethical defence issues. See Michael Partridge: 'Sir Arthur Hockaday', *Independent*, 1 September 2004.

Douglas Hogg, Conservative politician. He was minster of state for foreign and commonwealth affairs, 1990–95.

John Howe, deputy chief executive of the Defence Procurement Agency. He was a counsellor in the UK delegation to NATO, on secondment to the FCO in the early 1980s. Earlier in his career, Howe held a wide variety of positions on both the management and policy sides of the MoD, where he became the founding head of the Defence Arms Control Unit. His correspondence with Quinlan dates from his spell serving as private secretary to Defence Secretary George Younger in the mid-1980s.

John Hunt (d.2008), British civil servant and politician. He was cabinet secretary from 1973–79 – the first Roman Catholic to hold the post since its creation in 1916. He was created a life peer, with the title Baron Hunt of Tanworth, in 1988. He was well known for going to the High Court to try to prevent the publication of the Crossman Diaries on the grounds that they would reveal the inner workings of government.

Bruce Kent, prominent British disarmament campaigner. He was general secretary of the Campaign for Nuclear Disarmament (CND) from 1980–85 and is now CND vice-president and organiser of the Movement for the Abolition of War.

John Killick (d.2004), British diplomat and influential figure in Whitehall in the 1970s. He served in numerous high-ranking posts in the Diplomatic Service, including British ambassador to Moscow. He ended his career as British ambassador to NATO from 1975 until his retirement in 1979.

Patricia Lewis, deputy director and scientist-in-residence at the James Martin Center for Nonproliferation Studies, Monterey Institute of International Studies, California. She was director of the United Nations Institute for Disarmament Research (UNIDIR) from 1998–2008, and before that was director of the Verification Research and Training Centre (VERTIC) in London.

Donald Mackenzie MacKinnon (d.1994), Scottish philosopher and theologian, known for his analysis of intractable theological problems.

Alastair Mackie, *Vulcan* squadron commander who left the RAF because he became convinced the UK's nuclear deterrent was dangerous and deluded, a false virility symbol, like a 'stick-on hairy chest'. He is now vice-president of CND and a vocal campaigner for scrapping *Trident*. See Alastair Mackie, *Some of the People All the Time* (Brighton: Book Guild Publishing, 2006).

Victor Macklen, former director of atomic-weapons development at AWE. He headed the committee (established in 1967) that examined Soviet ABM systems and their implications for *Polaris*. The work of the Macklen Committee eventually led to the *Chevaline* project.

David McGiffert (d.2005), US assistant secretary of defense for international security affairs during the Carter administration. Quinlan knew him well from their joint involvement in the NATO HLG, which McGiffert chaired.

David Mellor, former Conservative Party politician. He was a Foreign Office minister in the Thatcher government, responsible for East–West relations and the Middle East.

Brian Midgley, former professor of political theory in the Department of Politics, Aberdeen University. He was the author of 'Nuclear Deterrents: Intention and Scandal', *New Blackfriars*, vol. 44, no. 519, September 1963 – a highly critical analysis of the ethics of nuclear deterrence.

Walter Mondale, retired US politician. He served as vice president under US President Jimmy Carter from 1977–81. He was the Democrat candidate in the 1984 presidential election.

Paul Nitze (d.2004), one of the chief architects of US policy towards the Soviet Union. He was the chief US negotiator in the INF Treaty and special adviser to the president and secretary of state on arms control in the Reagan administration.

John Nott, former Conservative Party politician. He was defence secretary in the Thatcher cabinet from January 1981 to January 1983 (succeeded by Michael Heseltine).

James O'Brien (d.2007), Bishop of Manaccenser and Auxiliary Bishop of Westminster. He assumed responsibility for Hertfordshire in succession to Bishop Christopher Butler. He was chair of the Committee for Ministerial Formation on behalf of the Bishops' Conference.

David Owen, British politician. He served as foreign secretary from 1977–79 in the Labour government of James Callaghan. In 1981, he left the Labour Party, then in opposition, to found the Social Democratic Party (SDP). He led the SDP from 1983–90.

Michael Palliser, permanent undersecretary at the FCO from 1975–82. In 1982, during the Falklands War, he served as special adviser to the prime minister in the Cabinet Office.

George Perkovich, vice president for studies and director of the Nuclear Policy Program at the Carnegie Endowment for International Peace – a Washington DC-based, nonprofit organisation dedicated to advancing international cooperation. He and Quinlan shared a deep interest in nuclear dynamics in South Asia (Perkovich is the author of *India's Nuclear Bomb*, which received the American Historical Association's Herbert Feis Award for outstanding work by an independent scholar).

Richard Perle, assistant secretary of defense in the Reagan administration from 1981–87. He took a hardline approach to arms control and disarmament, believing US strategic interests to be best served through seeking and maintaining US military superiority over the Soviet Union. He continues to play a role in defence think tanks in Washington DC.

William Perry, US undersecretary of defense for research and engineering during the Carter administration from 1977–81. He later served as US defense secretary under Bill Clinton from 1994–97.

Tim Renton, Conservative Party politician. He served as a minister of state in the FCO and Home Office, and as chief whip in the House of Commons in the Thatcher government.

William Thomas Rodgers, one of the four senior Labour Party politicians who defected to form the Social Democratic Party (SDP) in 1981. In 1987, he helped lead the SDP into a political merger that formed the Liberal Democrat Party, and later served as that party's leader in the House of Lords.

Paul Rogers, professor of peace studies in the School of Social and Political Studies, University of Bradford, UK.

He is the author of numerous studies on the risks posed by nuclear weapons, including 'Learning from the Cold War Nuclear Confrontation', in A. Dobson (ed.), *Deconstructing and Reconstructing the Cold War* (Farnham: Ashgate, 1999), and 'A World Not Yet Safe From Weapons of Mass Destruction', in F. Allaun (ed.), *A Labour Peace Policy for the Millennium* (Labour Action for Peace, September 1998).

John Roper, life peer and defence expert. He sat in parliament as a Labour Cooperative MP from 1970–81 and as a Social Democrat from 1981–83. He was editor of the Chatham House journal *International Affairs* from 1983–89 and was the first director of the Institute for Security Studies of the Western European Union from 1990–95.

Roger Ruston, freelance theologian who has worked closely on the Dominican Justice and Peace Commission and for the Christendom Trust (now the MB Reckitt Trust). Previously, he taught ethics and moral theology at Blackfriars, Oxford and at Bristol University. He is author of a number of publications on moral theology and issues of political justice, including *A Say in the End of the World: Morals and British Nuclear Weapons Policy, 1941–1987* (Oxford: Oxford University Press, 1989), and *Human Rights and the Image of God* (SCM Press, 2004).

Martin Ryle (d.1984), Nobel Prize-winning British astronomer and writer on nuclear disarmament. He believed that the world was heading for nuclear annihilation unless nuclear weapons were completely abolished.

Stephen Sackur, British television presenter and host of the BBC political discussion programme *Hard Talk*.

Andrei Sakharov (d.1989), Soviet nuclear physicist, political dissident and prominent human-rights activist. Awarded the Nobel Peace Prize in 1975 for his work advocating civil liberties and reforms in the Soviet Union. The Sakharov Prize, established in 1988 by the European Parliament for people and organisations dedicated to human rights and freedoms, is awarded annually.

Walter Slocombe, deputy US assistant secretary for international security affairs (1977–79); deputy under secretary of defense for policy (1979–81 and 1993–94); under secretary of defense for policy (1994–2001); senior advisor for security and defense to the Coalition Provisional Authority in Iraq (2003); and a member of the committee on the Intelligence Capabilities of the US Regarding Weapons of Mass Destruction (2004).

Walter Stein (d.1996) writer, critic and prominent Catholic moral philosopher. He held a research fellowship at Liverpool University and a lectureship in English Literature and Philosophy at Leeds University. He was a member of the Alternative Defence Commission (1980–88) and subsequently on the Social Defence Project and Nonviolent Action Research Project until his death. He edited and contributed to *Nuclear Weapons and Christian Conscience* (London: Merlin Press, 1961 and 1981), and was a regular contributor to *The Tablet*.

Caspar Weinberger (d.2006), US secretary of defense under Ronald Reagan from 1981–87. He is especially well known for the role he played in the US SDI initiative.

Brian Wicker, former principal of Fircroft College of Adult Education, Birmingham, and lecturer in the Department of Adult Education at Birmingham University. He has been concerned with the ethics of war and nuclear deterrence for many years and has been chairman/vice-president of Pax Christi since the 1970s. He served as chairman of the Council on Christian Approaches to Defence and Disarmament (CCADD) and has edited and contributed to several books, including *Britain's Bomb: What Next?* (London: SCM Press, 2006)

John Williamson, retired British economics professor and consultant to the UK Treasury. He coined the term 'Washington Consensus', which originally referred to a package of economic policy prescriptions intended to promote development in conflict-prone developing countries.

Stan Windass, writer on defence issues and author of *Christianity Versus Violence* (Lanham, MD: Sheed and Ward, 1964). His later work on East–West reconciliation led to face-to-face discussions with senior members of the Soviet political elite at his home in Adderbury. He wrote or edited two books in the 1980s: *Avoiding Nuclear War: Common Security as a Strategy for the Defence of the West* (London: Potomac Books, 1985) and *The Rite of War* (London: Potomac Books, 1986).

Francis (Frank) Winters, emeritus professor of moral theology and international relations, School of Foreign Service, Georgetown University, Washington DC. He served as a consultant to the Bernardin Committee and lectured on ethics and nuclear strategy at the Army, Navy and National War Colleges, the Department of State, the CIA and RAND Corporation. Among his many publications, he co-edited (with Harold P. Ford) and contributed to *Ethics and Nuclear Strategy?* (Maryknoll, NY: Orbis, 1977) and was author of *Politics and Ethics* (New York: Paulist, 1974).

Albert Wohlstetter (d.1997), US nuclear strategist. During his career, much of which was spent conducting research for RAND and teaching at UCLA, Berkeley and Chicago, he wrote extensively on nuclear deterrence, non-proliferation, ballistic-missile defence, military technology, and civil nuclear energy. He and his wife (the historian and intelligence expert, Roberta Morgan Wohlstetter) advised both Democratic and Republican administrations, including advising President John F. Kennedy during the Cuban missile crisis of 1962.

ABM	Anti-ballistic missile (ballistic-missile defence system. See ballistic missile, below).
ABM Treaty	1972 treaty between the United States and the Soviet Union on the limitation of ABM systems used in defending areas against missile-delivered nuclear weapons. The treaty was in force for 30 years until the US unilaterally withdrew from it in June 2002.
ALCM	Air-launched cruise missile.
ASLP	*Air-sol longue portée* (or air-to-ground long-range missile).
ASW	Anti-submarine warfare.
AWE	Atomic Weapons Establishment, the British nuclear laboratories in Aldermaston, Berkshire, where the warhead for the *Trident* II missile is produced and supported.
BAC	British Atlantic Committee (later became the Atlantic Council).
Ballistic missile	Missile which follows a sub-orbital flight path, during which it is usually only guided during the relatively brief initial boost phase. During subsequent phases the missile's course is generally governed by the laws of orbital mechanics and ballistics.
BW	Biological weapons.
CASD	Continuous-at-sea-deterrence, the British strategy of keeping at least one nuclear-armed submarine on patrol at any time in order to deter a 'bolt from the blue'. This policy, which has demanding operational requirements, has been in place since the introduction of *Polaris* in 1968.

CCADD   Council on Christian Approaches to Defence and Disarmament.

CD   Conference on Disarmament, a UN disarmament negotiating body in Geneva.

Chevaline   UK defence programme for the upgrade of the *Polaris* submarine-launched ballistic-missile system. The upgrade was considered necessary to allow the *Polaris* missile to defeat Soviet ABM defences around Moscow.

CND   Campaign for Nuclear Disarmament.

CPSU   Communist Party of the Soviet Union.

CTBT   Comprehensive Test Ban Treaty, a treaty intended to prohibit all nuclear-weapon test explosions and prevent further nuclear proliferation. It opened for signature in 1996 but is still not in force despite near universal adherence. Article XIV of the treaty requires ratification by 44 named states, some of which have yet to ratify.

CW   Chemical weapons.

DA-Notice   Defence advisory notice, known as a D-Notice until 1993, which restricts UK media reporting on sensitive defence issues.

DoD   US Department of Defense.

Double effect Term used to reflect the fact that the use of any kind of weapon against a specified target can have an effect that is intended (the destruction of the target itself) and one that is unintended (the destruction of people, facilities and land near the target). The debate over double effect is especially heated in relation to nuclear weapons, due to their indiscriminate destructive power.

Dual-key   Arrangement whereby US nuclear weapons are stationed in Europe. In the event of war, some of these weapons would be transferred to allied forces and delivered by allied aircraft, and could possibly be used in a war-termination strategy in response to conventional attack (NATO nuclear strategy has never ruled out first use, which should not be confused with 'First Strike').

Duff–Mason Report	1978 report produced by a senior diplomat and the Chief Scientist to the MoD, which focused on the minimum level of deterrence the UK needed to face the Soviet Union. Richard Mottram was secretary to the groups that worked on the report. He revealed that the work was overseen by Quinlan, who he said played an important part in the decision to opt for *Trident*.
DUS(P)	Deputy Undersecretary for Policy (also referred to as 'policy director').
First Strike	Massive, pre-emptive first use of strategic nuclear weapons in an attack intended to destroy an adversary's retaliatory capability.
FREEZE	Peace campaign, launched in the US in 1981. The goal was to get the US and Soviet Union to simultaneously adopt a mutual freeze on the testing, production and deployment of nuclear weapons and of missiles, as well as new aircraft designed primarily to deliver nuclear weapons.
FRG	Federal Republic of Germany (West Germany).
GLCM	Ground-launched cruise missile.
HLG	NATO High Level Group (see Appendix 1).
ICBM	Intercontinental ballistic missile.
INF	Intermediate-range nuclear forces.
INF Treaty	1987 agreement between the US and USSR which eliminated nuclear and conventional ground-launched missiles with intermediate ranges, defined as 500–5,500km.
IRBM	Intermediate-range ballistic missile.
JIC	Joint Intelligence Committee.
LRTNF	Long-range theatre nuclear forces (see *Pershing* II and SS–20).
MISC 7	UK cabinet sub-group tasked with nuclear decision-making.
MIRV	Multiple independently targetable re-entry vehicle (part of some nuclear-warhead delivery systems).
MLF	Multilateral Force, a failed US proposal to create a NATO nuclear fleet in the 1960s.

Moscow criterion   Targeting strategy underpinning UK nuclear doctrine for much of the Cold War, based on assessments that the UK should have the capability to independently strike the Soviet decision-making apparatus concentrated in the Moscow area (in order to destroy the Soviet leadership's capacity to remain in control of the Soviet Union in the event of a Soviet nuclear strike on Western Europe).

MP   Member of the UK parliament.

MRBM   Medium-range ballistic missile.

NFU   No-first-use, a commitment not to be the first to use nuclear weapons, including in a situation of escalating tension between adversaries.

NGO   Non-governmental organisation.

NPG   NATO nuclear planning group (see Appendix 1).

NPT   Nuclear Non-proliferation Treaty (1968), a treaty to limit the spread of nuclear weapons to additional states and promote nuclear disarmament among the five states that had already tested nuclear weapons when the treaty came into force.

NWFZ   Nuclear-Weapon-Free Zone, a specified region in which countries commit themselves not to manufacture, acquire, test or possess nuclear weapons. Regions currently covered under NWFZ agreements include Latin America (the 1967 Treaty of Tlatelolco), the South Pacific (the 1985 Treaty of Rarotonga), Southeast Asia (the 1995 Treaty of Bangkok), Africa (the 1996 Treaty of Pelindaba) and Central Asia (the 2006 Treaty of Semipalatinsk).

Pershing **II**   Mobile intermediate-range ballistic missile of the US Army, deployed at American bases in West Germany beginning in 1983 and aimed at targets in the western Soviet Union. It carried a single thermonuclear warhead with an explosive force equivalent to 5–50 kilotons of TNT. This class of missiles was eliminated by the INF Treaty.

PGA   Parliamentarians for Global Action, an international network of legislators whose aim is to promote peace.

Polaris   The UK submarine-launched ballistic-missile system, procured from the US, which entered service in the UK in 1968. The predecessor to *Trident*.

PTBT	Partial Test Ban Treaty (1963), a treaty prohibiting nuclear weapons tests 'or any other nuclear explosion' in the atmosphere, in outer space, and under water. It does not ban all tests underground, but it does prohibit underground nuclear explosions that cause 'radioactive debris to be present outside the territorial limits of the State under whose jurisdiction or control' the explosions were conducted.
PTBTAC	Partial Test Ban Treaty Amendment Conference (1991), a UN conference which many hoped would lead to a commitment to change the PTBT into a CTBT, but which ended in a stalemate when the US and the UK opposed the initiative.
PUS	Permanent undersecretary, the highest-ranking department officials in the UK civil service (now known as permanent secretaries).
RAF	Royal Air Force.
SACEUR	NATO Supreme Allied Commander Europe.
SALT	Strategic Arms Limitations Talks, bilateral arms-control talks between the US and USSR that led to two agreements during the Cold War: SALT I and SALT II.
SDI	US Strategic Defense Initiative, also known as 'Star Wars', a research initiative launched by the Reagan administration to develop a defence system based largely in space that would prevent missiles from reaching the US homeland.
SDP	Social Democratic Party.
SDR	1998 Strategic Defence Review.
SDSR	2010 Strategic Defence and Security Review.
Second centre of decision	Official role of the UK independent nuclear deterrent, which is arguably required in case an adversary 'miscalculates' that the US (and France) would not retaliate if the UK and/or its allies were attacked.
SHAPE	Supreme Headquarters Allied Powers Europe (headquarters of the NATO military organisation).
SLBM	Submarine-launched ballistic missile.
SNF	Short-range nuclear forces.
SNLE	*Sous-Marin Nucléaire Lanceur d'Engins*, a French nuclear-powered ballistic missile submarine.

SS-20	Soviet mobile intermediate-range ballistic missile (equivalent to the US *Pershing* II). It carried three independently targeted thermonuclear warheads, each with an explosive force equivalent to 250kt of TNT. Beginning in 1976, the missile was deployed at 48 bases in the Soviet Union, putting it within range of targets in western Europe and Asia.
SSBN	Nuclear-powered ballistic-missile submarine, such as the *Vanguard* class of four nuclear submarines, which entered service in the UK in 1994 and are likely to start leaving service from the early 2020s.
'Star Wars'	See SDI, above.
START	Strategic Arms Reduction Talks, successor to the SALT arms-control negotiations between the US and USSR, which led to two further agreements: START I (1991) and START II (1993). These agreements placed specific caps on US and Russian strategic nuclear weapons.
Strategic nuclear weapons	Nuclear weapons that are designed to inflict destruction on an adversary's civil, industrial and military infrastructure (to the extent that the country's survival would be in question).
SWP	Stiftung Wissenschaft und Politik, a research institute in Ebenhausen, Germany.
TASM	*Tomahawk* anti-ship missile.
TNF	Theatre nuclear forces, designed for use for specific military purpose in a limited theatre of operations.
Trident	Nuclear missile system used by the UK. See Appendix 2.
***Trident* II missile**	Missile with a range of over 4,000 nautical miles, procured from the US (the UK is reliant on the US for supply). The warhead for the D5 is produced and supported by the UK AWE, with US-supplied non-nuclear components.
TTBT	Threshold Test Ban Treaty (1974), treaty that set a ceiling of 150kt.
WE–177 gravity bomb	A free-fall nuclear bomb, which was carried by RAF *Vulcan* and *Tornado* aircraft and served in a tactical role.
WMD	Weapons of mass destruction (usually defined to include nuclear, biological and chemical weapons).

Publishing the correspondence of a senior member of the British civil service may appear an unusual undertaking given the role that most of them play out of the public eye, but Sir Michael Quinlan was no ordinary civil servant. At his memorial service at Westminster Cathedral he was described as the leading civilian thinker within the British government on defence policy, a key architect of British and NATO nuclear doctrine and strategy during the Cold War, and one of the most brilliant and influential nuclear thinkers of his time. He lived and breathed nuclear policy when the international system was dominated by the nuclear arms race; when analysts on both sides of the Iron Curtain feared a catastrophic third world war. Into this tense, divided world stepped the clear-thinking philosopher and strategist Michael Quinlan, who argued that the advent of nuclear weapons had made another major war unthinkable, and who believed that, as long as they were handled appropriately, nuclear weapons could play a stabilising role in East–West relations. His ideas about how that stability could be achieved shaped British nuclear policy for a generation, strongly influenced NATO strategy and doctrine, and were highly respected among nuclear decision-makers in the UK, the US and Western Europe.

Quinlan's thinking on nuclear ethics and strategy is laid out in extraordinary detail in the thousands of private letters he wrote when he was serving in key positions in the British Ministry of Defence (MoD) and elsewhere in the civil service. He wrote these letters in his spare time, filing copies of them – and the replies that he received – at his home. Before he died in 2009, he made it known that he wished for his correspondence to be published and for the letters to be archived in the War Studies library at King's College London. This book helps fulfill that wish; it is intended as a memorial to Quinlan, an important historical record of British nuclear thinking during the Cold War, and a contribution to current debate over the future of nuclear deterrence both in the UK and internationally. Quinlan clearly recognised the significance of his letters to current as well as past nuclear thinking, which was an important motivation in his desire for them to be published. As will become very apparent in the pages that follow, towards the end of his life he was acutely aware that the nuclear debate was shifting, that the rationale for maintaining nuclear weapons had changed, and that, in the months before he died, new energy was being breathed into disarmament debates, including among elite opinion-shapers in the US and UK. In his retirement, Quinlan played an important role in these debates: on the issue of whether and how the UK should replace *Trident*, on how multilateral disarmament should proceed; and on how a world of low numbers of nuclear weapons – and ultimately of zero – could be verified.

After Quinlan's death in February 2009, his family set about ensuring that his final wish was fulfilled, and with the help of Mark Fitzpatrick, director of the IISS Non-proliferation and Disarmament Programme whom Quinlan had known well from his time as a consulting fellow at the institute, helped provide the impetus that led to the launch of the Michael Quinlan Project in May 2010. I was recruited shortly afterwards to edit this book of Quinlan's correspondence, along with Josh Freedman, whose main task was to index and convert the thousands of letters into electronic format. Our first step was to collect the files from Quinlan's family home in Oxfordshire, where we spent an enjoyable morning discussing and going through them with Quinlan's wife Mary and his son, Tony. We learned while we were there that Kevin Tebbit, Quinlan's successor at the MoD from 1998–2005, had already been through the papers and removed any material that was considered potentially sensitive (that material is to be archived separately). Our second step was to assemble a group of Quinlan's contemporaries, whom we invited to become part of the project's advisory committee, to provide guidance on the book and first-hand insights into Quinlan's life and work. That committee has proved invaluable, helping to raise funding for the project as well as offering information and colourful anecdotes. Its members include: Lawrence Freedman, professor of war studies at King's College London; Jeremy Greenstock, retired British diplomat and former director of the Ditchley Foundation; Richard Mottram, Quinlan's successor as MoD PUS from 1995–98; David Omand, Quinlan's contemporary at the MoD and subsequently PUS at the Home Office; and Kevin Tebbit. I have also drawn on the insights and expertise of some critics of Quinlan's deterrence thinking, who have been equally helpful: William Walker, professor of international relations at the University of St Andrews, Scotland; Brian Wicker, author and Catholic moral philosopher; and Frank Winters, professor emeritus of ethics and international affairs at Georgetown University, Washington DC.

This introductory chapter provides a brief outline of Quinlan's career, an explanation of the core assumptions that underpin his thinking on deterrence, and some discussion of contextual matters that offer important insights into Quinlan's establishment role: the nature of nuclear decision-making in the UK and NATO; the relationship between civil servants, government ministers and society in general; Quinlan's Catholic faith and the involvement of church leaders in moral debates of the day, including over nuclear issues; and finally, some thoughts on Quinlan's mastery of the bureaucratic draft and what this means for his correspondence. The remainder of the book is divided thematically into three parts: the first includes letters on the logic and morality of deterrence; the second covers key strategic decisions in which Quinlan was closely involved (the 1979 decision by NATO to procure long-range theatre nuclear forces, and the 1980 decision by the British government to procure *Trident*); and the final part comprises correspondence on nuclear arms control and disarmament. Most of the official MoD communications associated with Quinlan's role during this period are not discussed (with the exception of a few key documents that have recently been declassified). Where it helps elucidate certain issues, Quinlan's published work is referred to, but the focus is on Quinlan's discussion of nuclear matters in his private correspondence, most of which occurs in response to letters from concerned individuals, many of whom wrote to him to explain why they felt strongly that nuclear weapons were dangerous, immoral or simply too costly. Naturally, this gives the book a certain flavour, with the majority of Quinlan's correspondents criticising British and NATO nuclear policies, and Quinlan – on most occasions – defending and justifying establishment positions and trying to persuade his correspondents of the case for nuclear deterrence.

Quinlan's career

Immediately after completing his national service in the Royal Air Force in 1954, Quinlan joined the civil service and moved rapidly up the ranks. He was private secretary to the chief of air staff from 1962–65 (a period that included the Cuban Missile Crisis) and in 1968–70 he led MoD work on the Strategic Arms Limitation Talks (SALT) and the Anti-Ballistic Missile Treaty (US–Soviet arms control deals). He was defence counsellor in the UK delegation to NATO from 1970–73, and then deputy undersecretary (policy) in the MoD from 1977–81, when the UK was engaged in the process of modernising its independent nuclear deterrent (via the *Chevaline* updating of *Polaris* and then its replacement by *Trident*). He led the MoD/Foreign and Commonwealth Office (FCO) team in the NATO work on the modernisation of intermediate nuclear forces in response to the Soviet deployment of the SS-20 missiles, and reached the highest rank in the MoD, that of permanent undersecretary (PUS) from 1988–92, just as the Cold War was ending. In between these positions in the MoD, he also served in senior positions in the Cabinet Office (1971–76), the Treasury (1981–82) and the Department of Employment, where he was PUS from 1983–87.

Quinlan referred to the MoD as his 'home' and was extremely disappointed in 1981 when he was transferred to serve as deputy secretary responsible for industry at the Treasury.[1] In a letter to his successor, John Blelloch, he referred to his transfer from the MoD as a 'deportation',[2] and for the next seven years, he made no secret of his desire to return. It must have been particularly difficult for him when in 1983, the position he most desired, that of PUS at the MoD, was given to Clive Whitmore and Quinlan was moved to the Department of Employment. It was a promotion – Quinlan was given the top job of PUS – but he yearned to return to his natural home at defence. Others understood and shared his frustration: a letter John Roper, MP, sent to Quinlan in 1983 ended with the words: 'I hope that, although your temporary abode is Employment, you will continue to think of yourself as a defence professional. The argument on these issues is too important for you to be out of it for long.'[3] And yet Quinlan did remain 'out of it' (in an official capacity at least) for seven years. And as the years passed he began to wonder whether he was out of it forever, as his letters to his counterparts in the US attest.[4] But then in 1988 he was sent back to the MoD, to his final post as PUS in what was to be the fulfillment of his ambition and his last official post.

After he retired from the civil service, Quinlan remained actively engaged in nuclear policy discussions. In 1992 he became director of the Ditchley Foundation, an institution established in 1958 to bring together transatlantic and other international experts for high-level discussions on public policy and international affairs. He was also appointed as a visiting professor at King's College London (he was in fact instrumental in the 1990 creation of King's College's Centre for Defence Studies while he was PUS) and as consulting senior fellow at the IISS. With greater freedom to indulge his interests and publish with fewer restrictions, he produced a number of highly regarded scholarly works on nuclear policy, arms control and the ethics of deterrence during his retirement, contributing to debates on the concept of a just war, the future of *Trident*, international disarmament, and the role of nuclear weapons in the post-Cold-War and post-9/11 world. However, above and beyond his impressive scholarly output during this period, Quinlan was probably best known for his high-profile opposition to the 2003 invasion of Iraq. He was not afraid to speak out about what he saw as a flagrant abuse of power, a 'precarious gamble' which he argued was 'not necessary, not prudent, and not right'. There were many aspects to the war that he objected to, not least as he saw it, the fact that ill-judged and immoral decisions had been pushed through by a coterie of Prime Minister Tony Blair's close associates without proper consultation of the Cabinet. He also strongly believed that the war was unnecessary strategically, insofar as Saddam Hussein could be deterred if he acquired WMD. Arguments for regime change offended his trust in nuclear deterrence as a means of achieving restraint.

Quinlan's criticisms of the Iraq invasion and his concerns about its detrimental repercussions for international relations proved to be very well-founded, but most would agree that the high point of his career, when he made his most influential contribution to policy discussions, came during his time at the MoD. Those who worked closely with him in the MoD point to his time as deputy undersecretary for policy (DUS(P)) – more commonly known as 'policy director' – from 1977–81, just as much as his time as MoD PUS from 1988–92, as the pinnacle of his influence, when his role in shaping British and NATO nuclear doctrine and strategy most closely matched his skills, abilities and interests. Many of the most interesting letters in Quinlan's private correspondence on nuclear deterrence were written during that period: 1977–92 (including and especially during the seven years he was not officially responsible for defence issues). For that reason this book on his correspondence primarily focuses on those 15 years, despite the fact that Quinlan's career was well established before his time as MoD policy director, and despite the fact his contribution to nuclear debates continued long after his retirement from the civil service.

Quinlan: 'master of deterrence'
Due to his unmatched grasp of nuclear strategy and influence on policy debates, Quinlan was known among his colleagues

in the MoD as 'Big Q', the authority on all things nuclear. It was a role and a reputation he enjoyed, because he firmly believed nuclear weapons provided the best means for maintaining peace and preserving human life and thus, for him, shaping British and NATO nuclear strategy and doctrine represented the ultimate role in exercising public responsibility. As he admitted, he was also attracted by the complex and abstracted nature of debates on nuclear strategy and doctrine, as well as those dealing with moral philosophy. His intellectual curiosity is very clear from his correspondence, which delves into questions of deterrence ethics and strategy in fine detail and with a rigour that leaves one in no doubt of his fascination for and enjoyment of the subject as well as his sharp intellect.

An explanation of Quinlan's thinking on nuclear deterrence will help lay the foundations for understanding his correspondence. In this, it is helpful to draw on the analysis of Lawrence Freedman, who distilled the main features of Quinlan's deterrence thinking into an easily digestible framework, outlined below.[5] The framework is underpinned by Quinlan's crucial assumption, which remained firm throughout his civil service career, that nuclear weapons were unlikely to be relinquished until the international system was transformed and conflict was no longer a feature of international relations. The first three features of the framework are straightforward: the 'nuclear age', dominated by mass-destruction weapons that use nuclear technology, was likely to continue for the foreseeable future; these nuclear weapons revolutionised warfare due to their huge destructive power, with the result that previous strategic concepts required extensive adaptation; and since nuclear war between major, nuclear-armed powers has not occurred, all thinking about nuclear strategy was speculative (although this does not mean one nuclear strategy was as good as another; despite the unknowns, Quinlan thought it was still possible to devise more and less reliable strategies).

According to the framework, because the possibility of conflict escalation and nuclear annihilation made conventional war between the major powers less likely, nuclear weapons also revolutionised strategic thinking. Despite this, war between the major powers was still possible (states exist in a competitive international environment) and the spectrum of force that could be used in any future major war included both conventional and nuclear weapons. Quinlan was nonetheless clear that, amid the stresses of warfare, nothing could be ruled out, including the risk that a conventional conflict could turn nuclear. There was, therefore, a close link between any major conventional war and nuclear war, because any war now had the potential to provoke nuclear use. Consequently, states must shape their strategy so as to act as a brake on tensions; restraint and war prevention were the order of the day. It was vital to Quinlan's concept of deterrence stability that this feature was understood by all states that possess nuclear weapons, and by states that relied on extended deterrence.

For Quinlan, strategic doctrines that treated nuclear and conventional warfare as separate categories divided by a 'nuclear threshold', and those that relied on a no-first-use pledge, lacked credibility and were in fact dangerous. He was concerned that if these doctrines were believed by the adversary (and were not considered 'bluffs'), deterrence could not operate as intended, whereas if states believed conventional war could escalate into nuclear war, they would behave in a more restrained and risk averse manner, thus contributing to stable deterrence. The objective for Quinlan and for others who upheld this view was to make it clear to the adversary that aggression would be met with a decisive response, but to leave the adversary uncertain as to what exactly that response might be, thus creating fear that the cost of aggression would be too high. Under the framework, the various levels of military force were therefore complementary and interdependent: all contributed to deterrence and therefore none could be ruled out.

Quinlan had also thought carefully about how deterrence could yet function against an enemy that was invulnerable to a disarming first strike. If, for example, the adversary possessed a submarine-based nuclear deterrent, there was no reliable route to victory in a war that escalated to a nuclear exchange. But this by no means made victory in nuclear war impossible – different configurations of nuclear weapons (of various yield, capability and range) could open up possible routes to victory, although the effect of their use would be speculative, and victory might be measured not by the physical elimination of the adversary, but by denying the adversary its political and strategic goals.

Finally, Quinlan believed operational planning for nuclear use in war was vital, in case deterrence failed in its ultimate goal of preventing the outbreak of hostilities and some form of intra-war deterrence was required. In this situation, nuclear weapons could serve a 'war termination' role, by making it clear to the adversary that it had crossed a red line and further aggression would not be tolerated.

According to Quinlan, then, the two major roles for UK and NATO nuclear weapons were thus war prevention, and, in the event that prevention failed and war broke out, war termination. During the Cold War, making deterrence work depended on the UK and its NATO allies developing a thorough knowledge of Soviet values in order to understand what its strategists would consider to be an unacceptable price for aggression (and thus what the allies should threaten or 'hold at risk' in their nuclear targeting). It depended on careful and effective communication: ensuring the Soviet Union understood what actions the allies considered to be unacceptable and that the consequences of crossing these 'red lines' would be immediate and dire. Here, Quinlan argued that the UK's independent nuclear deterrent served as a fall-back: if communication failed, and the Soviets 'miscalculated' that the US would not retaliate if Western Europe were attacked, the possession of independent nuclear forces by the UK and France would leave Moscow wondering how London and Paris would respond to Soviet aggression. This fall-back justification for the UK's non-NATO nuclear deterrent, known as the 'second centre of decision' argument, continues to be used by MoD officials as the main rationale for maintaining Britain's independent nuclear capability. (Some politicians also argue that nuclear weapons bestow prestige and ensure Britain's place at 'the high table'.)

Quinlan's arguments can be criticised on many levels, from his assertion that the advent of nuclear weapons has revolutionised warfare, to his contention that, as a last resort, nuclear weapons could play a credible war-termination role. Even his claim that nuclear weapons cannot be 'disinvented' – a view that softened somewhat over time – attracts counter-arguments by critics who believe this position is defeatist and fatalistic. As the letters included in this book will reveal, academics and strategists have picked over Quinlan's ideas and identified every potential weakness, a process that Quinlan appears to have relished. In most cases, he was able to defend his arguments against even the most able and well-informed critic, but there are some important exceptions, as a few of the letters on strategy and ethics reveal. The key point, however, is that he was able to convince a generation of officials and politicians in the UK and the US of the logic and coherence of his arguments. Long after the Cold War ended and the nature of the threat had changed, his thinking on nuclear deterrence continued to dominate nuclear policy in the UK.

In the Cold War context, the Quinlan framework outlined above is indeed persuasive, and so one does not need to search too long to explain his impact on the British defence establishment and on NATO nuclear doctrine during the period 1977–92. But there are other reasons for Quinlan's influence that go beyond his ideas about nuclear strategy: on the one hand, the role of senior defence officials in UK and NATO nuclear policy-making processes help account for his extraordinary impact; on the other, the particular qualities of the man himself were key to his influence – his integrity, moral accountability, courtesy, commitment to debate, and last but not least, his faith and ethical principles.

Nuclear decision-making in the UK and NATO

The extent of Quinlan's influence over British and NATO nuclear strategy and doctrine requires some understanding of the part that senior civil servants play in the policy process in the UK – a situation where the phrase 'knowledge is power' holds true. In Britain, the Official Secrets Act prevents officials from releasing information on government decisions, and even most members of the prime minister's cabinet are kept in the dark where nuclear issues are concerned. This extreme secrecy dates back to the origins of the British nuclear programme, to the 1947 decision by Prime Minister Clement Attlee and a small band of advisers to build an atomic bomb, without the knowledge of most of the executive branch of government, let alone Parliament and the public. Since then, although the veil of secrecy has lifted to some extent since the decision to procure *Trident*, most major decisions affecting the British nuclear deterrent are taken by the prime minister and a small group of key ministers: usually the defence secretary, the foreign secretary and the chancellor of the exchequer. Decisions made during these top-secret discussions are presented to the full cabinet for approval, and announced to

Parliament as a fait accompli. But it would be a mistake to assume that the individuals involved in this elite ministerial decision-making process are the only important drivers of British nuclear policy and doctrine. The select group of ministers take the ultimate decisions, but the information and analysis on which those decisions are based, and in fact specific recommendations on the most appropriate course of action, are provided by the policy directors and the highest-ranking civil servants in the Ministry of Defence and the Cabinet Office, with varying degrees of input from their counterparts in the Foreign and Commonwealth Office and the Treasury.[6]

Senior civil servants are far more influential in the policy decision-making process than most people outside government realise. This is partly because – unlike political appointees who tend to be generalists, come and go with each government, and have many diverse and competing demands on their time (such as attending meetings in the House of Commons, visiting their constituencies and attending party functions) – civil servants hold permanent appointments. Their official role is to develop expertise and an institutional memory for the executive branch and to provide it with the means to examine and implement policy on a continuing basis. The diaries of Richard Crossman, who was secretary of state for health and social security under Harold Wilson from 1968–70, shed some light on the relationship between government ministers and senior civil servants: Describing the period when he first took his position, he wrote:[7]

> **"**I felt like someone in a padded cell, but now I must modify this. In fact I feel like someone floating on the most comfortable support. The whole Department is there to support the Minister. Into his in-tray come hour-by-hour notes with suggestions as to what he should do. Everything is done to sustain him in the line offi-

> cials think he should take. But if one is very careful and conscious one is aware that the supporting soft framework of recommendations is the result of a great deal of secret discussion between the civil servants below. There is a constant debate as to how the Minister should be advised or, shall we say, directed and pushed and cajoled into the line required by the Ministry … Each Ministry has its own departmental policy and this policy goes on while Ministers come and go. **"**

The dependent relationship described by Crossman is significantly augmented in the highly esoteric and secretive realm of nuclear policymaking, where schedules for developing new weapons systems can stretch to decades, and where mastering the technical and political complexities associated with strategy and doctrine is extremely challenging. The result is that the line between the official support role of the civil service and the decision-making role of the ministers is sometimes hard to draw. By virtue of their long years spent honing their expertise, framing policy alternatives and advising government ministers, those in the most senior ranks in the civil service have the power to shape nuclear policy to an extent that few outside the most elite echelons of government fully appreciate (and to an extent that some find unacceptable[8]). There is no doubt that as policy director, Quinlan had a strong influence on the NATO nuclear modernisation plan of 1979 and the UK *Trident* procurement of 1980.

NATO decision-making adds another layer of complexity and opacity to the British nuclear policy process. Decisions on Alliance nuclear policy are taken by the Nuclear Planning Group (NPG), which is chaired by the NATO secretary general and staffed by the defence ministers from all NATO member countries (with the exception of France).[9] Policies agreed upon by the NPG are made by consensus and thus represent the collective will of the Alliance, but as in the case of national nuclear decision-making, the decisions of the political appointees are heavily influenced by career civil servants, who feed their recommendations on procurement, strategy and doctrine into the NPG meetings. Support for the NPG is provided by the NPG Staff Group, which serves as its secretariat, and more significantly, by the High Level Group (HLG), a body consisting of senior defence ministry personnel from the NATO member states, which is chaired by the US assistant secretary of defence for international security policy. It serves as the NPG's think tank. When it was first created in 1977 to study the Soviet build-up of theatre nuclear forces (TNF), the HLG was considered so successful that it was incorporated into NATO's permanent decision-making structure.[10] Its key attributes are that its members have the ear of the most senior political leaders in their own countries and have operational responsibility for defence planning within their governments. During his time as policy director at the MoD, Quinlan led the UK delegation on the HLG, and as his fellow delegates were quick to point out, his organisational skills and superior grasp of nuclear strategy and doctrine meant that the group was strongly influenced by his views during NATO deliberations on nuclear strategy. Richard Perle, Quinlan's counterpart in the US during the HLG discussions on modernising NATO long-range theatre nuclear forces (LRTNF), highlighted what he regarded as Quinlan's significant contribution in a letter he sent him on leaving the Reagan administration in July 1987:[11]

> **"** It is always difficult to bid farewell to a valued colleague. During the years we served together in the High Level Group, we were privileged to work towards the shared goal of enhanced Alliance security. This work was

immensely rewarding to me, as I am sure it was for you. We met each challenge with dedication and succeeded in strengthening NATO's deterrent capability, thereby advancing the cause of peace.

On the occasion of my departure from government service, I want to extend my best wishes for continued success in your career. Your past contributions have been most significant. I know your future contributions will be equally important. **"**

Understanding the role that senior defence ministry personnel play in the nuclear-policy process in the British government and NATO goes some way to help us understand the important influence the MoD policy director and PUS have over nuclear decision-making. To fully appreciate Quinlan's legacy for UK nuclear strategy and doctrine, however, we also need to explore the reasons for the high esteem in which he was held by defence officials on both sides of the Atlantic, in Europe and even in the Soviet Union. It is true that as PUS of the MoD, Quinlan held one of the most powerful defence positions in the land, and that in his stint as policy director, he played a pivotal role in discussions on *Trident* and NATO procurement. But others who have held the same high-ranking positions in the British defence establishment and NATO could claim to have had the same power and influence over nuclear decision-making. Yet Quinlan's status as the architect of British nuclear doctrine and strategy is widely recognised as unique, as discussions with his contemporaries and successors at the MoD confirm. Many considered him to be an intellectual giant and true master of his field. Lawrence Freedman, the leading British scholar on nuclear strategy and policy, explains that Quinlan 'helped give official [nuclear] policy a coherence and philosophical strength that it would otherwise have lacked'.[12]

Historian Michael Howard goes even further in his explanation of Quinlan's intellectual legacy, claiming that he 'taught our masters how to think'.[13]

The public debate on nuclear weapons

Despite the closed and highly secretive nature of nuclear decision-making in the UK, Quinlan believed that open debate about nuclear policy was important and necessary. This was something that set him apart from most of his contemporaries and one of the reasons his influence stretched far beyond government circles to schools and universities, church organisations, think tanks and non-governmental organisations (NGOs). His engagement with these groups, through public appearances at conferences and seminars, publications in journals and magazines, and his prolific personal correspondence, dramatically increased the demands on his time, so that often, despite his famous 'speed in dispatching business',[14] he must have sacrificed precious family time for his work. With four children to raise, that cannot have been easy for Quinlan or his wife Mary. But Quinlan enjoyed being in the public sphere. Like most public figures, he was not without vanity, and although constitutionally civil servants in the UK are accountable to ministers only and not to the public at large, he believed one of his most important responsibilities was to engage in wider debate about the logic and ethics of nuclear deterrence. It was an expression of his integrity, and his commitment to democracy and moral accountability.[15]

Other reasons for Quinlan's heavy involvement in nuclear debates were more pedagogical and strategic: he was eager to correct misinformation and to identify logical flaws in the arguments of those who criticised the doctrine of nuclear deterrence. Where critical issues of national security were concerned, there was no place for sentimental arguments or 'woolly thinking' –

one had to be disciplined and accurate in the use of evidence, logical in the application of theory, and measured in the choice of vocabulary. He was quick and sometimes even merciless in identifying weak arguments, because he regarded them as potentially damaging, particularly if those making them were in positions of influence in the church, education or advocacy groups.

There may also have been a more personal reason he was so dedicated to the public debate, stemming from his Catholic faith and his need to square his bureaucratic role as nuclear deterrence chief with the ethical dilemmas posed by nuclear possession and use. Some of his letters on these difficult issues verge on dogmatic, which may partly be due to his very direct writing style, but there may also have been an element of the author being determined to remain persuaded of the arguments he was relaying to the reader with such clarity and certainty. Some of the letters hint at this possibility – especially his letter to the prominent Quaker and scholar Sydney Bailey, in which Quinlan admitted that he wanted to believe, by virtue of his official role, that a nuclear strategy built around war prevention and war termination could be morally acceptable:[16]

> ❝ Let me admit first, as I did at the Canterbury conference, to a certain predisposition: I do not want to condemn possession of nuclear weapons. That predisposition, I recognise, may well be motivated in a significant degree by my particular situation – it would unquestionably be directly awkward for me to find myself driven to a conviction that having these weapons was ethically intolerable. ❞

The fact that Quinlan had to overcome tight restrictions to participate in the public nuclear debate makes his role in it all the more remarkable. One thing that his letters make absolu... , clear is that the volume of his contribution to the published literature would have been far greater if he had not been constrained by a combination of UK constitutional restrictions on civil servants on the one hand, and intense domestic political controversy over British nuclear policy on the other. His letters reveal that these constraints on his ability to publish increased significantly over the course of the 1980s, when the topic of information disclosure became a highly sensitive issue after a series of whistle-blowing incidents by civil servants critical of the Thatcher government.[17] Key developments included the review and strengthening of section 2 of the Official Secrets Act of 1911 (whereby disclosure of sensitive official information is a criminal offence) and a review of the duties and responsibilities of civil servants in the 1985 Armstrong Memorandum, which stressed that civil servants must be politically impartial and loyal to the government of the day, including where matters of individual conscience are concerned.[18] This increased scrutiny of the role of civil servants and their constitutional obligations coincided with a period of intense politicisation of the nuclear debate – a time when the issue became polarised between an anti-nuclear Labour Party opposition and a strongly pro-nuclear Conservative government, which was wary – perhaps even paranoid – about Soviet infiltration of the peace movement. The result was a period of heightened sensitivity over public disclosure issues, which limited Quinlan's capacity to fully engage in the public debate on the subject.[19]

These official restrictions were a source of frustration to Quinlan, which he occasionally vented to his correspondents. Before he could accept an invitation to speak or offer his work for publication, he had to seek official clearance from the Cabinet Office, and sometimes from government ministers themselves. On some occasions, permission was granted, but on others it was not. A letter Quinlan wrote in September 1985 to Professor Douglas MacLean and Professor Henry Shue of the University of Maryland provides some insight into the impact the official protocols had on his publications as the political divisions over nuclear policy heated up in the 1980s. He had received a letter from the professors inviting him to participate in an international study on nuclear deterrence and moral restraint, which he was clearly keen to accept. But he was unable to do so, except under the strictest conditions of anonymity, which prevented his contributions being published and his statements being attributed. He explained this clearly in his reply:[20]

> **"** The impediment is … a semi-constitutional one. As you will know, the UK civil service is a career service right to the top, and based accordingly on a strong convention of political neutrality. This means that its members – especially those at levels like mine – must not be seen to engage publicly in position-taking on matters of political controversy. This latter term is not further defined, but a pragmatic interpretation would be 'disputed publicly between the leading figures of the main political parties'. I was able – though even at the time this was regarded as unusually close to borderline – to secure in 1981 and 1982 the permission to give two public talks on nuclear deterrence … But since 1982 the position of the main opposition party here has moved and hardened in a way that makes it no longer plausible to claim that there is inter-party consensus on even the most general propositions about nuclear weapons policy. The view has been taken accordingly that I should publish no more. I say 'has been taken' because I have actually put the matter to the test on two separate occasions … Both pieces [that I wished to publish] were much liked at very

high governmental levels indeed, but opposition – on the constitutional grounds I have indicated – from a key senior Minister – led to refusal of permission. **"**

Earlier, in a letter to Richard Harries, dean of King's College London, Quinlan explained that the 'key senior Minister' who was blocking his publications was Defence Secretary Michael Heseltine, who 'took a strictly purist line on any notion of a senior civil servant uttering in public (even from an ethical rather than a political approach) on matters which were the subject of political controversy'.[21] Quinlan regarded these restrictions as 'narrow, tiresome and unnecessary' and was clearly pleased when, after Heseltine's resignation over the Westland affair,[22] he was able to publish one of the manuscripts in question (an article on the ethics of deterrence), albeit 'quietly' in the US journal *Theological Studies*[23] – a publication that was deemed to be low profile enough to pass under the radar.

These constraints and sensitivities were compounded by a further bureaucratic protocol: that of not treading on the toes of successors. When senior civil servants are promoted within a department or transferred from one to another, they are expected to genuinely 'move on' from their former role for the sake of their successor. Thus, when Quinlan was transferred from the MoD to the Treasury and then to the Department of Employment, the expectation was that he would not remain publicly engaged in defence issues. Similarly, as PUS, it would have been inappropriate for him to remain as deeply involved with day-to-day nuclear policy issues as he was when he held the position of policy director. Quinlan had to manage this situation very carefully, and it was one of the reasons he had to obtain clearance before publishing or publicly engaging in nuclear debates. A letter he wrote to his successor at the MoD, John Blelloch, highlights some of these difficulties:[24]

❝ As you know, since my deportation [from the MoD] in July 1981, I have, with your department's knowledge and acquiescence, continued to take a hand in discussion of nuclear deterrence issues by way of attending conferences, giving talks and the like – always, save a few instances all specifically cleared in advance with MoD, on 'Chatham House' or otherwise private basis … I am sure I must now bring this activity to an end. I have one more date to fulfill – a talk to sixth-formers at Downside School at the end of November – but I am taking on nothing else. **❞**

These combined constraints help explain why the volume of Quinlan's published output did not reflect his major contribution to deterrence thinking. Anyone interested in his true intellectual legacy will discover that much of it is hidden in the writing of scholars, politicians and church leaders, whose speeches and publications Quinlan contributed to on an unattributed basis, or via the copious feedback he provided on their manuscripts. This was his way of overcoming the restrictions of officialdom – most of his contributions to the nuclear debate were quiet and indirect, built up, layer upon layer, over many years of corresponding with the great thinkers of the day. When leafing through the thousands of letters he left behind, many of them providing detailed critiques of complex strategic and ethical debates, one is struck by his devotion to scholarship and knowledge. What is most striking is that, while in his official capacity he occupied one of the most demanding and responsible positions in the land, he was also privately engaged in an extremely active and highly demanding professorial role. That he was willing and able to balance these demands, and at the same time overcome the many constitutional and political hurdles that stood in his way, is the true measure of Quinlan's intellectual ability, dedication to his work, and his lifelong love of well-informed debate. A paragraph in a letter that Beatrice Heuser (a professor of nuclear strategy, who at the time was part of the War Studies Department, King's College London) wrote to Quinlan stands out in this regard, as it reveals that he was a gifted and entertaining speaker who drew immense pleasure from participating in public debate. Once retired, he reveled in his freedom to debate to his heart's content:[25]

> ❝ I can see that you are going to treat the assembled conference like formerly your Policy Planning Staff and you will doubtless appear as the benign professor, right answers ready, and we will all have to get up, stand straight and answer your questions in turn. Correct answers receive a stoic nod of approval; incorrect answers will trigger an elegant volley of corrections, pointing out all the inconsistencies of the view just uttered without any major clue as to where the right answer lies – until the stunned victim finally hits upon it after being chased intellectually by you into and out of every possible logical dead end along the way. I shall savour every second of this intellectual hunt, even if I am convinced that I too will be left behind panting and puffing as your mind runs ahead of everybody else's! ❞

Nuclear deterrence and the church

Quinlan has been described as 'the closest thing to being a Jesuit without actually being a priest or a monk'.[26] He was religious and, for a lay person, involved at a very high level in church affairs, especially in church debates over the morality of nuclear deterrence. His Jesuit education at Wimbledon College provided the foundation for his faith; it helped build the core values that led him to a life of service guided by strong moral principles. It also nurtured in him the powerful analytical skills that equipped him so well for policy work, and familiarised him with the philosophical literature that later drew him to debates over 'just war' and nuclear deterrence. As Freedman pointed out in his discussion of Quinlan's education, as a result of his time spent under the tutelage of the Jesuits, Quinlan 'had no problems with the notion that far from precluding rational analysis the unfathomable could set the starting point and provide a firm foundation … the challenge was to fit the logical structure that flowed from the starting premise, sustained by the core values, to the practical realities, contextual, political and technical, that must be faced in any consideration of appropriate policies'.[27] This clearly set Quinlan up very well for the esoteric debates over nuclear deterrence – discussions that, due to the absence of nuclear war, are unavoidably speculative, abstract, underpinned by enduring assumptions, and – some would also say – by leaps of faith.[28]

A significant portion of Quinlan's contribution to deterrence thinking can be traced to his participation in church debates on the subject, particularly in the early 1980s, when the Catholic bishops in the US publicly debated the ethics of deterrence and denounced first-use doctrines. As Quinlan's correspondence with senior figures in the UK Church demonstrate, he was extremely concerned about this development, which he regarded as misguided and wrong-headed, and he set about trying to ensure that the Catholic hierarchy in the UK did not follow the US lead. He did this by publishing his own arguments on the ethics of deterrence in the Catholic weekly, *The Tablet,* by corresponding with leading church figures, and by assisting fellow Catholics in the MoD and the FCO who were also engaged in similar outreach activities. The huge volume of Quinlan's correspondence on this issue is quite remarkable, and some of his letters hint at the reasons he devoted so much of his time to this campaign: there was a possibility that influential church leaders could sway the public debate in the UK against nuclear weapons, or at least against the nuclear doctrine that he had so carefully calibrated. In his eyes, this could have spelled disaster, leaving the UK and its allies vulnerable to Soviet aggression, and to Soviet attacks on the cherished values of the West. As Quinlan admits in some of his letters, these values included the religious freedom that was so close to his heart.[29] Intelligence assessments warning that the Soviets had launched a campaign of subversion through infiltration of peace and church movements no doubt added to his concerns, and helped motivate his own counter-offensive.

Quinlan's writing style and expertise

Quinlan has been called the master of the bureaucratic draft. In his writing and his speeches, he chose his words extremely carefully 'to say no more and no less than required … to convey meaning but not to demonstrate the erudition of the author or explode as a provocation in the face of the audience'.[30] As Lawrence Freedman points out, this muted style, so delicately tuned to make a point accurately and concisely, without any trace of sensationalism, makes his publications and letters more suited for the expert audience, 'who might recognise the allusions and appreciate the political context' and 'get more out of his work than one coming to it fresh'. This is true: Quinlan's letters are a rich resource for experts on strategy and ethics and would appeal to civil servants who would be more likely to appreciate his precise style (one colleague at the Treasury, for example, described his pleasure in reading 'compelling thoughts expressed in such meaning-packed sentences'[31]). But his style is not to everyone's taste and it is certainly not easily accessible to the general reader. His prose does suit the topic, however, given that nuclear strategy and the ethics of deterrence are heavy, complex and demanding subjects that require a high degree of intellectual rigour and commitment. And while the task of reading and understanding this book of correspondence presents a challenge to the non-expert, the importance of Quinlan's contributions to the nuclear debate, especially at a time when the role of nuclear weapons is being reconsidered, make it a worthwhile and rewarding experience.

PART ONE

The logic and morality of nuclear deterrence

For years within the MoD Quinlan was considered the authority on deterrence. Many of his colleagues came to be regarded as his disciples, having had his rigorous deterrence teachings drilled into them to the extent that they continued to seek his advice and to share his faith in the logic of deterrence long after he had retired. Likewise, some of his fellow representatives to the NATO High Level Group (HLG) sought his input on nuclear policy matters more than a decade after his involvement in the HLG had come to an end. Even outside government circles, Quinlan was one of the most powerful contributors to public debates on nuclear deterrence – particularly discussions within the UK Catholic hierarchy, which was strongly influenced by Quinlan's arguments in favour of deterrence. The letters in this part of the book reveal the key elements of Quinlan's deterrence thinking that so many of his contemporaries and successors found so compelling, focusing on his ideas on deter- rence stability, nuclear use and conflict escalation. There is a great deal of discussion of these themes in his correspondence, much of it addressed not to his 'disciples' but to his critics: a well-informed minority within the British establishment and the public at large that did not share Quinlan's faith in the logic of deterrence and were at pains to highlight its weaknesses. As the letters show, Quinlan was more than happy to respond to critics and followers alike, relishing the chance to correct factual errors, identify faulty logic and highlight false assumptions. He took every possible opportunity to feed his knowledge of nuclear strategy into the discussions, speeches and publications of scholars and practitioners in the UK, northern Europe and the US. His letters on deterrence logic provide a unique insight into his thinking on nuclear issues, underpinned by his unshakable belief that there was no acceptable alternative to nuclear deterrence in the Cold War era: without nuclear weapons, Western Europe could be forced to succumb to Soviet totalitarianism; with them, the prospects for Western Europe to retain its freedom and independence increased exponentially.

This part of the book also addresses issues of morality. Nuclear weapons create obvious moral dilemmas due to their huge destructive power, which pushes the limits of just war principles. Even a low-yield nuclear strike against an adversary's territory would almost certainly lead to massive casualties, including civilian victims. The question of whether nuclear weapons can fulfill the 'just war' criteria of discrimination and proportionality has therefore always been a contentious one, even among those responsible for formulating and implementing nuclear policy. Many deterrence advocates believe nuclear weapons present a paradox: on the one hand, the possession and potential use of nuclear weapons can never truly be morally justified; but on the other, maintaining a credible nuclear deterrent is a 'necessary evil'.

Quinlan did not share this view, and it is striking that he avoided using the word 'evil' and the phrase 'weapon of mass destruction' in connection with nuclear weapons. In response to questions over whether it can be morally legitimate to threaten an adversary with nuclear weapons and to be prepared to carry out that threat, Quinlan's answer was 'yes – depending on the circumstances'. If the alternative was to risk defeat by an aggressive, nuclear-armed totalitarian adversary, then nuclear possession and use was justified under specific conditions and within certain limits. In fact, he went further, and argued that in extremis it would be a *moral obligation* for the West to launch a nuclear attack against the Soviet Union, in order to maintain international peace and stability. This conviction provided the foundation for nearly everything he wrote on nuclear issues during the Cold War. In Quinlan's eyes, nuclear weapons were a terrible (though not 'evil') necessity; they posed the gravest of risks and appalling ethical dilemmas, but at the same time they provided the only assurance that Western freedoms could be protected.

Providing a convincing defence of his belief in the morality of nuclear deterrence (and especially nuclear use) was the biggest challenge Quinlan faced in his private correspondence, and he was fully aware that, in making his case, he sometimes skated on very thin ice. But it was vitally important to him that the ice remained intact. The reasons for this were religious as well as strategic: as a religious man, he wanted others to share his belief that his work on nuclear policy planning and the work of others involved in the nuclear infrastructure was morally licit; and as a nuclear strategist and career civil servant, he believed that the maintenance of a credible nuclear deterrent depended upon the shared belief in its legitimacy. Thus, for Quinlan, engaging in debates on deterrence ethics was just as important as participating in debates on nuclear strategy (although he would probably be the first to admit that he was on more solid ground in his contributions to the latter).

Due to the esoteric nature of the subject, the quiet and constitutionally constrained role of civil servants, and the social circles within which Quinlan moved, it was inevitable that the majority of people he engaged with on morality issues were part of a narrow circle of political and religious elites. Besides the letters from professors of philosophy and religious studies and from Jesuit teachers in the UK and the US, most of his correspondence engaged fellow senior civil servants in the MoD, FCO and Cabinet Office, as well as senior military officers and church leaders. Nearly all Quinlan's correspondents on deterrence ethics shared his Catholic faith and were concerned not only with the wider policy implications of nuclear debates for the Church and for government, but also, like Quinlan, with matters of personal conscience and responsibility. The letters in Quinlan's files show that he had a profound impact on these elites, sometimes turning deterrence skeptics into advocates, and encouraging those who initially favoured passive deterrence to share his moral and logical justifications for active nuclear planning and for potential nuclear use. Not all his correspondents were persuaded, however, and the most fascinating letters, some of which generated hundreds of pages of detailed exchanges, came from Quinlan's most consistent, determined and intellectually brilliant sparring partners. There were plenty of these on both sides of the Atlantic, but it is noticeable that Quinlan had far less success in influencing moral debates among religious and academic elites in the US than he did in the UK. It was in England and Wales in particular that he, probably more than any other lay person, was responsible for preventing church authorities from following the US Catholic bishops in condemning nuclear use of any kind, including counterforce strikes.

Deterrence logic

Quinlan viewed nuclear weapons as a strategic necessity. He firmly believed that the advent of such powerful weapons had revolutionised warfare, making the prospect of major war between the great powers so abhorrent that they would not risk confrontation with each other, including conventional war. His thoughts on this, which under underpin all his writing and thinking on deterrence, were summed up in a speech he gave at the Royal College of Defence Studies on 26 October 1982 (which he later used as the basis for a paper titled 'NATO Nuclear Deterrence Concepts', which he sent to US nuclear strategist Albert Wohlstetter in 1987):[1]

> **"** […] the advent of nuclear weapons has done something quite fundamental – not just a big shift in degree, but an utterly radical change – to the entire nature of war, and to the meaning of victory, in conflict at any level, not just the nuclear level, between powers or blocs possessing them. The result is that some of the old categories of military appraisal – and, for that matter, political appraisal – have simply ceased to apply … [This is because] nuclear weapons are not just new and nasty sorts of weapon requiring to be managed and exploited (or banned and forsworn) as adjuncts to or aberrations within the spectrum of military force, like dum-dum bullets or mustard gas. They are far too powerful and decisive, and so far too fundamental, for that. In effect, they stretch out the spectrum of force to near-infinity. In doing that they utterly change the character of the spectrum as a whole, and so the significance of all the individual components in it – even the familiar ones. We have to accept that though we can recognise subdivisions of the spectrum of force, and though concepts like thresholds and firebreaks can have their limited place, in the end no conceptual boundary can be reliably secure in practice amid the formidable stresses of any major armed conflict between East and West. Overwhelmingly, therefore, the key threshold

is the threshold of war – not nuclear war, or strategic nuclear exchange, or any such internal step within war. Escalation is not a certainty – far from it. But we do have to recognise and live with the facts, firstly, that there is no way of reducing to zero the risk of its continuing if it once starts; and secondly that it starts with the first bullet, not just the first atomic shell. **"**

The enduring nature of Quinlan's belief in this revolutionary, stabilising and war-prevention role for nuclear weapons can be seen in the speech he delivered to the Soviet General Staff in Moscow in November 1990:[2]

" The coming of nuclear weapons is not just another technological development in warfare like the invention of gunpowder, or of aircraft. It does something more fundamental: it carries the potential of warfare past a boundary at which many previous concepts simply cease to apply. The combination of nuclear explosive power, the worldwide delivery capability of modern missiles and the diversity and elusiveness of modern launching platforms makes available what is for practical purposes infinite destructive power, power that cannot be warded off or exhausted. And this has to change our whole concept of what war can be about ... War-making capability has reached and passed the limit of meaningful rationality. An unrestrained conflict between nuclear superpowers or alliances would therefore be not just an immense human calamity; it would be, in the strictest sense, a logical absurdity. **"**

To ensure that nuclear weapons prevented the recurrence of major war in Europe, it was vital that the system of nuclear deterrence was strong and credible; that nuclear-armed adversaries would not be tempted to exploit perceived vulnerabilities or test each others' resolve. For Quinlan and most of his senior counterparts in Europe and the US, nuclear burden-sharing and the pursuit of a common nuclear strategy and doctrine under the auspices of NATO was the most appropriate Western response. As long as NATO members, nuclear and non-nuclear, demonstrated to the Soviet Union that they would not accept defeat, and that they were prepared as a last resort to employ the full spectrum of their shared nuclear capabilities, from tactical to strategic, to protect their vital interests, major war between East and West would be prevented. This planning doctrine, which dates back to the early 1960s but to which Quinlan contributed significantly during his time in the MoD and HLG in the 1970s and 1980s, is known as 'flexible response'. It is worth detailing the doctrine's main elements here, as it crops up regularly in Quinlan's correspondence and is often the cause of confusion, even among defence experts. For Quinlan, the flexible-use doctrine, as set out in paragraph six of his Ebenhausen paper 'NATO Nuclear Deterrence Concepts', relied on projecting the West's readiness to use its weapons. The power of the West's own strategic armoury was so vast that aggression could be undertaken only if Soviet leaders believed that the West would at some point accept defeat without using all this power. NATO deterrence therefore sought to make it as difficult as possible for the Soviets to form such a belief, or dare to act on it.

Flexibility was the doctrine's second main principle. Possession of a full spectrum of options leading right up to the strategic level was believed to be essential to the credibility of the Western nuclear deterrent. It was a minimum-force concept, under which NATO sought to have available a set of response options from which to choose for dealing with the particular circumstances and form of any aggression. This did not assume first nuclear use; neither did it assume a graded ladder of pre-determined automatic escalation; on the contrary, it was supposed to offer flexibility. The rationale for flexible response ran as follows: the prospect of strategic nuclear response by NATO to levels of potential Soviet attack much below the strategic level lacked credibility and so could not reliably deter. NATO non-nuclear forces could not however be counted on to defeat all such lower levels of aggression, since they could have been overwhelmed either by Warsaw Pact non-nuclear (including chemical-weapon) strength, which many people judged to exceed NATO's in some key areas, or by Warsaw Pact non-strategic nuclear forces. Flexible response sought to close this gap in capability between NATO strategic nuclear capability and NATO non-nuclear capability.

Theatre nuclear forces (TNF or intermediate-range nuclear weapons) were needed for deterring Soviet military attack from starting at any level, to give evident and credible options for resisting levels of aggression (conventional or nuclear) too high for non-nuclear resistance to meet but not high enough to warrant strategic nuclear action. The aim of using TNF, if deterrence failed, was to reverse the initial Soviet calculation of the comparative advantage of aggression – to persuade the aggressor that the likely benefits of continuing were outweighed by the likely costs and risks, above all by the risk that the weight of military effort needed to pursue military success would reach the point at which NATO might respond with a major strategic strike.

Quinlan was convinced of the logic of flexible response, and the most compelling elements of his ideas on nuclear deterrence centre on NATO doctrine rather than on the rationale for or benefits of the UK's independent nuclear deterrent. The UK's nuclear forces were assigned to NATO to fulfil NATO roles, but the UK also established (and continues to retain) the operational independence of its strategic nuclear deterrent. Quinlan viewed the UK national deterrent as secondary to that of the Alliance; as performing a support role that added to the overall strength of the NATO deterrent. It is important to understand this aspect of Quinlan's deterrence thinking, as he did not share the view, popular in some circles in the British establishment, that the UK nuclear deterrent serves a symbolic role in maintaining British strategic and political independence and prestige. In Quinlan's mind, the UK deterrent served a very limited and specific strategic and political purpose: to provide a 'second centre of decision'. He explained this rationale in the 1980 White Paper *The Future of the United Kingdom's Nuclear Deterrent*, which he wrote when he was director of policy planning at the MoD:[3]

> **“** While the United Kingdom has every confidence in the American strategic guarantee, it is possible that at some time in the future, under circumstances that were different from those prevailing now, a Soviet leadership might calculate … that it could risk or threaten a nuclear attack on Europe without involving the strategic forces of the United States. If the Soviets were ever tempted to make such a horrendous miscalculation, the existence of an immensely powerful nuclear force (Britain's) would be an enormous complicating factor and a powerful argument for Soviet caution. **”**

Although Quinlan's belief in flexible response drew criticism on both sides of the Atlantic, his exposition of nuclear deterrence appealed to senior defence officials in the US, who found his arguments had a logical consistency that was lacking in US discussions on nuclear issues. Walter Slocombe, who was deputy under secretary of defense for policy from 1979–81 and served with Quinlan on the HLG, features prominently in Quinlan's files of correspondence, as the two men shared their thoughts on nuclear strategy and doctrine and exchanged papers that they had both written on the subject. An early letter from Slocombe to Quinlan, dated 24 September 1981 (after Quinlan had moved from the MoD to the Treasury) provides some insight into why these two defence officials saw eye-to-eye:[4]

> **❝** Your remarks to the York conference are eloquent. By chance, I had to talk to a Presbyterian Sunday School on 'The Nuclear Balance and Why We Need It' the day after I got your letter and I found your talk … extremely useful. It is perhaps one of the penalties of the allegedly more sophisticated and certainly more abstract discussion of nuclear weapons in the US that there is a real dearth of serious material on these fundamental issues. I am particularly stuck by the importance of confronting people with the problem of avoiding all large-scale war, not just nuclear war – and the terrible costs of failure to defend ourselves. Building on the introduction I received in the talk I gave (which referred to Hiroshima), I tried to introduce what I wanted to say by observing that the Second World War left us two awful legacies – the image of what nuclear weapons could do and, equally frightening, the memory of what a rampant totalitarianism meant for the nations and peoples on whom it turned its power. The problem is to continue to avoid both. **❞**

Subsequently, Slocombe regularly drew on Quinlan's arguments in his speeches. In fact, he joked in one of his letters that a speech he delivered to the Conference of the American Society of International Law in April 1982 was a 'clear infringement of

[Quinlan's] common law copyright'. This would not have troubled Quinlan in the slightest, as his move to the Treasury and the intensification of the nuclear debate in the UK meant he could no longer be seen to publicly engage on nuclear issues; allowing others to use his arguments and present them as their own was the easiest way for him to continue to influence deterrence debates. His voice comes through loud and clear in significant portions of Slocombe's speech:[5]

    " Whether or not we would have been better off over the years since 1945 had nuclear weapons never been invented, the question is academic. They cannot be disinvented. Nor, I suggest, can they be effectively – or perhaps even safely – abolished short of a transformation of international society that has no plausible chance of happening. Our task rather is to devise a system for living in peace and freedom while ensuring that these weapons are never used to attack or to coerce. The very complexity of posing the task is two-fold – not merely avoiding war, but avoiding it without giving up things almost equally as valuable as life itself – highlights a fundamental, but, on reflection, an obvious point: The complex horror of nuclear weapons has no simple solution. The scale of the horror makes it more, not less, important that we think clearly and realistically about how to prevent it.

    The system of deterrence amounts to saying to the Soviets that if they attack us we will resist: we will go on resisting until they stop or our strength fails: and our strength will not fail until we have inflicted on their society, their military power, and their political regime such great destruction that – however vast the losses to us and to the rest of the world – they will be worse off at the end than if they had never started. Indeed, they will have produced by their aggression the destruction of the very system they have invested so much in building and protecting.

Deterrence means getting that message across and getting it across so clearly that it is both remembered and believed to the point compelling restraint whatever the temptation – even provocation – they may feel; whatever opportunity – even danger – they may sense. **"**

Deterrence stability

Quinlan did not share the concerns of those who argued that nuclear deterrence was precarious and unreliable, at the mercy of decision-makers and uncontrollable superpower ambitions. On the contrary, nuclear deterrence had 'wide tolerance margins' because the consequences of confrontation were so high; it made even the most powerful states risk-averse, inducing caution in them and their non-nuclear allies. Nuclear deterrence was therefore an inherently stable condition. He argued that as East–West relations became less adversarial, nuclear weapons should be retained and that the goal should be to achieve stability at lower numbers. He made this point in an interview he gave to Scilla Elworthy, director of Oxford Research Group (ORG), in January 1988 as part of a study ORG was conducting on the nuclear beliefs of different groups of decision-makers:[6]

" I believe we're in a very stable condition now. We can probably make it marginally more stable, 99.95 can become 99.97. ... Though I find it very difficult, certainly in a timescale that's remotely relevant to policy now, to reach a condition in which nuclear weapons aren't there at all and don't play any part in the structure of the world so to speak, the structure of world organisation, I do think we can move to a situation where one doesn't talk of threat. In a piece coming out in May I've [argued] we have to have some of these things to make sure [warfare] stays safely cancelled out … I think we could organise an entirely stable and in a sense quiet military stand-off, which is what we're about, what we're trying to do at levels much lower than they're at now. **"**

He rejected what he saw as sensationalist, scare-mongering ideas of anti-nuclear groups who argued that deterrence was dangerous. For him, concerns about misperception and irrational decisions leading to nuclear confrontation were overblown, and signalled a lack of understanding of East–West deterrence dynamics:[7]

" While no human enterprise can be wholly free of the possibility of major glitches, I think we do pretty well. I think we will not have done well if all that communication about where our limits of tolerance lie had to be communicated in a crisis. We really need to have done all that communicating beforehand. On the whole I think we probably have. The Iron Curtain may be nasty but at least it is clear and I think it is very well understood that military acts which cross that – just to take one example – lead you into an utterly new game; and that's just a simple example, one would no doubt be facing a more complicated situation, but most of the communication of what is of vital interest has to be done beforehand. Now you can fairly argue that if despite all that we get into a crisis kind of mess, of which I think the likelihood is very low, some of that communication by definition will have failed to do its job. But given that both sides now have an utterly overwhelming interest in making sure we don't blow ourselves up (because we have the power to), I would be quite sanguine of how the essentials of communication would operate. No doubt there could be all sorts of glitches of one kind or another, the machine wouldn't work on the day, or the chap whose job it was to work it hadn't done his refresher course because he had flu six months ago or that sort of thing. But the system is I think quite well exercised, certainly within NATO. **"**

Later in the same interview, he went even further, explaining that even outside of the East–West context, in which communication was well-established, the likelihood that a 'loony' rogue leader would emerge on the international scene and provoke a nuclear crisis was so remote it was not worth worrying about:[8]

" [Nuclear deterrence] doesn't require that much rationality. It doesn't have to be a very sophisticated calculation on their side. It's pretty clear you can get blown up if you get it wrong. And the other thing is the rather general observation that we can't conduct human life at all unless we make sane minimal assumptions about rationality on the part of the people we're dealing with. You simply can't conduct life if you assume the total maniac. If you assume that if I go out and cross that road, some lunatic is going to mow me down with a machinegun, it's not mathematically impossible, but I just can't conduct life that way; and provided the risks are not very high, there isn't any option but to run all this business again on some minimal assumption of rationality … I doubt whether even Hitler would have gone blithely ahead and blown us all up. **"**

Not everyone shared Quinlan's faith in deterrence stability or his optimistic assessment of the low prospects of escalation if tactical nuclear weapons were used in a war-fighting role. When the nuclear debate in the UK heated up in the early 1980s, defence commentators voiced their concerns about British and NATO nuclear doctrine and the risks of miscommunication or misperception leading to a nuclear crisis. John Keegan, who was a journalist at the *Daily Telegraph*, made his views clear in a speech he gave to the Oxford University Strategic Studies Group, All Souls College, on 27 January 1981:[9]

> 66 It seems generally accepted that the gravest danger of an outbreak [of nuclear war] will derive from a misperception of the significance of responses to events with which a superpower will have no choice but to deal – threat to oil supplies, for example, or insurrection in satellites … Am I being too naïve in suggesting that what we really need for a secure world is an imaginative effort to … create some sort of [international] situation room in which the velocities of crisis could be brought back under control by the mutual evaluation of common intelligence reports and the exposition of the intended, rather than perceived, significance of governmental responses? A very senior Whitehall policymaker,[10] who was kind enough to give me an afternoon – no crisis that day – while I was preparing this paper told me that I am being naïve; that such a situation room would instantly become a clearing house of information retailed by the has-beens and nearly men whom the best and brightest would dump there. 'There would be nothing to do most of the time, so you wouldn't get the good people to go', he said. And I can see that. But I can also see that if we don't find some way of explaining ourselves across the nuclear

frontier a crisis is going to come which even the good people won't be able to steer by hand and the hotline, when misunderstandings will proliferate, menaces accumulate, and men desperate for some response to events will start to catch events on the wing and try to match them with the pictures in the drill book. Once that starts to happen, it cannot be long before a head of government finds himself with the word 'first' ringing in his ears and his hand on the oven door. And then it won't only be the cat which will get roasted. **"**

Similar questions over deterrence stability, which were attracting attention on both sides of the Atlantic, also troubled Jon Connell at the *Sunday Times*. He read – and found convincing – Paul Bracken's scholarly thesis on the risks of misperception leading to pre-emptive strike, and recommended Quinlan read his book.[11] Quinlan took his advice and after reading his arguments, sent Connell his response in a letter dated 18 April 1984. The letter, while acknowledging the seriousness and worthiness of the topic, amounted to a rejection of what he viewed as Bracken's overblown risk assessment:[12]

" I promised to read Paul Bracken's book, and I have now done so, albeit less continuously and reflectively than I should have liked. My general impression is that it is (for reasons I'll illustrate in a moment) overplayed; but the subject is a real and serious one which he is right in saying needs more attention – we (the West) probably do need to design the total system more consciously and positively for stability. The US [has] been working afresh in that direction since PD 59[13] and before; I'm no longer sufficiently up with the detail to have useful specific opinions on what more they could or should be doing.

Here are some reasons – very assorted, and in no special order – why I think Bracken overdoes things:

a) He constantly cites – seems almost obsessed by – the August 1914 analogy. Michael Howard has written well on this, and on its deficiencies. For example, the whole national mood in the relevant countries is quite unlike the jingoist bellicosity of those days; there is nothing now like the military instability resulting from the risks then of being left behind in the mobilisation race; there is nothing like the political instability resulting from the decay of old conglomerate states (consider the clarity of the Iron Curtain); and there was in 1914 no collective popular or governmental sense of the enormity of major war, let alone of nuclear war.

b) There seems to be an assumption that if a many-times repeated event like a DC10 flight has a substantial probability sooner or later of producing an unexpected calamity, an extremely rare or unlikely event (like getting into a major East–West conventional conflict) also has a substantial probability of producing an unexpected calamity if or when it does happen. The two situations are quite different in statistical logic.

c) The analysis largely neglects the real-life political context…

d) There seems a general assumption that nuclear conflict would be a matter of struggle for classical victory, conducted moreover in terms of very-short-notice decisions resting on finely-tuned assessments of (for example) damage, surviving forces and the like. This is unreal, to my mind.

e) There is a good deal of appeal to what Khrushchev said about pre-emption. Quite apart from the facts that Khrushchev was discarded as an adventurer, that the Russians and everyone else have had twenty years plus Cuba and other crises to learn from since then, and that what Russians say cannot simply be taken at face value, we should remember that Khrushchev had a force numerically hugely inferior and itself highly vulnerable to a US first strike. It would not be wholly surprising if he had indeed (for 'use or lose' reasons) been pre-emptively-minded. But things are very different now.

In short, apocalyptic inferences about the situation would be as inappropriate as complacent ones. **"**

Nuclear use

While he clearly believed in the stability of nuclear deterrence and its war-prevention role, Quinlan was not squeamish about discussions on nuclear use. In his view, it was illogical to argue that nuclear deterrence would work (and could be morally justified) only on condition that the weapons would never be used. As a last resort, if deterrence failed (an unlikely scenario, in his view, but still an important one to consider and prepare for) nuclear use might be necessary and justified to stop or limit an attack on the UK or its allies by a country he described as 'having objectives and political organisation which is deeply different from ours, with very considerable forces'. In other words, the limited use of nuclear weapons could serve a war-termination role if deterrence failed.

Due to restrictions associated with the Official Secrets Act, Quinlan was unable to publicly discuss targeting except in the broadest possible terms, but that did not stop him addressing the issue of how nuclear weapons might be employed in a war-termination strategy. Even during the time he was not officially employed at the MoD, Quinlan's expertise on this

subject was very much in demand among deterrence thinkers on both sides of the Atlantic and in Europe. In 1985, the
German nuclear expert, Uwe Nerlich, from the Stiftung
Wissenschaft und Politik (SWP) in Ebenhausen, FRG, invited
Quinlan to participate in a nuclear strategy project, a major
part of which would be 'to define what constitutes a range of
politically sensible employment options as distinct from retaliatory uses [of NATO nuclear weapons]'.[14] He wanted Quinlan
to develop what he regarded as justifiable options for nuclear
use in response to conventional military attack. He added that
he could think of 'few, if any [other people] who could do that
paper'. Quinlan declined the invitation, explaining that 'the
task of assessing what sorts of targets would achieve the best
blend of maximum damage to the Soviet State with minimum
havoc to civilians really calls for detailed assessments in which
I have no direct expertise; and what I happen to know of other
people's ideas on the matter mostly came to me some years ago
in very highly classified contexts'.[15] However, Quinlan's text
on NATO nuclear deterrence concepts, which he had contributed to an earlier SWP project and used in a speech he gave at
the Royal College of Defence Studies (RCDS) in 1982, is quite
illuminating on the subject of potential NATO use of theatre
nuclear forces in a war termination role:[16]

> ❝ NATO recognises the theoretical possibility of using TNF
> in a purely demonstrative role – over the sea, perhaps, or
> in open country – with no direct effect on Warsaw Pact
> operations or capabilities. In the main, however, NATO
> has judged that the aim of dissuading the Warsaw Pact
> from continued aggression would have to be sought
> through action which had substantial military effect,
> even though that effect would be only a means to the
> political end and could not in itself be finally conclusive.

The concept is that NATO's nuclear action should try to compel Soviet leaders to address fresh and dangerous decisions, and to weigh the consequences. Nuclear action which Soviet Leaders could readily choose to ignore militarily – which left them, for example, free to continue all their successful operations unchecked – might not compel this crucial re-appraisal.

We need to consider what sort of fresh decisions NATO TNF action might seek to force upon an aggressor. In principle the bigger the new step required by a decision to continue aggression, the more obviously dangerous it would be and therefore the better chance that the aggressor would prefer not to take it. From this standpoint, the ideal role of NATO action would be to deprive him of the military ability to continue aggression in its initial form, so that if he wished to continue he would have to raise the level of conflict sharply, with all the attendant risks. In some settings this 'ideal' option might be available; but in others – such as major land/ air conflict in Europe – achieving it could not prudently be counted on, as NATO's own extensive studies clearly showed a good many years ago. The reasons why that is so include the great size of Soviet forces; their possession of large TNF of their own; the nearness of their homeland resources for sustaining or resuming operations; and the likelihood of heavy damage to NATO's own territory. In such circumstances NATO could not sensibly expect its TNF to change a losing military situation into a winning one. The maximum realistic option for the military effect of TNF would then be something like imposing a substantial setback or delay, rather than tactical defeat, upon Warsaw Pact operations at the existing level. But NATO's capability must be clearly adequate to achieve at least something of that order – with anything less we risk leaving a hole in our deterrence.

What all this means in terms of military capability (weapons and delivery systems and deployment) is that NATO needs to have assured means – that is, means able both to survive before launch and to penetrate after it – of putting down some nuclear firepower reasonably promptly and accurately, in a controlled manner and on a modest but significant scale, in any broad theatre of operations – including support areas – where it may plausibly find itself resisting attack on its vital interests at a level which non-nuclear force could not be sure of repelling. But that firepower need not, and in many areas in practice cannot, be capable of fundamentally reversing the course of operations; and nowhere can it be capable of removing entirely the enemy's power to hurt us further if he chooses to accept the risks to himself of doing so. **"**

Although Quinlan was sensitive to the moral dilemmas of nuclear use, he did not accept the arguments of those who drew a distinction between nuclear deterrence and nuclear use. He was asked for his thoughts on this subject during his 1988 interview with Elworthy, to which he replied: 'I don't understand the distinction [that some people draw between deterrence and defence]. It's a bit like the distinction between deterrence and war-fighting. It always strikes me as stripped down, fundamentally bogus.'[17] He went on to explain the reasons he believed this to be the case:[18]

" Weapons deter by their capability for use when the chips are down and if they have no possibility of use then they can't deter. If deterrence fails, as it were at the first level, if the Russians look us in the eye and march, then the weapons are there to be used to defend us and in the nuclear age, to defend us not by disarming the foe, as in past times, but by persuading him that he has miscalculated the risk and our resolve; in that sense nuclear weapons would be for defence. They can't provide a physical guarantee that we cannot be annihilated. They would be there for use and a use which was directed to ending conflict before we had lost things we regarded as vital ... for example, if [the Soviets] overrun Germany and France, we have ourselves suffered a colossal and I would think an almost decisive defeat – and therefore it seems to me entirely possible to entertain the possibility (given that you would entertain the possibility of using nuclear weapons at all, and a lot of people wouldn't buy that) of for example the use of British tactical weapons in the course of the battle in Germany. I wouldn't rule that out; an awful decision to have to take, as all these decisions are; one might decide on the day that 'not tonight Josephine' was the right answer. 🙶🙶

Quinlan's belief in the potential war-fighting roles of sub-strategic nuclear weapons hinged on his conviction that nuclear use would not automatically lead to escalation and all out nuclear war. He explained this in a private, confidential letter to John Roper, MP in 1983, which he had sent him in preparation for a speech the latter was due to make to the House of Commons in response to a Green Paper on nuclear deterrence.[19] He made two important points: firstly that NATO strategy was not based on the early use of nuclear weapons, but 'as the FRG habitually puts it: on use as late as possible, as early as necessary'; and secondly although 'no one supposes that limiting nuclear war is an easy or safe concept, or that nuclear weapons can win the war for NATO in terms of military capability', Quinlan and NATO decision-makers believe that 'escalation is not a certainty' and that 'sensible policy can maximise the chance of avoiding or arresting it'. Once started, therefore, Quinlan believed a nuclear war could be stopped at a certain point; and that it would not necessarily escalate beyond the use of tactical or sub-strategic nuclear weapons. He elaborated on this point during his interview with Elworthy, explaining that, while no one knows what would happen in a nuclear conflict, because 'no-one has any experience of nuclear war', the likelihood was that a nuclear conflict would not automatically escalate in a 'physical process like a chemical chain reaction'. Such claims, often made by anti-nuclear activists, failed to take into account the fact that once subjected to a nuclear strike, the Russians would be forced to think twice about the objectives of their military aggression, and whether it was worth the immense physical cost of continuing to pursue them:[20]

> **"** If what we are faced with were to be the certainty of [all out nuclear war and obliteration] then clearly we hoist away at the white flag … But the hypothesis is nonsense in a sense because it ignores the fact that the Russians are people too, facing decisions and on the day, if for example they march and we face overwhelming conventional force we have to assess certainly the risk that the use of nuclear weapons will carry us up all the way but also the effect upon them and on what they think. That seems to me to be at least an option. It seems to me it must be the case that they will have embarked upon this aggression on the assumption that we will not reply with all our armoury, the more armoury we reply with the

higher the likelihood that they will say 'Oh God, we got it wrong … we didn't think it would be like this, let us stop'. **"**

Quinlan's views on the subject of nuclear use were widely shared within the MoD and Cabinet Office, the NATO HLG, and among senior US defence officials. But Lynn Davis, an American defence expert who worked both in government and academia and was involved in the HLG, appears to have resisted his intellectual spell, and was always willing to push Quinlan to address the weak points in his case, or at least to acknowledge the full implications of his particular exposition of nuclear strategy. Perhaps because of this, Quinlan appears to have considered Davis his intellectual equal. Her comments on the article he wrote on deterrence, sent to him in a letter dated 29 February 1984, show the contribution she was able to make to his work thanks to her experience in academia and her astute, probing questions. His article set out his thoughts on why under certain conditions (such as the invasion of Western Europe by the USSR) the use of nuclear weapons in a war-termination role could be strategically appropriate and morally justified. As the letter shows, Davis was fascinated by his ideas, but was also keen for him to explore them in more depth, and urged him to tackle more openly and in more detail the thorny issues of strategy, targeting and escalation:[21]

" I find the part [in the article you wrote] on 'The Morality of Possible Use' the most interesting. This is because it is clearly the most controversial as well as the issue which has received the least attention.

… You say that 'in this new situation, a nuclear super-power or alliance attacking another can rationally do so only on a judgement that the other will at some point give way without using his full strength'. Do you mean judgement about giving way? Could political leaders really ever come to that judgement? It seems to me that political leaders will be required to come to a different judgement: that there is no acceptable alternative to the use nuclear weapons with this as the objective: to force the other side to desist from his aggression. Political leaders could indeed come to that judgement without being able to say with confidence that the other side will be prepared to give way. If this is the case, then what political and military leaders will need to decide is whether and how to seek the objective – to force the other side to desist from the use of force, short of all out nuclear war. They would not have to judge that the aggressor will in fact give way.

You mention the criteria of indiscriminate and disproportionate damage. I have read many different arguments on this subject. Can you be any more specific as to what criteria we should use? Obviously, desisting short of all out nuclear war is a necessary condition, but is it sufficient? Is demonstrative use what you have in mind? If not, you might say what would be required both to lead to a change in the policies of the other side and to meet the criteria of discriminate and proportionate damage. More specifically, what difference will it make what weapons are used, what targets are selected, and what scale of attack is undertaken? I think I know your answers but your reader will wonder about all these issues.

You challenge the argument that any use of nuclear weapons will lead with high likelihood to general holocaust. Isn't it the case that such statements are often made with the purpose of serving deterrence – to try to raise the risks of all-out nuclear war. Would you have political leaders say anything else? If so, what? A separate question is whether political leaders can afford in the West to admit publicly that a nuclear war could be limited? Look at what happened to Reagan and Haig. I think you should address these questions and note that the reason we hear the argument that nuclear war will escalate is in part because we thought it served deterrence and was necessary domestically. I also think the statements reflected a healthy, and appropriate, skepticism as to what the prospects for nuclear escalation would actually be.

In your argument on the potential use of nuclear weapons, aren't you assuming that one side (our side) would see the need to pursue our goals through the use of nuclear weapons – but that the other side would rather give up his original goals than respond or escalate through the use of nuclear weapons? That is certainly possible and the arguments you use are plausible. But don't you need to admit that this is what you are positing would have to happen?

Additional evidence for your argument that pressures will exist in the direction of desisting from further conflict is the degree of caution that nuclear weapons by their existence have introduced into international politics since 1945. But these pressures really go against what most people seem intuitively to believe. And certainly against what the military can be expected to recommend. I think you ought to address these beliefs, why they exist, and how one might go about changing them. For success in what you are advocating will depend on political and military leaders relying on your arguments, not on their intuitive beliefs.

> Finally, you state … that 'if weapons cannot be used they cannot deter'. I think what you mean is that if the weapons will not be used they cannot deter. They could still deter as long as they have the capability to be used and uncertainties existed as to whether they would be used. **"**

Quinlan replied in a letter dated 12 March 1984 that: 'on substance, I recognise the force of all your comments'.[22] He could see the places in his text where he needed to 'say more' or express himself 'more clearly or exactly'. However, he decided not to elaborate because he and Davis had arranged to meet in the not too distant future and he preferred to respond more fully to her critique in person.

No-first-use debates

Quinlan believed no-first-use proposals were dangerous, and that they could undermine deterrence stability. In his view, in the East–West context, deterrence would only be stable as long as it was credible. Once credibility begins to unravel, deterrence could fail. Stability therefore depended on the allies resisting the temptation to adopt no-first-use pledges – as long as they were able to do this, 'current stability [would have] very large tolerance margins'.[23] As Freedman explained in an article he sent Quinlan when the no-first-use debate was gaining momentum, Freedman arrived at the same conclusion concerning the misguided nature of no-first-use – although, as he explained in his letter, he had arrived at that conclusion for different reasons. Whereas Quinlan argued no-first-use was unwise because deterrence is dependent on a credible threat of nuclear use to prevent conventional and nuclear war, Freedman argued that a no-first-use doctrine lacks strategic credibility because 'war is so indeterminate that no firm predictions can be made as to its likely course' and 'therefore no established limitations, even if acceptable and desirable to both sides, can be guaranteed to hold'.[24]

The no-first-use issue became an important focus of Quinlan's attention during the period 1982–84, when it was hotly debated in parliament. It was during that time that Quinlan provided the politician Lord Mark Birdwood with persuasive arguments against no-first-use proposals for a speech the latter gave in the House of Lords on 21 March 1984. The fact Quinlan was corresponding with Lord Birdwood while he was PUS at the Department of Employment, and when his official obligations as a civil servant placed particularly strong restrictions on his freedom to engage in the public nuclear debate (due to intense politicisation of the nuclear issue), is an indication of his concern over no-first-use debates, which appealed to a public that was increasingly anxious about nuclear confrontation. In a letter Lord Birdwood wrote to Quinlan two days after he had made his speech to the Lords, he enthused that:[25]

> ❝ Without your in-put I would have had precious little to say, so I will always be in your debt. I am returning the two papers you lent me and you will see from Hansard which I also enclose that I lifted a whopping chunk of 'No-first-use' in the middle of my speech. I hope you don't mind the mutilation in red of the section I used but it is still readable.
>
> Three of the other speakers in the debate were clearly certifiable but, as you hoped, Michael Stewart [the Labour politician who served as Foreign Secretary under Prime Minister Harold Wilson] gave a quite excellent presentation; rational, balanced, vigorous; he has got a very attractive intellect. I was only disappointed that

the reports on the radio didn't lift any quotations from what he had to say, homing in, instead, on several of the more emotive phraseology that I had included. The Fifth Estate can behave very like a jackdaw sometimes. 🙶

The speech itself, which he gave on 21 March 1984, comprised a rousing defense of deterrence, which, though at times more colourful than Quinlan's own very careful and precise prose, clearly owes more to him than simply the 'whopping chunk' on no-first-use that Lord Birdwood referred to in his letter:[26]

> My Lords, the noble Lord who initiated this debate[27] is to be commended for his sincerity. The whole debate is founded on sincerity, and the question which it begs is founded on delusion. That little contribution I can make I hope will introduce reality.
>
> Unpalatable though it may be, the reality of deterrence … is that holding and maintaining in balance numbers of nuclear warheads is not unstable. The truth of the matter is that this situation is inherently stable and that the existence of numbers of these weapons available to both super powers is at the heart of this stability. Of course, no sane person can morally defend this satanic arsenal.[28] There is nothing honourable about the bomb. But Pandora's box is open; we cannot close it. The thermonuclear genie is out of the bottle and we cannot put it back in.
>
> … I wanted to achieve two things by taking part in today's debate. The first was to emphasise this belief of mine that for a variety of reasons nuclear deterrence when mutually practised is stable now and getting more stable. [The second was to demolish the arguments of disarmament advocates] … But the one-sided disarmer

comes in two strengths. The real vintage stuff supposes
that the conscience of ideologically antagonistic nations is
somehow alerted by sacrificial self-denial. This is simply
rubbish. I do not think that it is particularly dangerous
rubbish but it is rubbish. A far more insidious, subtle and
better argued case comes from those parties in the shape
of the no-first-use concept. It is persuasive, honourable
and does not ask for NATO to throw down its arms and
it is very, very dangerous. I propose to demolish it.

Like all nuclear jargon, no-first-use needs a little
explaining. It is that a firm undertaking should be given
that the West, and the East for that matter should in
no circumstances whatever be the first to use nuclear
weapons. This proposition has often been urged by the
Soviet Union, though its military tactical doctrine and
training actually stress pre-emptive action. It is a theme
which has been vigorously taken up by some Western
commentators. The first article in this month's *Scientific
America* is an elegantly argued case in point. I am not
talking about first strike, which is the idea of a massive
pre-emptive operation. That is not a NATO option and
could never be.

Another misconception is that NATO has a policy of
first use. That is not so. NATO has a policy of not accepting the conquest of any of its homelands. The scale and
the nature of the armouries, as I said a little earlier, are
such that both sides now dispose of effectively boundless physical force. This fact changes fundamentally the
significance of any military operations between them. It
sets quite new and intellectually very difficult problems.

Classically, the professional military aim in major war
has been to deprive the adversary of effective capability
for further action, but this has become an unattain-

able aim. The only possible purpose of the defender's operations at any level – conventional as well as nuclear – must now be to induce the aggressor to desist by placing plainly and credibly before him the prospect that further aggression will be met, not by surrender but by resistance at a level which will sooner or later cost the aggressor more than he can afford to pay. Given the two-way fact of boundless force, the aggressor could have embarked upon aggression only on an assessment that the defender was afraid to use his capability and would prefer to lose rather than do so. The longer and the more resolute the resistance, the more pressure on the aggressor to recognise that his initial calculation was mistaken and that for his own survival – which is ultimately just as much at risk as that of the defender – he must back off.

NATO clearly recognises this central idea, the aim of inducing an essentially political reappraisal, not pursuing the mirage of military victory as the centrepiece of its nuclear planning. The concept is without question an uncomfortable one, turning, as it fundamentally does, upon intention, judgment and resolve, rather than clear-cut physical force.

We have to recognise, however that no other concept of military resistance can be available. The risk of escalation is sometimes cited as a key argument against first use. It is inherent that escalation is always a possibility and never a certainty; but the risk bears upon both sides and both must reckon with it. That arises with any act of resistance at any level, since escalation begins with the first warlike act. If the existence of this risk is regarded as an overriding argument, it tells against any use of nuclear weapons, not just against first use, and indeed against any Western military resistance at all. The logical inference would be that the only rational policy, in the face of a nuclear capable potential aggressor, is pacifism and willingness to take all its consequences. The seduction of no-first-use is a notion of honour; the reality is that we are saying, 'Whatever you take, you keep'.

During the same period, when debate over the future of the UK national deterrent and its position within NATO was at its height, Quinlan also provided John Roper MP with assistance in preparing comments on a Green Paper[29] on nuclear policy, which was due to be debated in the House of Commons. The letter shows that among British defence officials as in the general debate, the issue of no-first-use invited controversy and conflicting interpretations. A letter from Quinlan to Roper, dated 5 January 1983, shows this very clearly:[30]

> **“** I promised, too long ago, to send you – on a private and Chatham House basis – some thoughts on the Green Paper. As you know, there is a great deal in it that I admire; I concentrate now essentially on points of disagreement or question. And as I undertook, I look at it simply as a defence professional; I am well aware that your answer to several of my comments might recall that it is a political document which has, legitimately, to be addressed to several audiences and to do a job of salesmanship and attention-getting.
>
> The comments are in the Annex herewith. I haven't wasted space on arguing *Trident*; if I were to do so, I would concentrate on the question of what practical alternative there is in the long term once one accepts – as by implication you do – that Britain should not decide to get out of the independent business.

I offer a few other bits of paper, on the same Chatham House basis – a note on No-first-use; notes on how much is enough for UK strategic capability (relevant to paragraph 2 above), and on whether such a capability can be credible; a copy of a talk at Ampleforth which is now my main piece on the ethical side; and a copy of a talk at St George's House.

You mentioned to me that in his comments to you Arthur [Hockaday] had repeated his assertion that 'we are in a de facto no-first-use situation today'. Let me explain my difficulty with this. It has a beguilingly simple present-indicative air. But it is of course highly compressed shorthand for something far more complex, conditional and predictive. Unpacked, I take it to be saying something like this: 'With present force level and deployments and present tactical concepts, whatever kind or level of non-nuclear (including chemical) aggression the Warsaw Pact undertook, and however profound the nature and significance of any defeat this aggression seemed about to inflict upon NATO, NATO would under no circumstances use its nuclear weapons'. This seems to me an extraordinarily confident assertion to make; and I do not believe it is well-founded.

I am sending a copy of this letter to Arthur so that he may if necessary correct my unpacking; but I am not burdening him with all the attachments. **"**

One of the interesting revelations in this letter is the disagreement between Hockaday and Quinlan on the issue of no-first-use. Hockaday was not prepared to accept that the UK or NATO would ever be first to use nuclear weapons in a conflict, whatever the circumstances, even though its official doctrine did not rule out the possibility in the interests of shoring up deterrence credibility. Quinlan was deeply unhappy with this position of bluff, which he regarded as being at odds with NATO strategy. He referred to the no-first-use concept as 'fuzzy-minded rubbish' – a phrase Hockaday appears to have found quite amusing, as the following extract from his letter of 4 January 1983 reveals:[31]

> **"** I believe that popular support for nuclear deterrence could more easily be mobilised: (a) if nuclear deterrence was viewed in an overall East–West context of total deterrence rather than in a nationalistic context which torpedoes at a stroke our support for non-proliferation; (b) if more emphasis was placed on the proposition that nuclear weapons are vitally necessary, but at the same time valid only as deterrents to the use of nuclear weapons by others; (c) if consequently it were brought out that we are in a de facto 'no-first-use' situation but will remain so only as long as there is a balance; (d) if we heard from the Americans less rhetoric about the need for new systems to 'restore superiority' (in the 1960s it was recognised that despite American numerical superiority the Russians had strategic parity, so what has the Russian counter-programme achieved except to foster in the United States hallucinations of vulnerability to total first strike?) and rather more emphasis upon the search for a first step which hopefully would be reciprocated but even if unreciprocated would not endanger security but would put the political onus where it belongs. I thought the Pope [John Paul II] got it about right in his New Year Message.[32]
>
> I had better comment at this point on the passage in your lecture which in effect calls into question propositions (b) and (c) above. This is where you ask why, if first

use is incredible because of its irrationality, second use should be any more credible when it is equally irrational. This is a fair question in logic; but empirically I think you underestimate the difference in enormity between taking the first step of irrationality and proceeding from the first to the second step. Experience shows, especially in modern wars involving whole nations with Governments subject to popular pressures, that once the Rubicon is crossed rationality soon flies out of the window. We have seen this in demands for total victory and unconditional surrender; but perhaps a more directly relevant example is the strategic bombing campaign against Germany, which was not a very rational way of using military resources in terms of damage to the German war effort but which was primarily seen as the only way for a time open to us of hitting Germans in response to their raids on Rotterdam, Coventry, London etc.

A good deal of the above constitutes indirect comment on your [RCDS] lecture, but I must also refer to a few passages in which I feel that you are unfairly getting at my old chief [Lord Carver]. In paragraph 20 you say:

'The line is that NATO first use cannot be a rational option; that we should therefore formally renounce the possibility; and that we should build up our non-nuclear forces in a way that makes it unnecessary. Some eminent names have espoused all this. It is nevertheless fuzzy-minded rubbish'. In actual fact it is only the second of those three propositions that is fuzzy-minded rubbish, for the reasons which you set out; and it is very interesting that, although you and I both winced at hearing Mike Carver advocate a 'no-first-use' declaration when he addressed the IISS, he made no mention of it in his book *A Policy for Peace.* 🔊

Hockaday ended his letter with:[33]

> **"** P.S. Since writing the above I have seen the summary in
> *The Tablet* of Mike Carver's talk to CCADD[34] in November,
> which I missed because I was abroad. I note that, while he
> did not specifically propose a 'no-first-use' declaration,
> he did indicate that he would see certain advantages in
> one. I cannot therefore exempt him completely from the
> charge of talking fuzzy-minded rubbish in this area! **"**

Hunting down the 'fuzzy-minded rubbish' that was being used
to support no-first-use arguments occupied much of Quinlan's
time in the 1980s. He was often blunt in the feedback he gave
to journalists and television producers who covered the issue,
determined that the public debate should not be dominated by
what he saw as the illogical but emotionally appealing rejec-
tions of nuclear use. This comes across very strongly in the
letters he wrote to Jon Connell at the *Sunday Times*, in response
to his call for a change in UK and NATO nuclear doctrine.
A letter dated 13 February 1986 picks Connell's argument to
pieces in typically frank and concise style:[35]

> **"** As you probably expect, the largest area where I
> disagree with you concerns the question whether and
> how nuclear weapons are usable. I do not for a moment
> suppose that I shall budge you on this; but I enclose
> another private piece from a few years back to illustrate
> further my own approach. In the terms of that piece, I
> regard you and Carver as Ptolemaics,[36] trying to think
> about nuclear weapons in a wholly outdated framework
> of analysis. Part of your difficulty, I submit, is that if you
> were right you would have proved too much, because
> you are left without any coherent theory at all for the

use of nuclear weapons, even in retaliation. There has to be some concept of possible use otherwise deterrence cannot work; what exactly, in your thinking, is that concept? The generalised label 'retaliation' won't do; you have to think through what exactly is the nature and purpose of the use. If you've no answer, you have no deterrence; if you have an answer, you then have to explain (and I think you'll find you can't) precisely why this answer makes sense exclusively of retaliatory use and cannot possibly do so of first use. I do not say all this as a debating rejoinder; it lies absolutely at the heart of the matter, and unless you think it through you are simply not facing the issues.

The other major difficulty in your approach, in my view, is that having – as you suggest – decoupled nuclear weapons entirely from non-nuclear ones (including C[hemical] W[eapons]?) you then fail to produce any credible theory of how NATO – given the facts of geography, politics, social system and so on – is going to be confident of dealing successfully with a determined Soviet attack. You indicate an assortment of directions of possible improvement in NATO's non-nuclear posture; but you do not assess in the round what real chance these have of redressing the balance, especially in face of the likelihood of Soviet counter-improvements. What, in your concept, is to happen if NATO loses at the conventional level? And given that your answer (presumably 'Accept defeat') is proclaimed in advance by your whole analysis, what does this do to deterrence? **"**

Quinlan's correspondence shows that no-first-use remained a controversial issue as the Cold War drew to a close: while Quinlan continued to believe in the strategic soundness of not ruling out first use and avoiding a strategy of bluff, other senior officials continued to question his unbending rejection of no-first-use pledges. A letter to Quinlan from Andrew Edwards (undersecretary at the Treasury) dated 20 June 1988, argued:[37]

> 66 You may be right that deterrence which is pure bluff in the sense that the nuclear country is absolutely certain that in no circumstances whatsoever would it use its weapons, is neither practically nor morally sustainable. What is perhaps no less important, however, is that deterrence which comes extremely close to this position – which even approaches asymptotically[38] to it – may I think be eminently sustainable and indeed desirable.
>
> The leaders of a nuclear country may be unable to imagine any realistic set of circumstances in which they would consider nuclear use justified but remain nevertheless fractionally less than one hundred per cent certain that such circumstances could never arise. In such circumstances a policy of retaining deterrent forces could still, I believe, be morally sustainable.
>
> Interestingly, I think that your own conception of a fairer world in which the great nations regard war as having 'no place among policy options' may itself approach asymptotically to the position which you initially wish to describe as morally untenable?
>
> I think also that one must not under-emphasise the extent to which a decision to use nuclear weapons raises moral issues going far beyond a decision to possess the weapons. 99

Academics who challenged Quinlan's position were equally forceful, most of them, like Edwards, offering critiques based on ethical rather than strategic objections. Professor Michael Kaiser, of St Anthony's College, Oxford, was one of the exceptions, believing that the UK and NATO's refusal to adopt a no-first-use pledge was strategically risky. In his letter to Quinlan, dated 7 June 1984, he makes this point very powerfully, based on discussions he had had with Soviet strategists in Moscow:[39]

❝ Thank you very much for your letter of 2 June, the enclosed exchange of correspondence with Walter Stein and the revision of your note on the ethics of nuclear deterrence. Let me first comment on your observation on my earlier letter to you.

By chance the day before your letter came John Williamson telephoned me about an economics article and, learning of my recent trip to Moscow, solicited an article for *The Tablet*. It is due to the discussions at the Anglo-Soviet Round Table last month that I am clearer in my mind on what I wrote to you.

The first day of the Round Table was as always (I've attended six of the eight annual sessions) devoted to security matters and the Soviet side (which included General K. Mikhaylov who had participated in most of SALT and START) made an expected call for 'no-first-use'. [Conservative Party politician and author] Alun Chalfont believed (and so stated) that the Soviet view compounded two meanings – a preemptive strike as well as the no use before the other side. The anxiety which the Soviet leadership has about the short (10 minute) warning time of a Europe-deployed *Pershing* compounds with that of a preemptive strike and it seemed to be far more weighty than that about no-first-use strictly defined. One of the other Soviet participants claimed that the USSR had withdrawn its missiles from Cuba because it realised how seriously the USA regarded the danger of a preemptive strike with a ten-minute or so warning time.

I was guilty in my letter to you, and in my thinking then, of confusing the two constraints. A solemn undertaking to renounce any preemptive strike would, in my assessment, at a stroke wipe out a major ground for Soviet suspicion. At the Moscow talks, Jim Eberle [former Commander-in-Chief Fleet and Director of the Royal Institute of International Affairs] did all he could to explain that no NATO scenario exists which requires it to deliver a preemptive strike – but, such is the profundity of Soviet fear of the West (of which I emphasise here my understanding), that these and similar averments count for nothing.

What I went on to say in my letter to you coincides with the acceptance in your commentary that 'we can never take it for certain, whatever is said beforehand, that losers will accept non-nuclear defeat in obedience to treaties or promises'. The USSR would know that victory by conventional arms in the NATO area could evoke the nuclear response it fears, but to still its fears over the short warning time, NATO must renounce a trip-wire use. The latter is so close to preemptive strike that NATO must disown that strategy. As the discussion on 23 November and the public debate makes clear, the corollary is a credible conventional defence at the Warsaw Pact/NATO interface. If, as you say 'the notion of a purely conventional deterrent system in face of nuclear force is unreal' so is the non-deployment of nuclear force in unequal conventional struggle.

Your Annex B on 'No-first-use' accepts that Western leaders facing conventional defeat would have to consider whether to disregard a 'peacetime promise' and argues as a secondary factor that that defeat might be rendered more likely by massing conventional forces in a way that would be vulnerable if first use was anticipated.

The scenarios you reject … are those which the USSR cannot bring itself to believe impossible. NATO's declaration of no-first-use would be the confidence-building measure the USSR most seeks. Walter Stein, in his letter to you recognises that 'no counterforce capability … could avoid being perceived as a first-strike threat by the other side'. I would say that a no-first-use promise is the best guarantee that the adversary could expect to disabuse him of the threat of a preemptive strike. You criticise in your reply to him that he throws all counterforce in with a preemptive strike: but if our military adversaries in the Kremlin are doing just that, is not our first practical duty to disabuse them? Such an action is morally good to the extent that it reduces the risk of morally-abhorrent nuclear conflict. **"**

Continuity and change in Quinlan's deterrence thinking

Quinlan's basic assumptions about the strategic rationale for nuclear weapons remained constant during the Cold War, with very little change from the time he served as policy director at the MoD to his promotion to MoD PUS as the Cold War drew to a close. This continuity is evident in his correspondence, and was clearly expressed in the interview he gave to Elworthy in January 1988, during which he explained his conviction that nuclear deterrence was vital for major war-prevention and was becoming part of a global conflict-prevention system:[40]

❝ It seems to me substantially agreed by both major powers that war is simply not on, there's a very elaborate and over-expensive apparatus to brandish the reasons why it's not on, but it seems to me that – and this would be almost in my vision of what the future will be – that we want to move to a situation where though there will always be adversary relations of one kind or another, people just accept that war is cancelled out, it simply is not an option for the conduct of business ... I think they both have to recognise that because there is an infinity of power on both sides, war has become in the strictest sense an absurdity. War is a contest of strength. If strength is infinite on both sides – and that is what nuclear weapons and the means of delivery on both sides have done – a contest to find out who is stronger is patently logical nonsense. It seems to me that the model we have gone a long way towards, which we now need to entrench for the rest of time ... Now alas that's not going to stop other countries which haven't reached this *reductio ad absurdum* situation from fighting; the evidence is painfully around us in many parts of the globe. But certainly as between major powers that seems to me where we are and where we had better get used to enjoy being because there isn't anywhere else to go. **❞**

As the end of the Cold War drew closer, Quinlan made the same point in his official capacity as PUS during an address to the Soviet General Staff in Moscow in November 1990.[41] His speech was considered a singular moment in Cold War history. Here was Quinlan, a key architect of NATO Cold War nuclear doctrine, explaining the West's philosophical justification of nuclear deterrence directly to the adversary, which would have seemed unthinkable just a few years earlier. His key objective was to communicate as clearly as possible that nuclear weapons should not be renounced below a threshold of 'significant numbers of each side at both the strategic and non-strategic levels', because even in a world in which relations between East and West had warmed, nuclear weapons still had a vital war-prevention role to play. They could not be relinquished because they could not be disinvented and they had made war between the major powers – including conventional war – an absurdity. He stressed that nuclear weapons should therefore remain 'a prudent and positive element in the construction of a dependable international system for preserving peace'. In the same speech, he restated his fundamental belief in the stability of nuclear deterrence; the non-automaticity of escalation (which he described as not a 'set of mindless spasms but a sequence of human choices which are not predetermined'); and in the unreliability of no-first-use pledges.

Despite his consistent and enduring belief in nuclear deterrence, Quinlan was not resistant to new thinking on the subject, and when he retired from the civil service in 1992, he threw himself into nuclear debates with gusto. By this time, ideas about the future of nuclear deterrence had begun to shift among academics, many of whom argued that the economic and political costs of retaining nuclear weapons could no longer be as easily justified as they could when the UK and NATO faced a powerful Soviet adversary. Increasingly, Quinlan's ideas about deterrence stability were challenged by those who had previously grudgingly accepted nuclear deterrence as a necessary evil. In the post-Soviet multipolar world, nuclear dynamics might be much more difficult to manage: communication between multiple, competing powers would be more challenging; horizontal proliferation pressures could be stronger; new nuclear-armed states might emerge that had neither the infrastructure nor the experience to handle nuclear weapons safely and securely. In this new international context, nuclear weapons lost some of the aura they had developed during the Cold War. But despite this, Quinlan remained convinced that nuclear weapons could play an important war-preventing role in the post-Cold War world. The changes at the international level meant it was more important than ever that they were carefully handled, that numbers were reduced to minimum levels, and that lessons drawing on four decades of nuclear experience were learned by the nuclear-weapons states (and where appropriate, shared with nuclear newcomers).

At King's College, Quinlan was in regular contact with Lawrence Freedman and Beatrice Heuser, scholars who shared his interest and expertise in nuclear strategy. Quinlan's correspondence during this period sheds an interesting light on the extent to which the new strategic environment and his immersion in academia were challenging his assumptions about nuclear deterrence, and the extent to which he accepted new thinking. A letter from Heuser, dated 3 October 1992, gives some insights into the types of intellectual challenges he faced, as the chief threat faced by the West seemed to be shifting from the USSR to the Soviet nuclear-inheritor states, and to regionally ambitious 'rogue states', such as Iraq under Saddam Hussein.[42] At the time of writing there were a number of new international non-proliferation priorities: the First Gulf War had recently been fought and had uncovered an advanced nuclear-weapons programme in Iraq; international negotiations were under way between the US and Ukraine to encourage the latter to peacefully relinquish the nuclear weapons it had inherited from the USSR; and strong suspicions existed over North Korea's nuclear activities, as well as those of India and Pakistan, which seemed to be edging to the brink of a nuclear arms race. In all, it appeared that the post-Cold War international environment would not be a benign one, but at the same time, it was unclear how nuclear strategy and doctrine developed during the Cold War could be adapted to serve in a war-prevention or termination role in the new international context. Ideally, NATO nuclear forces could be used by the strong states to deter and check the ambitions of rogue states, but how would this be achieved? Heuser had serious doubts about the transferability of stable deterrence to the new world order, and she expressed these concerns in her letter to Quinlan:[43]

> **"** Do you remember my unsubstantiated claim over lunch that I felt the classic and the new nuclear strategies, in existing side by side (just as the threats will exist side by side for a while) undermined each other? The classic one being defined here as Quinlanism – a Whitehall term I have joyfully adopted! – up to 1990. The new one is the *dissuasion du fort au faible* (deterrence by strong states of weak states) – I prefer that term to North–South, as the *faible* may well be the Ukraine or [Belarus] one day, unless you equate South with Third World (at the IISS conference in Zurich last year Lawry [Freedman] pointed out that that would make South Korea part of the North and North Korea part of the South…). My argument revolves around first use threats. The critical part of Quinlanism that applies here (woe is me if I get this wrong) is the NATO threat to use nuclear weapons regardless of whether the enemy has used them or is about to use them (and, one might say, the threat would have to be made even if he did not possess weapons of mass destruction if his conventional superiority could not – and might still not in future – be balanced by Western conventional forces alone). The use, and I have learnt my lesson, would aim at stopping the war, and would be made in defence of vital interests … The

threat of use by us would be credible because we would be close to desperate when resorting to it as our vital interests are at stake ... This is presumably why Britain insisted in the inclusion in the London Declaration[44] of July 1990 that there should be 'no circumstances in which nuclear retaliation in response to military action' could be 'discounted', even if their use was more remote (your doing?).

In a potential second Gulf War scenario where the other side has nuclear weapons, our vital interests would be decidedly at stake, and nuclear escalation would be most likely to harm us. If confronted with a nuclear power whose vital interests would then be at stake unless we talk about pure battlefield use which I know we both disapprove of totally (and thank goodness so does [Pierre Bérégovoy, the French Socialist leader who served as prime minister of France under François Mitterrand from 1992–93]). As we agreed – you after some hesitation – it would presumably be in Western interests to communicate a no-first-use pledge in such circumstances in order to limit the level of conflict and prevent the other side from becoming desperate. Our 'no circumstances discounted' declaration negates that directly.

Admittedly, there are other conceivable scenarios for *'dissuasion du fort au faible'*, e.g. the direct nuclear threat by Libya against Italy. The absence of common land frontiers is important though, because such a threat could never form part of an escalating conventional war unless one imagines barbaric hordes crossing the Med with thousands of boats. So again, classical Quinlanism doesn't seem to apply.

I suppose an armed clash between Kazakh and Turkish forces or Ukrainian and German forces in the context of military conflict in and around the area between them would present a hybrid problem of deterrence by the strong of the weak – and these eastern nuclear powers might not be that weak either if they somehow hang on to their ICBMs and manage to target them. But you see the drift of my argument.

As you note yourself in your most recent (and once again thoroughly stimulating) paper, the resulting logic by which our nuclear arsenals should now be restructured is still not quite recognisable – and again I would argue that this is the case because of the co-existence of a (hopefully) moribund and potential nascent threat and the conflicting strategies required to meet them. Thus the deployment of nuclear-capable aircraft on the territory of threatened friends/ allies may visibly reinforce our commitment and may also be needed for Third World madmen who have persuaded themselves that unseen submarines don't exist. Yet the deployment of nuclear-capable aircraft might also invite first strikes or otherwise unduly increase tensions in a conflict (Gulf War against nuclear Iraq) which we are trying to keep limited. Against a Russia-turned-Nazi Germany, we would undoubtedly need something like the ASLP;[45] against Saddam we probably would not because we might not want to introduce nuclear-capable aircraft into the war in the first place because of the concerns just mentioned. Even a nuclear-capable *Mantis* [unmanned combat aircraft] would be a problem, as you would not be able to use it even in its conventional mission in a Gulf War against a nuclear Iraq because news of its launch might lead an enemy to panic – a good old crisis (in)stability problem. 🗭

Quinlan's reply was dated 7 October 1992 – just a few days after Heuser's letter. In typical Quinlan style, he sent her a concise list of comments in response to her questions, which hint at a certain resistance to her line of reasoning, and a belief that nuclear weapons could indeed play a stabilising role in a world where the primary threats are ambitious rogue states, such as Iraq. He urged her not to generalise too much about rogue threats, as each needed to be addressed on a case-by-case basis. There is a sense in his letters of the period that he accepted that NATO nuclear deterrence had become a more complex affair in the post-Cold War world, and that there was a lot of work to be done on how to make it operate effectively:[46]

> I mildly dislike the WMD term – while accepting that it has become established as a term of art with a fairly exact ambit – because the weapons are not capable *only* of 'mass destruction', a term which in ordinary usage carries condemnatory implications (indiscriminateness etc.).
>
> No, I didn't specifically influence the terms of the London Declaration; but I would have agreed with the point, and I suppose some of my disciples (if such a species exists) might have had proper doctrine in mind from being ground down by me.
>
> I suspect that you may be compartmentalising or classifying Gulf-War-type episodes a little too neatly. In such situations, I would not necessarily be keen to advertise or admit that I did not regard the issues at stake as being of the first importance to me; and partly for that reason I would not assume automatically that a no-first-use declaration would be in my interest – it might, as I conceded, but then again it might not; I would prefer to judge the matter case by case in all the circumstances of

the time and place. It would not necessarily be the case that the-West/the-goodies had clear effective superiority at the non-nuclear level; even in the Gulf War case, had Saddam gone straight on to seize the huge Saudi bases *Desert Storm* would have been very difficult to mount. And – separate point – it might not be good for deterrence, even intra-war, to offer the other side assurance that the conflict would be limited. In the Gulf case the reasons for re-affirming (as Britain and France effectively did) the Negative Security Assurance had, I believe, more to do with reassuring their own publics about morality than with signalling to the adversary.

I think your madmen not believing in submarines are a shade far-fetched. But the more important point in my argument is that the US will have plenty of capability, visible and invisible (including serious carrier-based capability, which we and France cannot hope to match) and I doubt the reality/importance of 'second-centre' requirements in counter-Saddam scenarios. I would pay a bit for ASLP on such a ticket, but nowhere near what it is likely to cost – the premium is likely to be disproportionate (in terms of opportunity cost elsewhere in the defence programme) to the particular risk insured against. But there is of course more to talk about here. **"**

The morality of nuclear deterrence

At the height of the debates over the logic of nuclear deterrence in the 1980s, Quinlan and a number of fellow senior establishment figures (who shared his Catholic faith and interest in defence ethics) aired their concerns about the morality of nuclear weapons in a series of elite debating forums. The work of some of these forums, such as the Pembroke Group and the Council on Christian Approaches to Defence and Disarmament

(CCADD), feature prominently in Quinlan's letters and shed an interesting light on the tensions between the public role and individual conscience of those responsible for nuclear policy-making.

The Pembroke Group, in particular, played a key role in establishment debates over deterrence ethics. It was set up in the early 1980s by the then chaplain of HMS *Pembroke*, and consisted of serving and retired civil servants and military officers. The fact that Quinlan was a founding and active member of the group is hardly surprising, given the group's focus on the complex intellectual debates over 'just deterrence'. The group's members were united by the fact that they were all Christians who shared current or past responsibility for maintaining British defence, but most importantly, they all agreed that nuclear deterrence was required to maintain peace and stability in the East–West context and that 'however unwelcome in ideal terms such a situation may be and however important it may be to maintain a constant aim of moving eventually to a different one, the Christian conscience cannot reasonably be required to reject it out of hand'.[47] Beyond this fundamental pro-deterrence posture, members of the group differed over how deterrence should be analysed and understood in terms of Christian theology and traditions of Just War, and which aspects of the moral debate should 'most usefully be stressed by pro-deterrence Christians in dialogue with others'.[48] Among the group's prominent members (some of whom exchanged letters with Quinlan over a period of many years), were Hugh Beach (a retired army general, author and adviser on defence issues, and much later, a leading disarmament advocate), John Blelloch (Quinlan's successor in nuclear policy planning at the MoD), Leonard Cheshire (a retired group captain in the RAF, author and leading philanthropist), David Fisher (an MoD policy planning official who left to study deterrence ethics at Oxford University), David Goodall (a career diplomat who was attached to the Cabinet Office in the early 1980s); Richard Harris (dean of King's College, London), and Arthur Hockaday (director-general of the Commonwealth War Graves Commission).[49] In common with Quinlan, members of the Pembroke Group wanted to believe that the direct and indirect support they provided to the UK's nuclear infrastructure was morally defensible. They felt a burden of responsibility for the defence of the UK and its allies; were troubled by the ethical dilemmas raised by nuclear deterrence; and were passionately committed to their professional roles.

Reading through the letters, one is left in no doubt that Quinlan was deeply loyal to the British political and defence establishment and to his job as part of the nuclear policy elite, and that his contributions to debates on deterrence ethics need to be understood in this context. 'Let me admit' he explained in a letter to Sydney Bailey in 1979, 'I do not want to condemn the possession of nuclear weapons. That predisposition, I recognise, may well be motivated in a significant degree by my particular situation – it would unquestionably be directly awkward for me to find myself drive to a conviction that having [nuclear] weapons was ethically intolerable'.[50] A few years later in another letter to Bailey, Quinlan confirmed his main goal in debates over the morality of nuclear weapons, was to 'legitimise [nuclear] planning and possession', due to the key role he played in the British establishment.[51] This was a sensitive subject for Quinlan and the other members of the Pembroke Group, and one that at times put them in an awkward position among Catholics who were not part of the establishment, some of whom accused them of putting their career interests before their religious faith. This message is politely but firmly relayed in a letter from the Catholic philosopher Brian Wicker shortly after Quinlan retired from the MoD in 1992:[52]

❝ Are there not ethical demands which of their nature take precedence over any 'role' we may have been called to play? The usual way in which this tension is coped with in a pluralistic society is to say that these are matters of the individual's private moral stance – so that the difference between you and me on the morality of (say) nuclear deterrence is interpreted as a difference between our private views. I am sure you are right that the British civil service is rather good at making allowances for such individual moral scruples, by interpreting them as 'private'. It is a civilised and humane – perhaps an essentially pagan – way out of the difficulty. But it seems to me that a Catholic cannot be satisfied with this way of 'privatising' crucial problems. **❞**

Quinlan may have found this letter uncomfortable to read because he recognised that the moral case that he used to defend deterrence (though influential thanks to his powers of persuasion, his remarkable intellect and his tireless efforts to engage sceptics) was actually stretched rather thin, but unlike other members of the Pembroke Group, he never admitted this in public.[53] Moreover, he was conscious of the concerns expressed by some intellectuals that 'the Christian Establishment has been rather ready to acquiesce in or even promote the policies of whoever happens to be Caesar'.[54] Nevertheless, he still took comfort from the fact that the highest church authorities – including the pope and the archbishop of Canterbury – had accepted nuclear deterrence as morally legitimate and that relatively few senior figures in the Catholic hierarchy had spoken out against it. When a Catholic military officer confided in him about his own private qualms about nuclear deterrence policy, Quinlan used this point about church acquiescence to reassure him, adding that 'I do not at all suggest that that absolves the individual conscience from being concerned about the issue; but it is a reasonable and reassuring point which the individual is entitled to regard as a factor in his own appraisal'.[55]

Double effect

Quinlan was always at pains to point out that deterrence ethics should be understood within the broad context of international security. Because of this, reaching a decision on whether nuclear possession and use is morally licit depends on analysing circumstances that change over time – it is not a 'moral absolute'. This raises extremely complex questions that have no clear right or wrong answers; rather than asking whether the direct and immediate impact of nuclear use against an adversary is right or wrong, broader questions have to be taken into account. For example, could threatening an aggressive, nuclear-armed adversary with nuclear attack – or even resorting to limited nuclear use against that adversary – prevent an all-out war that could lead to appalling suffering, perhaps on the scale of the Second World War or worse? When confronted with an aggressive, nuclear-armed adversary, would the risks to the lives, welfare and freedoms of a state's inhabitants be proportionately greater if that state chose to disarm rather than to retain a credible nuclear deterrent? These types of questions probe the issue of whether, in certain circumstances, it can be right to do or threaten to do something that would normally be considered morally wrong, if the overall purpose (that is, the intended consequence) of the action is morally good. They also lead to parallel, even more complex ethical questions over where to draw the line in assessing whether an action is good or bad: how much 'collateral damage' (unintended civilian deaths) can be justified in certain circumstances? If the collateral damage is foreseen due to the nature of the weapons employed (unintended but inevitable), can it still be regarded as morally licit? In 'just war' theory, some (although certainly not all) moral philosophers argue that unintended civilian deaths can be deemed acceptable according to the principle of 'double effect'[56] – a principle that dominates Quinlan's letters on deterrence ethics.

Quinlan made his own position on double effect very clear in an exchange of letters with Sydney Bailey in 1981:[57]

> **❝** I do regard it as wrong (I think without qualification) to make non-combatants (leaving aside the problems of defining that term) the deliberate object of attack, in the sense of attack whose point is, and whose success depends upon, their killing. I believe however that their killing can be accepted if it is the incidental effect of attack directed to other and legitimate ends, provided that that incidental effect is both kept to the minimum feasible and not disproportionate to the legitimate effect sought. I suspect, from what you have said from time to time ... that you and I would differ in that you would, and I wouldn't, regard a certainty of 'incidental' killing as making an attack illegitimate whatever its proportionality. **❞**

This comment, sent in a letter from Quinlan to Bailey on 9 February 1981, triggered a volley of letters between the two men on the subject of double effect, and led Bailey to seek feedback from Quinlan on a paper he had written titled 'Christian Perspectives on Nuclear Weapons'. Quinlan read the paper and sent his response in a letter dated 5 May 1981:[58]

> **❝** The words used on this subject [of double effect] are important, and difficult. As I read your passage, you

proceeded on the basis that 'foreseen' = 'not accidental' = 'intended'; and that the double effect concept does not legitimate the acceptance of intrinsically evil results if they qualify for this threefold description of whatever may be their proportionality to other (good) results of the action in question. I confess to not having looked up Aquinas or subsequent authorities on the subject, but this is not quite my understanding of double effect. As I view it … the key distinction is between what is purposed ('willed') and what is, albeit perhaps clearly and certainly foreseen, not purposed. Just for example, if I wade in the river in order to get to the other side, getting my feet wet is foreseen but not purposed; what I purpose is to be on the other side, and getting my feet wet is unavoidable in the circumstances but not of the essence. By contrast, if I wade in the river for the fun of paddling, getting my feet wet must be viewed as purposed – it is then of the essence … I realise that it may not always be easy to judge instantly what is of the essence and what is not.

[In] the nuclear case … in my terms, the collateral damage – by radiation or otherwise – is not willed or purposed … It is not of the essence to my purpose of (say) destroying the Soviet Northern Fleet base that I kill a lot of citizens of Murmansk, though I fear I certainly shall. It follows, on my theory, that I am entitled to weigh consequences like their death and wider fall-out in the scales of proportionality (in which I do not for a moment question, they must weigh heavily) and not to regard them as automatically and absolutely ruling my action out of court (as I take your argument to claim) on Just War principles … Does this, I wonder, shed any light or in any way close the gap between us?"

As the letters reveal, the abstract nature of the topic leant itself to the use of analogies, which are often disturbing, as in Bailey's reply to Quinlan, dated 13 May 1981:[59]

> **“** I was grateful for your letter of 5 May which I shall of course treat as personal. I think on reflection that I have not done justice to your position, but I admit that I have always found the principle of discrimination more easy to apply than that of proportion because the latter is, to some extent, subjective, and also because of the possibility of escalation (which, admittedly, may be the moral responsibility of an adversary unless he was left with no rational alternative). Your analogy about crossing the river is not very exact (and probably not intended to be) because there can be no moral objection to wet feet. A more exact analogy would be if an old person had collapsed on a dark road at night: what undesirable effect would it be right to risk in order to prevent an on-coming vehicle from crushing the body? Would I risk one death to save one life? Probably yes, if the first were only a risk and the second a virtual certainty. Two deaths? Perhaps. Three? Probably no. If there were time, I might consider the relative values of the various lives at stake, though I admit this becomes hazardous.
>
> What if the on-coming vehicle was a fire engine and to stop it would have unforeseeable consequences? It might be going to extinguish a fire on the clothes of an IRA terrorist who had ignited himself while committing a criminal act, or the fire might be at a maternity hospital. This would be a difficult predicament.
>
> Or consider a situation which I and my colleagues faced in Asia during the war at a time of famine. As there was not enough food for all, we had, in effect, to

decide who should live and who should die. After much thought, we concluded (contrary to our instincts) that the children and the elderly must die so as to have a chance of saving those who would grow next year's crops and bear the next generation of children. This decision was especially poignant as the young and the old seemed to be relatively 'innocent', whereas among those we tried to save were a small but-unidentifiable number of profiteers and hoarders. The deaths of the young and the old were unintended by us, but were inevitable, in the same sense as some innocent deaths from nuclear radiation would be.

Perhaps my second example about the fire engine is not helpful as it is too speculative. My first and third cases are better, especially the first, as one would probably resolve the matter (as you do over the indirect effects of nuclear weapons) by applying the principle of proportion in some rough way – though in the third case not simply counting the number of those who would live and those who would die, but attaching more importance to some lives than others, though not more value.

My first case seems to confirm your position. Although there is some number of deaths which would be too great just to save the one injured person: different people might draw the line at different places, but all would draw it somewhere. Other things being equal, the logical number is probably between one and two, though other things are not always equal.

The difficulty in nuclear war as I see it is this. Every scenario which I have seen (though you have seen many more) predicts more non-combatant casualties than combatants if account is taken of collateral damage, including local and global fallout, even in the case of limited nuclear attacks directed wholly against military targets.

Now I admit that this does not quite resolve the matter, because nuclear war would have so many unforeseeable consequences. So there is something left for us to discuss over lunch on 28 May, even if this exchange of letters has carried our discussion a stage further. I like to think that we do not part company even when we disagree, since we both understand very well the painful dilemmas which the other faces. **"**

After many letters back and forth, Quinlan eventually persuaded Bailey that it could be morally legitimate to conduct a nuclear strike that resulted in massive civilian casualties, depending on the circumstances. But Quinlan was not happy about the language that Bailey and others, such as Arthur Hockaday, employed to explain their acceptance of the double effect principle: that it may be right to do something intrinsically immoral, or even evil, in the pursuit of peace.[60] Quinlan saw this as a contradiction in terms, and moreover, as presentationally awkward in terms of persuading others of the moral underpinnings of nuclear deterrence. He made this clear in a letter to Hockaday, dated 19 February 1981. Hockaday had sent Quinlan an essay that he had written for CCADD on the ethics of deterrence, in which he had made the point that nuclear possession and use 'may contain an element of moral evil' but may be a morally acceptable price to pay if it was 'the most effective way of securing the twin objectives of preventing war and checking political aggression'. Quinlan responded:[61]

" As you know, I have basic conceptual difficulties about the whole shape and structure of your complex and subtle argument about intentions. My difficulties reflect,

I suspect, some fundamental differences in intellectual formation. I do not believe that good ends can justify bad means; nor do I believe in the possibility of situations in which we have no choice but to commit some kind of moral evil, in the sense of sin. **"**

Hockaday agreed in principle with Quinlan's point, but in a letter to Bailey (which he copied to Quinlan), he explained that in practice it did not stand up to scrutiny: civilian deaths, though an unintended side-effect of nuclear strike, would be inevitable and foreseen due to the nature of nuclear weapons, and therefore the principle of double effect, if strictly applied, could not provide a convincing moral defence of nuclear use.[62] He conveyed this argument directly to Quinlan in a subsequent letter, asserting that 'something which is not good, and may indeed be to a greater or lesser extent evil, may nevertheless be right'.[63] Quinlan, however, was not prepared to accept this language, which made him uncomfortable, as his letter of 24 May 1982 to Hockaday reveals:[64]

" [I use] 'morally legitimate' (or 'licit') as effectively equivalent to 'right'. I use the good/bad distinction less than you do partly, I think, because in all this it is right/wrong rather than good/evil that seems to me the immediately operative question; and partly also, perhaps, because I find in myself a vague reluctance to pin the specific label 'evil', in however qualified a sense, to an action which may be ([assumed]) in some circumstances not merely permissible but obligatory.

I fancy that we do not actually disagree about the relation between proportionality and discrimination. I regard the death of non-combatants as in itself an unqualified evil. But like other consequences, good and evil, of a given act, it then falls to be brought into the further – and in a logical sense I would say superior – calculation of proportionality, on double-effect lines. I would however go on to say (in accordance with my understanding of double effect) that this comparative calculation is legitimate only if the two sets of effects, good and evil, stand in genuinely parallel relationship, not if the evil effect is directly and essentially a necessary (therefore purposed) means to the achievement of the good effect. **"**

'Megadeaths' and morality

Outside of the Pembroke Group, debates over the ethics of deterrence were equally complex, but not always as sympathetic to Quinlan's establishment views or as easily deflected by his grasp of language and logic. In the person of Walter Stein, Quinlan met his match: a devout Catholic of equal intellect, an eye for detail and nuance, and a passion for the subject of deterrence ethics. The difference was that Stein bore no responsibility for defence policy and was very much on the opposite side of the morality debate to Quinlan: he was essentially a pacifist; an ardent critic of nuclear policy; and a leading expert on the moral illegitimacy of nuclear use. He and Quinlan engaged in a comprehensive analysis of the ethics of deterrence in 1983–84, writing some of the most painstakingly detailed and intellectually stimulating letters in Quinlan's files. In fact, some of Stein's individual letters ran to over 20 pages of small, single-spaced type, and combined would have amounted to a book-length manuscript. After they had chased each other in and out of every moral corner in the nuclear debate, Stein proposed to Quinlan that they find a publisher for their letters. This possibility was clearly important to him, partly because he had invested a huge amount of time and effort in their intellectual exchange, and partly because he felt the letters 'have more than private significance', in that people concerned with nuclear ethics (especially church leaders in England and Wales) were in danger of becoming 'too familiar with one side' of the debate (that is, Quinlan's).[65] Stein put the question of publication to Quinlan several times over a period of years, but Quinlan felt too constitutionally constrained to agree, and in any case could not foresee a suitable outlet for their exchange. However, Stein's extraordinary letters and his desire for them to be published were probably on Quinlan's mind for a long, long time, and may have been one of the reasons that Quinlan wanted his correspondence to be published after his death.

It is hard to do justice to the Quinlan–Stein exchange without publishing it in its entirety, and without including the two papers on which they based their debate, but unfortunately that is not possible here due to their length. Still, it is worth extracting some of their discussion of nuclear escalation risks and the ethical bearings of their assessments, as it was a subject they returned to again and again, and which seems more than any other issue to have underpinned Stein's rejection of the notion that a nuclear strike – even if it was counterforce rather than counter-city – could ever be morally licit. The following extract is taken from one of Stein's longest and most detailed letters, dated 15 April 1984:[66]

❝ The issue of escalation – which of course underpins the whole issue of strategic use – has two main aspects: the assessment of escalation risks and the ethical bearings of these assessments … Though I take your point about this not being a matter that can simply be left to the 'experts', the evidences of scientists and strategic analysts and practitioners in this matter are extraordinarily challenging, in very precise ways – not indeed as proposing 'certainty' but high probabilities. And when someone as prominently associated with 'limited nuclear war' policies as [US Secretary of Defense] Harold Brown ... had written: 'The odds are high, whether weapons were used against tactical or strategic targets, that control would be lost on both sides and the exchange would become unconstrained', this cannot be taken as less than an enormously weighty index of the state of the question ... the burden of proof [of whether escalation would occur following a nuclear strike] remains on those who assert that meaningful limitation is possible', and it cannot be said that your paper provides such proof. Indeed, though you dissent from the bishops' estimate of the escalation risks as 'high', you yourself, at one point, are led to characterise them as 'grave'. Your *Tablet* paper, moreover, observes that NATO policy is to maximise the possibility that an aggressor 'when met by a nuclear response' may 'back off rather than take the risks of going on' – 'while at the same time continuing to recognise that whatever we do it will remain no more than a possibility'. Whatever we might do then, that is. What we do, or do not, do now is quite another matter. And it cannot be easy to justify, here and now, the exposure to risks whose avoidance, in certain future contingencies, 'will remain no more than a possibility' – 'whatever we do'. (I do not see why such risks should not be described as 'high', or 'very high'.)

Beyond this matter of assessing escalation risks in themselves, there is, however, a crucial ethical point, relating to the argument's structure. The premise of your discussion is that escalatory risks can be morally relativised - that it 'cannot be rated an absolute difficulty' since 'it has to be weighed against the difficulties inherent in other positions'... Now, an escalating nuclear war, tending to loss of control, would not merely be a unique horror; it would be a unique moral horror. Who would be responsible for this horror; and when would this responsibility primarily have been incurred? In view of the escalation risks, 'whatever we do', the decisive moral responsibility can only be here and now: a catastrophe would be largely the consequence of our present choices. A plea that we had to weigh these choices against other possible consequences if nuclear deterrence were lacking would therefore not be morally admissible (in the way certain 'occasions of sin' may be accepted in order to achieve some proportionate good or prevention of evil). For the escalation risks of deterrence are at once (i) unique in their physical and moral enormity and (ii) deliberately irresponsible in their mode of acceptance. (The fact that 'no-one knows with certainty how politicians and soldiers will react in the unprecedented situations in question' and that, more generally, 'we do not know the answers with certainty' is an integral part of this irresponsibility). An acceptance of nuclear deterrence foresees - and may even make use of – the strongest possibility (at the other extreme of 'no more than a possibility' in the sense quoted above) of reciprocal loss of control: a game of escalatory 'chicken' – among unparalleled pressures of time, shock and uncertainty, and with critical vulnerabilities of command and control systems. If control were thus to be lost it would not be relevant to plead: this is not what we intended. In accepting the terms of the game, however reluctantly, and pursuing a course known to tend towards catastrophic loss of control in the circumstances envisaged, one has passed far beyond any mere 'occasion of sin': one is already in a state of conditional consent (parallel to, but not equatable with, the concept of 'conditional intention') to the evils built into the strategy as conditionally inescapable consequences of its adoption: one has already made the only decisive choices that one may ever be in a position to bring to bear in these matters. A strategy which implies that in certain circumstances this could, 'whatever we do', result in large-scale nuclear warfare, and quite possibly (in the words of the Pontifical Academy of Science, 1982) 'trigger major and irreversible ecological and genetic changes whose limits cannot be predicted', is here and now locked into a calamitous moral disorder.

All this holds quite apart from the recently discovered perils of a 'nuclear winter'. At the least, however, it must now be added that, among the matters 'we do not know with certainty' is the question of whether, and at what level of nuclear warfare, this consequence might ensue – stressing that, it appears, a quite restricted level of warfare could suffice to precipitate it. A strategy now known to be at least liable to such an outcome – ensuing from present choices, at a threshold we do not know with certainty – cannot avoid reckoning with this ultimate epiphany of transgressed limits.

These perspectives themselves preclude any attempted return to a moral justification of nuclear deterrence in terms of a just use of nuclear weapons. The factual risks and, especially, the structure of moral acceptances relating to these risks, leave no room for a moral purgation of 'strategic use'... Most critically, [this] includes the radical rejection of any idea of sanctioning 'limited nuclear war'; and so, with the utmost special urgency, any strategic doctrine or weapons system contemplating 'first use' (not merely, though of course including 'first strike'). The essential plea of your paper, that we must continually say Yes to the idea of some 'limited' version of nuclear war is precisely what is most centrally ruled out by [this moral position]. **"**

Quinlan replied to Stein on 31 May 1984. He accused him of falling into the trap of many deterrence sceptics – that is, a failure to address the consequences of unilaterally relinquishing nuclear weapons in face of the Soviet threat, which Quinlan regarded as the main path that Stein's argument was clearing. Quinlan explained that, given his past responsibility for nuclear policy and planning, his own moral reasoning was heavily conditioned by the real-life dilemmas confronting Western decision-makers, and by his desire to contribute to 'developing better moral understanding and direction *within* deterrence' rather than debating whether nuclear weapons, which in any case could not be disinvented, were morally licit. Nevertheless, he complimented Stein on his 'long and powerful letter':[67]

" [You] make an impressive case against regarding any use whatever of nuclear weapons as morally tolerable. It is at least as tellingly developed as (perhaps indeed more so than) any other I have ever read along these lines. I do not believe it is, even within its own confines and concepts, quite as watertight as you suppose, and I offer later in this letter assorted argument accordingly; but, within those, I think I would be tolerably ready to agree that your position might well be – to adopt the term I believe lawyers use of a preferred opinion in respect of an issue not seen as capable of formally conclusive resolution either way – 'the better view'. But the key reality is, in my judgement, that this issue cannot be handled in a compartmentalised way; and when it is set in a broader context, your position encounters much graver difficulty than you seem to admit.

[…] It seems to me illegitimate to assimilate accepting 'a tendency towards [which I take to mean a risk of] loss of control' to 'choosing to put oneself out of control', as [you do]. My position does not require or entail surrender of control … My concept of nuclear action does not in the least suppose or allow that decision-takers cease to be moral actors in the stress of war. [Your use of the phrase] 'deliberately irresponsible' … is a caricature. That leaders may forget their moral sense is certainly a risk, but not one that points to an absolute conclusion for all situations. There is a non-zero probability that a man who gets into a fight will lose his temper and kill his adversary; but moralists do not regard that as pointing to absolute prohibition of the right of forceful self-defence. At the same time, though, my position fully accepts that, come the event, decision-takers would have to weigh the escalation risk in their particular circumstances (which could vary very widely); and it might be their duty, on certain specific judgements, to accept the consequences of non-use rather than run that risk.

Can we really say of any temporal risk in this sort of context that it is absolutely to be eschewed irrespective both of probability and of alternatives? Consider an example. To lose one's life may be as conclusive and absolute a temporal disaster for the individual as for a community to undergo nuclear attack. To send my young daughter to the shops for a loaf of bread entails some risk – extremely low, but not zero – of this absolute disaster: of her being killed as she crosses the road. I accept that sort of risk for her because absolutely to reject it would be to stultify her life; there is, inescapably, an implicit comparison of alternatives and of their probabilities.

You speak of nuclear war as a unique horror, and a unique moral horror. The same might be said of global conquest by an atheistic totalitarianism possessed of super-power force and modern technology of repression. And my course is, in my judgement and that of many others, far less likely to lead to the former than yours is to the latter.

[…] I am astonished by your claim of 'a mass of powerful, detailed evidence' that the chances of avoiding catastrophic escalation are low. I am at a loss to know what 'evidence' could justify so strong an assertion across all conceivable scenarios ... I cannot help recalling that I have been a nuclear planner myself; and moreover that our understanding of nuclear warfare is a developing process. Much that would have been common supposition among planners in the 1950s would now be as commonly rejected by their successors. This real evolution of thinking and understanding as time passes is, by the way, one of the reasons why evaluation of the possibility of moral use of nuclear weapons cannot rest simply on observation of past practice, much of which has undoubtedly been of inadequate moral sensitivity. I repeat accordingly that there is no escape from the need to think hard on our own account, not just to rest on quotation (which in these untested matters can be found to sustain almost any opinion). There is indeed a general point here, going wider than just the escalation issue. Forty years is a short time in the intellectual history of any complex and difficult issue breaking the bounds of previous concepts and not easily refined by accumulating experience, as the whole development of (for example) Christian theology surely shows. We have to live with the knowledge of nuclear weapons for the rest of time; and even if the technological possibilities were static (which of course they are not) the development of thinking, especially moral thinking, about them must be expected to have a long way to go. You are entitled to look coldly and warily at what the history of plans and statements has actually been; but it would be strange to suppose, as your argument often by implication seems to, that this limited past period (which has itself seen much evolution of thought …) establishes the full content of the subject. The task I am particularly anxious to contribute to is one of developing better moral understanding and direction within deterrence – which would undoubtedly be likely to mean change in practical policies and planning – in this long perspective. **"**

Stein was not willing to accept Quinlan's 'practical morality' or his acceptance of what Stein regarded as a morally indefensible risk of nuclear escalation, potentially resulting in what Hockaday sometimes referred to as 'megadeaths' (a term Quinlan disliked). Stein referred to Quinlan's arguments over the moral legitimacy of nuclear use as a 'limitless overstretching of proportionality' to the extent that he feared 'something has gone wrong with our sense of proportion'. His discussion of the topic is striking – particularly his conclusion that nuclear planners must somehow have become numb to the horrors of nuclear war, from the moment of the initial explosion to the long-term impact of radioactive contamination. He refers to this process of numbing as the 'bitch-goddess of historical necessity', by deference to whom, when assessing the likely death-toll from weapons use, the nuclear planners 'are prepared to add a nought or two without all that much thought'.[68] In a letter of 24 April 1984 Stein expands on this disturbing point:[69]

“ On the level of quantitative judgement [of proportionality – i.e. how many civilian deaths are morally acceptable], there is the problem of the unavoidable imprecision characterising such judgements. But this does not mean that the matter is meaninglessly open. You yourself stress that collateral harm could run to 'very large numbers of deaths'; and suggest that, whilst 'almost everyone would agree that a hundred million non-combatant deaths would in any circumstances be disproportionate', an acceptable 'cross-over point between proportionate and disproportionate' along 'the immense spectrum between a hundred and a hundred million' might involve deaths to a number you do not spell out but which might be 'very large' – within the range of a spectrum that is certainly very large. One must also note your reference to the 'tens of millions of deaths' and 'immeasurable other loss and suffering' under tyrannies such as Hitler's or Stalin's: 'The price of defeating Hitler was enormous – many millions of lives, including a substantial propor-tion of non-combatants – yet most Christians would agree that it was not "disproportionate"'. I shall return to this reference presently. But it does not seem clear how far below the level of 'tens of millions' – or a hundred million – you would ultimately require your calculus of strategic proportion to be arrested (or indeed why this should not exceed the round number of 'a hundred million'). The [US] bishops seem on much safer ground – are bringing to bear a recognisably human scale – in denying 'that nuclear war can be engaged in with toler-able human and moral consequences' and specifically, declaring: 'It would be a perverted political or moral casuistry which tried to justify using a weapon which 'indirectly' or 'unintentionally' killed a million innocent people because they happened to live near a 'militarily significant target'.

The re-establishment of an authentic human scale is our era's most profound need. Not merely in matters of warfare – though most inescapably manifest in these – it is the cumulative radical erosion of such a scale that has brought mankind to the condition of which the Vatican Council said two decades ago: 'The whole human race faces a moment of supreme crisis in its advance towards maturity'. The American bishops have earned the exacting right to cite this pronouncement: they have made a start on translating it into concrete practical judgements, reversing the enormities of our age's limitless consequentialism and strategic permissiveness. They are calling a halt to the process D.M. MacKinnon, as far back as 1954, described as 'the bitch-goddess of historical necessity', breeding habits of mind which, 'where the number of human beings destroyed by a particular weapon is concerned', are prepared 'to add a nought or two without all that much thought'. Simply in repudiating such thought-forms the bishops' voice impinges with an intense prophetic authority. But they also get down to indicating the relevant human limits, underwritten by Christian tradition, with a suitably telling down-to-earthness.

Your own paper initially notes that nuclear weapons have not merely intensified the horrors of war in line with previous technological leaps but 'carried the potential of warfare past a boundary condition at which many previous concepts ceased to have meaning'. Accordingly, we have arrived at the 'reductio ad absurdum of war capability'. And yet you proceed to search for ways and means of transcending this 'boundary condition' – of reducing this absurdity to something less than absurd. It is hardly surprising that this leads you into self-cancelling perceptions both of this 'boundary condition' itself and of the associated crisis of moral limits.

Thus, against the bishops' central denial that nuclear war could be humanly and morally tolerable, your argument strives to reclaim nuclear war as a morally tolerable (or even morally necessary) option. Even in face of their specific denial that the 'indirect' or 'unintentional' killing of 'a million innocent people because they happened to live near a militarily significant target' could make moral sense, you would, in certain contexts, reaffirm a possible acceptance of such killings, in terms of 'proportion'. This specific implication of appeals to proportion is crucial – though your argument nowhere directly confronts it. Whilst it is the issue of escalation that measures the ultimate physical and moral nihilism of nuclear war, it is its *locally disproportionate harm to civilians* that already transgresses decisive traditional frontiers.

These frontiers had already been gravely breached in such raids as Cologne and Dresden – as well as, of course, the atomic raids on Japan. And it is vital not to allow the escalatory perspectives of nuclear war to diminish our sense of the gravity of such *localised* versions of the sanctity of non-combatant rights. The danger is not merely that such a blunted alertness might more easily accept the earlier stages of nuclear use (as well as accepting conventional violations, as in Vietnam) but that it might altogether disable the cutting-edge of 'discrimination' and misconceive – and so neutralise – the relevant 'proportionality' judgements.

Thus your argument starts by acknowledging that, even in defence against totalitarianism, only combatant forces may be 'directly' attacked. It then rightly stresses that the incidence of a measure of 'collateral' ('unintended' or 'indirect') harm to civilians need not transgress a morally valid discrimination', provided this harm is 'proportionate' to the actually intended effects. But in indicating the measure of such a proportionality, in the nuclear contexts envisaged, the argument hugely widens the focus: from *effects on the targeted areas, and associated collateral effects* to the *overall strategic effects of the war*. This is how the war against Hitler is brought into the argument – as a pointer to an acceptable 'price' of defeating a totalitarian opponent … The example is certainly relevant to any cost–benefit weighing of future possible conflicts. But as a measure of proportionate collateral harm to civilians in specific attacks on combatant targets, such an over-all focus can only befog the issue. The extreme quantitative elasticity of generalised 'collateral' harm thus implied (with only that highly indefinite 'cross-over point' somewhere below a hundred million non-combatant deaths defining its limits) perilously eludes the impact of discrimination imperatives. **"**

Quinlan's policy planning response to the moral dilemmas posed by nuclear deterrence was to engineer a subtle shift in UK nuclear strategy away from deliberate 'city-busting'. But this shift did not satisfy those who, like Stein, were suspicious that it equated to window-dressing; intended to appeal to deterrence sceptics who were troubled by the possibility of civilian megadeaths. Even critics who were not as convinced as Stein that limited nuclear use would lead to escalation wanted more information on targeting and firmer estimates of the impact on civilians of a nuclear strike. They felt that, without this information, they were unable to reach any firm conclusion on whether UK nuclear policy was morally licit. That Quinlan was constitutionally constrained from divulging these details was a source of frustration for some of his correspondents, including Brian Midgley of Aberdeen University. He had heard Quinlan speak on deterrence ethics at a private seminar, and had this to say in response:[70]

> **"** In your talk and in our conversation afterwards, you seemed to me to be trying to extract a controversial advantage from your unwillingness to argue from the actual nuclear policy and the actual system of preparation [for nuclear use]. You seemed to suppose that it would suffice to speak in general terms against a vague background of various theoretically possible states of affairs which do not actually obtain. **"**

Quinlan replied that he sympathised with Midgley's concern over the lack of public information, but that he was unable to offer specifics. His letter of 29 September 1980, in which he addresses the morality of the UK's targeting policy, makes this very clear:[71]

> **"** ... I am afraid I shall have to continue to seem obscure or shifty or both. I simply do not regard myself as free to add to or enlarge upon what the Government has officially said – which is very little indeed. Both the most recent and I believe by some margin the fullest statement is what is in the *Trident* Memorandum, particularly paragraph 12. I realise that you believe you know or can reliably deduce that our planning has been of a kind incompatible with [even a generous interpretation of] what could be morally legitimate. I cannot tell you whether in my view it has been, is or will be so.

You can observe that I continue to work in a job which involves me at the centre of these matters. I have to leave it to others to guess whether that reveals by implication something about the shaping of policy, or merely something about me. **"**

Midgley regarded Quinlan's response as an unacceptable evasion of the issue at stake, as he expressed in a letter dated 7 November 1980:[72]

" It is clear that, so long as you intend to remain in your present post, it is not practicable for you to enter into public disputation about the moral aspects of the Government's nuclear deterrence policy. Moreover, in view of the stance you adopt (against the background of your interpretation of the Official Secrets Act etc.), it seems to me that you are not really in a position to engage in a fully intelligible private and confidential discussion of these matters. If you seek to persuade the English hierarchy that you are right in thinking that the present policy is legitimate, without being able to tell them (say) whether your real argument is similar to that of A.L. Burns or similar to that of L.L. McReavy, you are more or less asking them to accept your own private moral theology on trust without their being able to check it for themselves. In your position, I should conclude that, unless and until I considered myself able to discuss matters more freely, I was not in a position to advise anybody outside the government service, even on a private and confidential basis. **"**

But even after Quinlan left his policy-planning position, he was still constrained by the Official Secrets Act, in its reviewed and tightened form. The resulting lack of transparency in his discussion of targeting thus remained an issue, which cropped up regularly in his correspondence throughout his career in the civil service. Brian Wicker, then principal of Fircroft College in Birmingham, found the transparency issue to be especially irksome, and suspected it masked a moral fudge over targeting. His letter dated 16 June 1987 puts this starkly:[73]

> " [...] There is one point on which I feel some further push ought to be made and this concerns public knowledge about nuclear targeting policies. I don't know what you think about this as a former MoD official but it seems to me that it is no longer necessary (in a world of ever increasing transparency) or justifiable for governments to hide their real purposes behind secrets concerning targeting when, as you say, that point is absolutely crucial to the public's ability to assess the ethical claims that are made on their behalf. It seems to me that history, especially recent history, teaches us not to trust governments always to do the ethically right thing, and as a tax payer I want to know whether British weapons are targeted on Moscow housewives or not. The recent defence White Paper makes it pretty clear that they are, even if not 'as such' or 'essentially'. Do you think there is ever likely to be a greater degree of openness about this matter? Is it not the case that the Russians know about it already? "

Quinlan replied on 3 August 1987 that:[74]

> " The matter of targeting is one that even now I can address only warily. I have a lot of sympathy for your basic point; but for assorted reasons I doubt whether governments, at least in this country, can realistically be expected to

go beyond saying what principles (positive or negative) guide or constrain their plans. This is of course not inconsistent with HMG saying rather more than it has done hitherto (paragraph 12 of the *Trident* memorandum of July 1980 is the [current exposition]). The Russians know what we *could* do, and that is (as I read it) what this year's White Paper, like previous ones, addresses. I have no reason to think that they know, separately from what they see of our capability, what we actually plan to do, which might of course cover a range of alternatives varying with circumstances. I recognise of course that this complicates moral evaluation on our own side. **"**

In this reply to Wicker, Quinlan was hinting at the fact UK deterrence has always been dependent on uncertainty; keeping the adversary guessing over whether an aggressive action on its part could prompt a nuclear response. Maintaining such uncertainty – which strategists insist is crucial to the credibility of the UK's nuclear posture – makes it strategically nonsensical for the government to be transparent about its targeting and intentions. Quinlan was therefore in a difficult position: he understood the need for openness to address questions of morality, but at the same time he was not only constrained by the constitution, he was also hemmed in by a doctrine of uncertainty which, for strategic reasons, prevented him from divulging the information on which moral assessments depended. No doubt, deep down, he was also uncomfortable about the genuine fudge at the heart of UK targeting strategy, because most militarily significant Soviet targets were located close to population centres in Moscow and elsewhere; and in 1979–80, senior MoD officials (including Quinlan himself) had secretly agreed that a figure of 10 million Soviet deaths was an acceptable (that is, proportionate) price to pay for UK independence.[75]

'In the soup': deterrence ethics and the US bishops

As is clear from the exchange between Quinlan and Stein, the US bishops became deeply concerned with deterrence ethics in the late 1970s and early 1980s. After three years of intense deliberations (which took place in an ad hoc committee that was set up by the church to consider the morality of nuclear weapons), they rejected all forms of nuclear use as unconditionally wrong. At the same time, however, they proclaimed that the temporary possession of nuclear weapons was morally acceptable, as long as nuclear-armed states sought to disarm over the longer term.[76] This position was set out in a pastoral letter, which was published in May 1983 and widely discussed among the Catholic hierarchy around the world. Quinlan followed the US bishops' debate with a mixture of surprise and alarm: surprise that the US bishops pinned themselves to an official position that he considered so plainly illogical that it landed them 'in the soup' intellectually; alarmed that, due to their influence on questions of morality, the US bishops could sway opinion across the Atlantic and potentially undermine UK and NATO deterrence. At the time, Quinlan corresponded frequently with Jesuit faculty members in the School of Foreign Service at Georgetown University, Washington DC. One prominent faculty member – a Catholic theologian named Father Francis (Frank) Winters – was especially closely involved in advising the US bishops, and it was through him in particular that Quinlan tried – but ultimately failed – to inject some of his famous Quinlan logic into the ethical deliberations of the US church hierarchy.

Quinlan had been uneasy about the ad hoc committee's first major interim report (released in November 1981), because it had denounced nuclear use as illegitimate except in the narrowest of circumstances – for example, as a demonstrative 'warning shot' against an unpopulated target. As far as he was concerned, this was strategic nonsense.[77] But as the US bishops' debate continued in 1982–83, it appeared to be taking a more radical turn – apparently influenced by the theological publications of US experts on moral theology, such as Winters, who cautioned that the bravura of the newly ensconced Reagan administration could lead to a riskier nuclear doctrine. In mid-1981, Winters had published a colourful article called 'The Bow or the Cloud',[78] which was filled with dramatic references to nuclear instability. He claimed that the US arms-control community had suddenly lost its nerve; it had a 'sense of the opening of an abyss', a 'dizzying glimpse of nuclear destruction lying just underneath the surface of international politics'. According to Winters, this was because the first 100 days of the Reagan administration had opened some people's eyes, for the first time, to 'the politics of assured destruction'. While Winters saw this as an opportunity for the US Catholic hierarchy to influence government policy towards greater unilateral nuclear restraint (short of unilateral nuclear disarmament), Quinlan saw things differently. He set out his concerns in a letter to Winters dated 17 March 1982.[79]

> ❝ […] perhaps I could elaborate a little on the difficulties I see in the concept of maintaining possession of nuclear weapons, but partnering this (in order to solve perceived ethical dilemmas) by a sincerely-meant renunciation of use in any circumstances. These difficulties are, at the ethical level, of two kinds, one conceptual and the other more concrete; and I then have a further difficulty about deterrent efficacy.
>
> My conceptual ethical difficulty is, in essence, that your position seeks to couple two components which I find extraordinarily hard to reconcile in any valid way. On the one hand you want to intend sincerely the abso-

lute renunciation of use; on the other you are very keen that this renunciation should not really be believed because if it is believed deterrence fails. How could you meet the argument that if you sincerely meant renunciation you should give up the weapons, and that the basis for keeping them could only be a desire deliberately to reduce the credibility of your renunciation, or to keep open the option (for which on your own ethical theory there could never be a legitimate basis) of withdrawing it, or both? I am not sure that there is a formal logical incompatibility between the two components if they could be taken purely in the abstract ([but as I argue below] they cannot be). But I do judge that Christian consciences generally would regard the juxtaposition as intolerably disingenuous; and that so strained a rationale for possession could not provide a stable foundation for the ethical acceptance of deterrence, especially over a long period. And you will know from my earlier piece that I believe there to be no realism in hopes that arms control is going to dissolve the nuclear dilemma in any near timescale.

My other ethical difficulty – which sharply heightens the first – concerns the matter of preparation. A deterrent stance is not just a combination between an inert inventory of hardware and a government declaratory policy; it involves a very large number of people, at many levels, in preparing to use the hardware – training, exercising, planning, supplying and so on. On your concept, all these people would be preparing (at the Government's direction) to help do something which the government had undertaken never to do. Quite aside from the intolerability of this to the individuals directly concerned (in itself a decisive objection, in my view) the whole process would amount to the expression of a lie on a massive scale – either the preparation would be bogus or the renunciation insincere. The nature, and indeed the positive intent, of one of them would inescapably be to mislead, by conveying an impression directly contrary to that purportedly given by the other.

I believe therefore that the stance you suggest is ethically unsustainable. Even if it were tolerable for the Christian conscience there would remain the practical consideration that its effect could only be to weaken deterrence, by encouraging the adversary to suppose that military aggression might be allowed to succeed. Whether it would in practice change his perception enough to tilt his conclusions decisively is not measurable; I would comment only that I prefer not to increase risk in this crucial area. But this is anyway, in a sense, a secondary matter from the standpoint of central ethical analysis. **"**

In response, Winters sent Quinlan a memorandum that the US bishops had asked him to submit to the ad hoc committee.[80] In it, he confirmed his belief that the US bishops should condemn all nuclear use, partly in the hope that US moral leadership on the issue would inspire similar moves in the Catholic church in Europe. Winters's letter was dated 29 March 1982, which shows that Quinlan's reaction was swift. His reply to Winters, dated 13 April 1982, contained the two general points outlined below, plus numerous specific points, one of which referred to some of Winters's analysis as 'an evasive cloud of words':[81]

" I admit to being now in something of a quandary, especially in a private correspondence between friends (and scions both of the Society, for I went to the same Jesuit school as my sons now attend). You write with manifest care and sincerity, and conspicuous personal courtesy; so I am tempted to send a bland commentary, picking up just a point or two here and there and stressing the many points on which we are at one. But that would not be wholly candid, nor a service to truthful dialogue. So at highly uncomfortable risk of again sounding harsh or arrogant or both, I pluck up my courage to tell you that I believe your analysis, for all its merits, to be misconceived in very fundamental respects; and that it seems incapable of reform in what I would regard as any successful way without uprooting some of your most basic assumptions, explicit and implicit. To compound my crime, I have to say that much the same comment applies to what I understand to be the position taken up by Cardinal Krol [the archbishop of Philadelphia] and in some measure by your bishops' Conference itself.

I illustrate these outrageous opinions in the attached point-by-point commentary on your draft. But let me pick up here the two most fundamental themes of my disagreement.

Firstly, I believe you do not surely identify and grasp the true nature of the underlying problem, and how utterly new and fundamental it is. Nuclear weapons have transformed the whole business of military force; and they have done so irreversibly. Arguments which are predicated, openly or not, on some supposition that they can be effectively disinvented, or that non-nuclear strategies can be found to seal off their existence, are built upon sand ... even if we persuaded all states to agree to abolish nuclear weapons, and if we got dependable verification to match that agreement (both these being in reality far-fetched suppositions) we would still have to recognise the fact – humanly as near certain as most things can be – that if major conventional war broke out, World-War-II-style, both sides would feel bound to race to recreate nuclear armouries – they simply could not afford to do otherwise. The knowledge cannot be expunged; and there is no way of making it unusable. We cannot dependably create for the rest of time a world in which major states go to war with one another yet are certain not to use nuclear weapons; we have to aim rather at a world in which major states recognise that they simply must not go to war. The best thing we can at present do with nuclear weapons is to harness them firmly to that crucial aim.

My second main theme concerns the possible use of nuclear weapons, and is closely related to the point made in [my response to] 'The Bow or the Cloud?' I do not believe it necessary to condemn outright, as Cardinal Krol apparently does (but Vatican II[82] did not), everything that could naturally be covered by the term 'strategic use'. But once one does accept that condemnation, any line of pro-deterrence argument attempting to maintain close logical rigour, like your own, seems to me to be inescapably fighting a losing battle, forced from one contorted sophistry to another in the attempt to avoid a conclusion which practical commonsense moves you (as it does me) to regard as unreasonable. In any customary field of intellectual inquiry I should regard this situation as pointing plainly to the need for sharply re-testing the starting assumption – in this case the blanket condemnation.

I recognise the weight of the judgement you make, as an observer of the US political scene, in [your letter].[83] To say that I have heard comments like these often before in

NATO's history, for example at the peak of the 'Mansfield amendment'[84] pressures a dozen years ago, is not to dismiss the point. My hope and belief is that the reality of our common interests, alongside the unreality of any radical alternative, will continue to sustain the essentials of the Western security structure. But that will, I fully accept, need a difficult and continuing process of public explanation and persuasion, on both sides of the Atlantic.

I ask you to accept that both the candour of my main comments, and their doubtless tiresome length, are motivated by a keen awareness of the importance of the issues – and the importance also that the authorities of the Church (particularly in your country, given the gravity of its global responsibilities) speak with the utmost prudence of approach, thoroughness of understanding and wisdom of judgement. I am frankly much relieved that on this colossally difficult and novel issue, where Christian ethical debate and analysis is manifestly still in uncertainty and development, my own bishops [in England and Wales] have not gone so far out on a limb as yours. On that impertinent observation I had better close!**"**

Winters's immediate reaction was to reject Quinlan's assertion that 'we have to aim [for] a world in which major states recognise that they simply must not go to war'. He wrote to Quinlan two weeks later, stating that 'no such world does or ever could exist' hence his belief that policy had to be underpinned by the assumption that 'war is virtually inevitable'.[85] For Winters, in such a world, preparing for nuclear war was dangerous and immoral.

In their Pastoral Letter of May 1983, the US bishops came out in favour of Winters's moral argument condemning all nuclear use – a radical departure from their interim draft of June 1982, which had advocated no-first-use but allowed retaliatory use.[86] The key concern that had swayed them against limited nuclear use, including demonstrative nuclear strikes, was that of vulnerable command and control – the potential for nuclear escalation leading to uncontrollable nuclear war. They had deemed that there was a high risk that any nuclear exchange would irreversibly disrupt the command and control network that links national command centres to field commanders (as well as to the adversary), which they believed could culminate in the destruction of the northern hemisphere. Their assessment was not that this apocalyptic scenario was inevitable, but that – based on expert literature and testimony – it was a 'less than improbable' outcome of any nuclear exchange. It was this assessment that led them to decide that nuclear use was incompatible with human freedom and therefore immoral.

The following month, Winters sent the bishops' letter to Quinlan, along with an article he had written about it for *The Month* titled 'The American Bishops' Warning on Nuclear War: "Abandon Hope All Ye Who Enter Here"'. In his article, he claimed that the bishops' letter comprised an unconditional rejection of the pragmatist approach to nuclear use espoused by Quinlan and others, based on the bishops' belief that it could not be justified according to Just War principles and therefore amounted to a 'moratorium on morality'. In the short letter that he attached to his article, Winters admitted – no doubt with tongue in cheek – that he was so exhausted by the debate that he was forced to retreat to his spiritual exercises. 'I am all bishoped out', he explained. 'Please pray for me.'[87]

The bishops' letter became a subject of discussion among the members of the Pembroke Group, who largely concurred with Quinlan's view that the bishops' conclusions were seriously flawed.[88] The core argument that nuclear use must always be wrong, while possession of nuclear weapons for deterrence purposes could be justifiable, simply could not stand up in practice or logic, as Quinlan had explained to Winters on numerous occasions. The same concerns prompted Albert Wohlstetter to publish a critique of the bishops' letter in the monthly magazine, *Commentary*,[89] which Quinlan shared with other members of the Pembroke Group. Quinlan enclosed the piece in a letter to Hugh Beach, dated 1 August 1983, along with a note that read: 'As you'll know [Wohlstetter is] regarded as inclining to the hawkish, and he is indeed further to the right (forgive the shorthand) than I would wish to be in tone and sometimes on substance, as with [anti-ballistic missile] ABM defence. But it seems to me a pretty good article, and most of the blows he lands on the US Catholic bishops are well-directed.' Quinlan followed this up with a letter to Wohlstetter, praising him for his piece in *Commentary*, which he 'read with pleasure and admiration' and which he regarded as a 'contribution of major importance'. He added that he was 'drawing attention to it in the various circles in which I still maintain a (low profile) presence in these matters'.

It turned out to be the beginning of a five-year conversation between Quinlan and Wohlstetter, during which they regularly exchanged their writings on nuclear ethics and strategy, as well as the work of others. As they saw eye-to-eye on the subject, their letters were short and to the point, with little in the way of debate. Both men were deeply concerned about the potential impact of the bishops' letter on nuclear deterrence, because it was attracting the attention of theologians worldwide, some of whom were making it their mission to sway public opinion against nuclear weapons and in addition, were targeting policymakers with their moral critiques of nuclear doctrine. Quinlan and Wohlstetter regarded the debate over the controllability of a nuclear exchange as particularly dangerous, as it led to simplistic and one-sided risk assessments and spawned a torrent of scholarship that they believed exaggerated the risk of catastrophic nuclear war. A letter from Wohlstetter to Quinlan, dated 26 January 1984, highlights the common ground between them:[90]

> 66 I have just received and read through your latest piece on nuclear issues and it reminds me of why I have regretted that these pieces of yours have to be private productions. It's very good indeed.
>
> I am attaching my exchange with critics from the December *Commentary*, which should help bring you up to date on the debate on this side of the water, as of last month. Bill O'Brien [ethics professor, Georgetown University] and James Turner Johnson [professor of religion and politics, Rutgers University] have been two of the best participants in the debate. O'Brien I am sure you are familiar with. Johnson looks to be the likely successor to Paul Ramsey [ethics professor at Princeton University] as the best Protestant moralist. I'll be glad to get you some of their papers if they would interest you.
>
> On the military side, there has been a flood of writing that pretends to show that it is impossible to limit damage to civilians or to prevent command and control from vanishing in favor of allowing anyone who is near a nuclear weapon to launch it. This dangerous nonsense is the greatest contribution to unilateralism. I know you are familiar with Desmond Ball's writings on the subject. On this side of the water, John Steinbruner, Paul Bracken, Wolfgang Panofsky and Spurgeon Keeney are among the many writers of such nonsense. It should be high on the agenda of those of us who oppose unilateral

disarmament to publish a discriminating and careful demolition of this literature. **"**

The Church of England and Wales: uncomfortable fence-sitters

As far as Quinlan was concerned, Wohlstetter was preaching to the converted: the need for a 'discriminating and careful demolition of the literature', including the pronouncements of the US bishops, was high on his agenda. A good deal of his private correspondence during the 1980s was dedicated to this task. To Quinlan's dismay, the Scottish, German and Dutch bishops[91] had condemned all use (and threatened use) of nuclear weapons, giving a major boost to the disarmament movement in Europe and to the US Catholic bishops, and he believed it was vitally important that the church hierarchy in England and Wales did not follow in their footsteps. Quinlan's letters provide a fascinating insight into the efforts he made to ensure that this did not happen: his input – albeit quiet and unattributed – into the deliberations of the Bishops Conference of England and Wales appears to have been critical in their decision to 'sit on the fence' on the issue of deterrence ethics. After three years of debate, the bishops of England and Wales decided to defer pronouncement on the morality of nuclear deterrence, except to declare that nuclear deterrence is not an adequate long-term formula for peace and to make ambiguous statements over the issue of nuclear use. This was despite the high profile and forceful arguments of theologians such as Roger Ruston, who argued publicly that the bishops of England and Scotland should go further than their US counterparts and condemn not only the use but also the possession of nuclear weapons as immoral.[92]

Quinlan engaged with numerous church leaders in England on this subject during the 1980s, but the main focus of his attention was the Commission for International Peace and Justice, which was responsible for the Episcopal Conference of the Roman Catholic Church in England and Wales. He kept in close contact with the General Secretary of the Commission, Robert (Bob) Beresford, who kept him informed of developments among the church hierarchy, and sought Quinlan's advice on all nuclear matters. In early 1982, Beresford sent Quinlan a draft statement on nuclear weapons, which was written by the chairman of the Justice and Peace Commission, Bishop James O'Brien. O'Brien had been deeply affected by the anti-nuclear arguments of Ruston and the anti-use stance of the US bishops and had drafted the statement in the hope that the Episcopal Conference would adopt it. The statement referred to a 'profound disquiet among thinking people [in the UK] concerning the morality of even possessing nuclear weapons' and the function of the bishops' conference to 'bring the light of Christian faith to bear on these issues, thus offering guidance to fellow Catholics, and indeed to the nation'.[93] Crucially, O'Brien argued that if there was a high risk that nuclear use could lead to escalation and nuclear war, 'that use would have to be condemned'. The draft prompted Quinlan to contact O'Brien to point out the flawed logic of the arguments being made by Ruston and others, leading to an exchange of letters in the months leading up to the bishops' conference.

O'Brien, who was keen for all views to be aired, encouraged Quinlan to publish a rejoinder to Ruston's arguments. Quinlan may have been tempted to accept O'Brien's invitation, because he admitted himself (although not to his church contacts) that Ruston's anti-nuclear arguments presented 'one of the more formidable statements of the ethical case against deterrence'.[94] But as Quinlan's letter of 23 June 1982 indicates, he felt constitutionally constrained and urged O'Brien to accept his advice on an off-the-record basis:[95]

" As you will know, Bob Beresford and I have talked from time to time about the expression of differing views among Catholics about the ethical issues raised by the possession of nuclear weapons. I have the impression from him that you yourself would prefer, both on general discussion-fostering grounds and with a view particularly to deliberations by the Bishops' Conference later this year, that Father Roger Ruston's forceful expression of one viewpoint should not have the field to itself; and that the question has arisen of whether I could make some matching contribution. I write now to explain my position on this, and to offer a limited suggestion.

Reluctantly, I am convinced that I cannot regard myself as free simply to mirror the Ruston pattern by writing for publication. This is not because I am ashamed of my views, nor because their expression need bring in confidential material, or anything like that. The difficulty lies in the constitutional convention – not in any way peculiar to the defence field – that civil servants should not avoidably become publicly associated with views on politically controversial issues. I was given, exceptionally (and only just), permission to speak in public or semi-public to the York civil defence conference last July and in the Dunamis lecture series earlier this year … Since the two permissions were given, the political environment has changed in a distinctly relevant way, in that (as I see matters) the front-bench Labour position no longer falls clearly within a broad consensus in favour of Western possession of nuclear weapons. In this altered situation for me now to undertake public authorship of a substantial new pamphlet on the issues would be out of the question.

At the same time, though I respect the force and sincerity of Father Ruston's views, I should be uneasy if there were any risk that leaving them to be the only ones that had received extended presentation might dispose the bishops to underrate the weight of other views. Would it be of value, I wonder if I put together a written account of my own approach for circulation to the bishops as a private document? I would envisage, by this, that the material could be drawn upon freely but not published as a whole[,] nor attributed to a particular document or author (it would be usable, in short, under what the jargon calls 'Chatham House' rules). I recognise that this would fall a good deal short of the ideal, not least in that my presentation would not be available to be tested by way of public scrutiny and argument. In the circumstances, there is no complete way round this disadvantage; but I would have no objection if, by way of alleviating it, my completed product were shown (on the same private basis) to some likely critics.

I would not want to commit myself to undertaking this task – stimulating though it would be – unless it were thought likely to be of reasonably significant consequence as an input to the bishops' work. Could you let me know candidly whether you would like me to have a shot at it? And, if so, the date by which you would need to receive the product? Given other current tasks, I could not easily meet a deadline earlier than September. **"**

O'Brien replied in a letter dated 30 June 1982 that he understood the constraints on Quinlan, and suggested that one way around the problem would be to publish the US bishops' Pastoral Letter at the conference, to ensure that Ruston's forceful views were not the only ones that were aired. One can only imagine Quinlan's expression as he read O'Brien's suggestion. In any case, he followed up with a letter to Beresford, in which he

tried to steer him away from submitting O'Brien's draft statement to the conference:[96]

❝ You explained to me on Tuesday morning that the main
immediate focus of your work on nuclear issues was the
framing, for further consideration, of a possible draft
statement which Bishop O'Brien might put before the
Hierarchy's conference in November [1982]; and that
you would therefore be glad of any early comment on
the material attached to your letter to me of 21 April.

I enclose at Annex comments on particular points in
the text (please forgive me if my phraseology seems at
times a bit tart). A good deal of my general view about
it can be inferred from these comments; but perhaps I
should draw it together. I think one must ask oneself
carefully what exactly the document is for. To give an
overview of the issues and considerations? Hardly that,
I take it – the complexity of the issues makes it, in my
view, impossible to do such a thing in anything so short
as three pages. To arrive at a definitive statement of the
Bishops' conclusions? Not that either, presumably – they
hardly seem in a position yet to pronounce categorically
for or against Western possession of nuclear weapons,
and the draft indeed does not purport to do so in any
explicit way. To offer some observations as guidance
to help carry debate forward? Perhaps; but if that is the
aim, it is important not only that the observations should
be pertinent, accurate and fair in themselves, but that the
choice of them should in the round give a reasonably
balanced picture of this unquestionably difficult subject.
With respect, I do not believe the present material, even
if detailed adjustments were made to iron out particular
flaws, is even close to satisfying this last requirement. I

look in vain, just for example, for any recognition that nuclear renunciation – which many if not most readers will take as the general direction in which the document points – may carry enormous practical consequences which would themselves be of deep moral concern ... I am sorry if all this seems unconstructive, but I judge it right to speak frankly ... **77**

Although Quinlan did not engage publicly with Ruston on the ethics of deterrence, he made sure that his critique of Ruston's pamphlet 'The Morality of Nuclear Weapons' was well known by those in the most senior positions in the Catholic hierarchy in the UK (and it is also clear from his correspondence that he kept senior officials in the MoD, FCO and Cabinet Office informed of these activities[97]). He engaged at length on the subject with the archbishop of Westminster, Basil Hume, who regarded the arguments for and against nuclear deterrence as 'a ghastly problem', which he found very difficult to untangle.[98] Quinlan sent the archbishop a long and detailed analysis of Ruston's anti-nuclear arguments, which he admitted were coloured by the fact that he was 'strongly predisposed towards justifying the system [of nuclear deterrence] and accepting the establishment view of the East/West scene', and 'not remotely as learned and well-read as Fr Ruston in the ethical literature'.[99] Still, Quinlan made his own case very forcefully, focusing, in part, on the implications that the unilateral renunciation of nuclear weapons by the UK (and surrender to the Soviet Union) would have for individual freedoms and for the Catholic Church. These concerns lie at the heart of the following extracts from his Ruston critique:[100]

66 The pamphlet evades or understates the reality of our problem in [a] crucial respect. I have not yet discovered

in this long and closely-written document a single reference to the fact that many if not most Christians believe,
with much evidence to support them, that the system
of totalitarian communism is immensely unjust and
unfree, has a considerable record of forcible aggrandise-
ment, has virtually never let a people go once seized, and
has taken the lives of many millions of people. [Ruston
indicates] that what resistance to a totalitarian aggressor is fighting for is simply 'political independence'. This
seems a grossly inadequate way of referring to a range
of possibilities to which in recent memory events from
the Stalinist repressions and Auschwitz onwards give
reality. The conclusion about nuclear weapons which
the pamphlet claims is an absolute one, to be accepted
irrespective of time and circumstance; and it therefore
purports to be valid for all time even if we were to face,
for example, a neo-Hitler armed with nuclear weapons.
The text nowhere confronts the implications of what it
requires – that Christians should be prepared to leave
nuclear weapons and any similar scientific discovery to
be wielded, uncountered, solely by the unscrupulous
and the aggressive.

Fr Ruston is of course fully entitled to his own opinions, which are plainly different from mine, about the
availability of alternative defence arrangements, about
the nature of potential adversaries, about the likelihood
of their coercing us if they had nuclear weapons and we
had not, and about the gravity of totalitarian conquest.
But if contrary opinions on these matters of non-ethical
judgement are widely, sincerely and not unreasonably
held (as they plainly are) any ethical conclusions to
which the Church may lend its authority must allow for
the possibility that these contrary opinions are right. If

they are, the practical consequences of an outright and
for-all-time condemnation of the possession of nuclear
weapons would be enormously grave. This then imposes
a very special burden of proof upon the proposed absolute conclusion – it should not be accepted unless it is
established with very great assurance. **"**

In response to Quinlan's analysis, Archbishop Hume confessed
the he was 'still not clear as to whether the possession of the
nuclear thing as a deterrent is morally in order or not' and he
asked for further information.[101] Quinlan was happy to oblige,
sending him enough material to keep the archbishop busy on
a nine-hour flight, along with a letter in which he reassured
him that that he need not come down on either side of the
fence on the morality of nuclear deterrence, but instead could
reasonably choose to sit on the fence.[102] 'Contrary opinions
may reasonably be held', he explained. '[I do not contend]
that the Church's authorities should endorse mine in place of
[Ruston's]'.

Quinlan was one of a number of senior civil servants in
the UK establishment who were trying to steer the Catholic
Church hierarchy on the nuclear issue. He and a circle of fellow
Catholics in the MoD, FCO and Cabinet Office coordinated their
combined assault on the US bishops' letter, exchanging letters
among themselves that discussed their strategy and tactics
for influencing church leaders, and also the substance of their
pro-deterrence arguments. The letters of one civil servant in
particular, a British diplomat called David Goodall (who at the
time was attached to the Cabinet Office) feature prominently
in Quinlan's files. Like Quinlan, Goodall was well connected
in the Catholic Church and was keen to see that it did not turn
unilateralist. In a letter dated 14 January 1983, sent by Goodall
to John Chick of the FCO and copied to Quinlan, Goodall laid

out the details of a meeting he had attended with the bishops of England and Wales, at which he had given a speech that he had written with Quinlan's assistance (the week after the meeting, Goodall wrote an handwritten letter to Quinlan to thank him, explaining that 'I can assure you that I wouldn't have got to first base without your help'[103]). Goodall's report on the meeting sheds interesting light on the Catholic civil service network of which Quinlan was a key part, and especially on its efforts to influence the church debate on deterrence ethics:[104]

> **"** [...] My impression is that no more than two or three out of the thirty or so Bishops who were [at the meeting] are outright unilateralists, notably Bishop Butler and Bishop Guazzelli (East London). But these are both much respected by their colleagues, the former as a theologian and elder statesman and the latter for his lively and forceful personality. Several more are waverers (including, I think, Bishop O'Brien, the Chairman of the Justice and Peace Commission); and there is a significant group which is satisfied that nuclear deterrence is both sensible and morally justified. This includes the Bishop of Salford, Dr Holland (also a theologian), and Bishop Mahon (West London). The majority are, I should judge, somewhere in between: they recognise the force of the practical and prudential arguments for the Government's present policies and want to be convinced that they are morally justified; but they are genuinely puzzled by the complexities of the problem. They are worried by the moral arguments, and aware of the mounting anti-nuclear pressures from sections of their flock. The Pope's pronouncements have clearly had a steadying effect against any trend towards unilateralism: at the same time most of the bishops feel that his qualified acceptance of

nuclear deterrence as licit for the time being is heavily conditional on progress being made towards nuclear disarmament, and that Britain, whose national deterrent they see as somewhat marginal to NATO's, ought to be in a position to give some sort of lead in this direction. (I expended a lot of energy in dealing with questions directed towards probing the feasibility of 'leading by example'.) They seem to have been impressed by a presentation which they had received the previous day from Dr Paul Rogers of the Bradford University School of Peace Studies, who had apparently argued in favour of Britain conditionally offering to abandon *Trident* (and *Polaris*) in return for some matching move from the Soviet Union. Dr Rogers had also produced facts and figures purporting to show that technological advance was accelerating, and that by the 1990s it would be possible for either side to destroy the entire military capability of the other (including submarines) in a single first strike, thus undermining the basis for deterrence; and that this lent great urgency to the need for early progress on arms control/disarmament.

On the level of principle, the bishops were predictably wrestling with the morality of conditional intention: i.e. could it ever be right to have the intention to commit a morally monstrous act, however justifiable and desirable the objective. Another problem (not bearing directly on the nuclear issue) which clearly loomed large for those of them with first-hand experience of the developing world was the morality of devoting so much of our resources to defence at a time when many millions of people in the Third World are starving.

In the winding up session, the point was made that they would need a public line to take in response to the

Church of England working group's report ('The Church and the Bomb'); and the question was raised (by Bishop Butler) whether they should try to produce a considered pastoral document along the lines of the American bishops' draft letter. The cardinal's response to this was extremely cautious: he pointed out that there was as yet no unanimity of view among them on the subject and that it seemed unlikely that they would be able to reach a consensus. It would be a mistake to 'canonise' the Church of England report, which had not yet been debated in the Synod: until that happened it only had the status of a draft. Before contemplating anything along the lines of the American bishops' document, it would be essential to explore the thinking of the French and German bishops' conferences, both of whom had so far been notably cautious in their utterances on the subject. Meanwhile it would be up to individual bishops to decide the line they should take with their people in relation to the forthcoming 'Peace Sunday' on 30th January. The cardinal also commented that the contributions which they had heard from the two moral theologians (one unilateralist and the other not) had been disappointing and relatively unhelpful. The two lay contributions had been more illuminating, and they needed to seek a good deal more expert advice before trying to form a definitive view.

It seemed to me in the light of the discussion that the crucial area for most of the Bishops is the extent to which deterrence is stable; and the extent to which it really is the only sure way of avoiding the outbreak of a world war, nuclear or otherwise. Bishop Butler said that if it could be shown to be certain that deterrence would work, and that therefore the conditional intention to use nuclear weapons would never have to be realised, his objections would fall. Bishop Holland replied that certainty was not to be found in nature, and that the tradition of the Church back to Aquinas was that the certainty required for moral judgements was derived from what would happen in the generality of cases. On this criterion one could be reasonably certain 'that no government, whether Soviet or otherwise, would risk aggression in the face of nuclear deterrence: and the circumstances in which the West might have to use nuclear weapons would consequently not arise. The question of a conditional intention to do evil was therefore irrelevant. I rehearse this rather esoteric exchange because (a) it clearly impressed the other bishops and (b) it suggests to me that the arguments to concentrate on in dealing with the Roman Catholic bishops are the ones repeatedly emphasised by Michael Quinlan, namely that deterrence is inherently stable rather than precarious; that the whole objective of the exercise is to maintain peace; and that abandoning the nuclear deterrent would be destabilising and calculated to increase the risk of war. The more evidence we can produce to support these propositions, the greater the likelihood that the Roman Catholic bishops will refrain from giving collective support to the Peace Movement in its present form.

A final point worth recording is the very favourable reactions of the bishops to their recent call on the Foreign and Commonwealth Secretary. Both the cardinal and the archbishop of Liverpool told me privately that they had been impressed and gratified by the seriousness with which [Foreign Secretary] Mr [Francis] Pym had listened to them and by the attention he had paid to the concerns they had expressed. The cardinal was particularly anxious to emphasise that he and his colleagues had wanted only to register their anxieties, not to lay down the law; that they recognised the heavy responsibilities the government carried for defence; and that the hastily cobbled together document which they had left with Mr Pym was in no sense a statement of the bishops' considered views, but simply an indication of the sort of feelings which were current among the Catholic community. **"**

As Goodall's report explained, the most senior figures in the Catholic Church hierarchy in England and Wales were sitting – somewhat uncomfortably – on the fence on the issue of nuclear deterrence, which was as much as Quinlan could have hoped for. But a few prominent bishops who were unhappy with this apparent acquiescence broke ranks and went public with their concerns. Goodall's letter mentioned Bishop Basil Christopher Butler as one of the most outspoken critics; he, like Bruce Kent, was personally appalled by the idea of nuclear use in all its aspects, and used the broadsheets and the Catholic magazine *The Tablet* to criticise UK nuclear policy and rally support for change. Goodall, Quinlan and others did what they could to fend off these attacks, often writing to the editors of the publications in question to point out logical inconsistencies, error and hyperbole, and to the authors themselves to explain why they believed their arguments were weak, misleading and damaging.

An exchange of letters between Quinlan, Goodall, Bishop Butler and the editor of *The Tablet*, John Wilkins, in mid-1983 shows this defense mechanism at work. Wilkins had published a leader article by Butler in *The Tablet*, titled 'The Dubious Basis of Britain's Defence', which had described British nuclear policy as immoral on the basis that it '[relied] heavily on the first use of nuclear weapons'. He went on to claim that a wide range of high ranking military leaders, including former chief of the British Defence Staff, Field Marshall Lord Carver, 'believe that such first use of nuclear weapons could not ultimately be restricted, but would inevitably lead to a full-scale nuclear exchange which would mean world genocide'. The leader prompted Goodall and Quinlan to write to Wilkins, expressing their displeasure. Goodall explained that he was shocked that *The Tablet* would publish such a flawed and inaccurate analysis, and declared that it was in danger of 'climbing on a bandwagon without any very clear understanding of the direction in which it is [heading]'.[105] Quinlan wrote that 'I have to tell you with candour … that I found the piece in last week's *Tablet* disappointingly superficial – even, in some ways, wild'.[106]

Although, as his correspondence shows, Quinlan's role in Church debates on the morality of nuclear deterrence was significant (it was also clearly approved of and even encouraged by senior figures in the MoD, FCO and Cabinet Office[107]), Quinlan took offense at any suggestion that the bishops on either side of the Atlantic had succumbed to political pressure to tow the establishment line. His sensitivity to these kinds of allegations was expressed in a letter to Brian Wicker, dated 30 September 2008. Quinlan and Wicker had been engaged in a long and detailed exchange over deterrence ethics, including over a piece that Wicker had written on the subject, entitled 'True Hope and False Gods'.[108] In his paper, Wicker had argued that the Church in some countries supported nuclear deterrence despite its immorality and implied that they did so because they had been too easily swayed by the arguments made by government officials. In a letter to Wicker, Quinlan made it clear that he was not prepared to accept the allegation, which he argued was baseless:[109]

" I do not plan to engage further in dispute about the argumentation on nuclear weapons which you deploy in the revised version of your paper 'True Hope and False Gods'. In my judgment prolonging this long-drawn-out debate between us has become a waste of time.

There is however one particular element in your paper which in my view ought not to be let pass. This is your assertion ... that the teaching of the Church in nuclear weapons was 'badly compromised by pressure exerted on bishops' conferences to say, or not to say, things determined by governments'. The words 'badly compromised' inescapably imply that bishops wrongly gave ground to these pressures; and [one of the footnotes in your article] plainly attaches the allegation to the US bishops in particular.[110]

You provide no evidence for this grave allegation. The fact that the bishops gave a hearing (rightly, I suggest ...) to those democratically charged with responsibility for the security of their peoples in no way means that improper concessions must have been made to the views heard.

[...] What did notably influence the US bishops, as you are surely aware and is indeed public knowledge, is that Cardinal Casaroli discussed with their representatives a draft of 'The Challenge of Peace', and moved them toward a significantly less anti-nuclear stance than had featured in the draft. I hardly think that you will have regarded that as improper pressure? Or that you will repeat in this context the insinuation you made some years ago in *The Tablet* – equally without evidence – that Pope John Paul II himself, in his utterances, yielded wrongly to political pressure? "

In his undated response, Wicker replied 'If I have written anything which is unfair to the US bishops in their compilation of "The Challenge of Peace", I unhesitatingly withdraw it. I certainly did not mean that (in your words) "improper concessions" were made by the bishops under pressure from government'.[111] He closed with an explanation of his concerns:

> ❝ As you know, I think that there is no way that the strategy of nuclear deterrence can be reconciled with the church's fundamental teachings about the immunity of the innocent from intentional attack. This is why I think that further reflection on the Church's role as Sacrament of the future is so important. However, I want to say again that I did not intend to imply that the bishops 'wrongly gave ground' in rewording their text in the light of what the experts said. The trouble is that what resulted was ethically unsatisfactory – as perhaps in the situation of 1983 it could not avoid being. This is part of what I mean in my paper that this situation was tragic. ❞

In the end, despite the frustration that sometimes creeps into the exchanges between Quinlan and those who challenged the morality of Cold War nuclear deterrence, there was less divergence in their beliefs than many will have realised. It is true that Quinlan spent much of his time defending UK and NATO nuclear strategy through the notion of practical morality, but some of his letters hint that beneath his apparent conviction, a personal struggle to reconcile his role with his faith was never far from the surface. This comes through in a letter Quinlan wrote to Winters in March 1982:[112]

> ❝ Let me conclude by acknowledging, in fairness, that nuclear weapons set the Christian conscience problems

of extreme difficulty; and I know of no position, whether for or against deterrence, which does not have to face somewhere along the line extremely awkward questions [...]. **"**

For Quinlan, the scales tipped in favour of nuclear deterrence during the Cold War because, as he commented to Beresford (quoting the pope): 'our grappling with the issues of security has to remember Auschwitz as well as Hiroshima'.[113] This fundamental belief in the need and responsibility to defend basic freedoms from the horrors of totalitarianism helped keep his moral doubts at bay. But in the decades following the collapse of the Soviet Union, Quinlan's confidence in the nuclear future began to wane, and by the time of his death, he was beginning to question some of his own assumptions. In fact, even though he never shifted from the pro-nuclear to the anti-nuclear camp, it is striking how some of the questions and concerns raised by Quinlan's most determined critics became the focus of his attention in his final years.

.

PART TWO

Strategic decisions: LRTNF and *Trident*

Some of the most fascinating letters in the Quinlan files date back to 1977–81, when he was director of policy planning at the MoD. It was a period in his life when his professional role perfectly matched his interests and skills; when he had the luxury to focus his attention on the intricacies of nuclear strategy and demonstrate his mastery of the subject in the British defence establishment and the NATO High Level Group (HLG). It was during this time, when the Cold War was at its height, East–West tensions were escalating, and fear of catastrophic nuclear war was peaking, that Quinlan contributed to two key nuclear developments: the 1979 decision by NATO to deploy long-range theatre nuclear forces (LRTNF) [1] in Western Europe, and the 1980 decision by the British government to procure *Trident* from the United States. Quinlan's contributions to the official discussions and negotiations that led to these decisions are widely regarded by his contemporaries and successors as representing a high point of his career, and as one of his most important legacies.

The first half of the following discussion of strategic decisions is devoted to Quinlan's correspondence on NATO

LRTNF. It explores his role in the NATO HLG and his subsequent attempts to dampen down the escalating tensions that accompanied LRTNF deployment. Through the highs and lows of the period, he defended the 1979 decision as strategically and politically necessary, dismissing critics' allegations that it was part of a US plan to acquire a disarming first strike or nuclear war-winning capability. But as his correspondence will show, he found it difficult to keep the debate on the best ground, and the Reagan administration's announcement of its Strategic Defense Initiative (SDI) in March 1983 only added to these difficulties. At times, Quinlan appears to have felt frustrated by what he regarded as the poor quality of the debate, doubly so because his involvement in the HLG meant he knew first hand that the conspiracy theories surrounding the 1979 decision, which were being exploited very successfully by the Soviet propaganda machine, were false. This adds colour to his usually precise and measured writing style: a tinge of irritation here and a flash of sarcasm there; little reminders that the High Priest of Deterrence may have been one of the most intellectually brilliant and influential civil servants of his generation, but he was also very human.

The second half of the discussion of strategic decisions shines a light on Quinlan's thinking on *Trident*, from his role in the crucial procurement studies of 1977–79, to the post-Cold War period, when Quinlan had retired from his position as PUS at the MoD but remained influential in debates on *Trident*'s future. As is the case throughout this book, the official communications associated with Quinlan's role during this period are not discussed. Where it helps elucidate certain issues, published official documents are referred to, as are Quinlan's publications on the subject, but the focus is on Quinlan's discussion of the *Trident* decision in his private correspondence, most of which occurs in response to letters from concerned individuals, who felt strongly that Britain's independent nuclear deterrent either lacked a strategic rationale, was dangerous and immoral, or was simply too costly for the UK to maintain.

Readers who are new to the subject may benefit from reading the appendices before reading the letters included in this section of the book, as they set out important background material for the non-expert: key facts and figures and important terms and concepts associated with NATO nuclear forces (appendix 1) and the British independent nuclear deterrent (appendix 2).

NATO long-range theatre nuclear forces

NATO has always been a difficult alliance to manage. Disagreements between its members over the future of the Alliance and the new Strategic Concept, which were on display at the November 2010 Lisbon Summit, reflect the difficulty of building consensus among a diverse group of states, with different priorities. These challenges have grown since the Cold War ended, but official documents show that the Alliance has always been plagued by divisions, especially over nuclear issues. The reasons for this have varied as the strategic context has changed and the Alliance has expanded, but in the context of East–West confrontation Quinlan had no doubt about the core strategic and political difficulty, which was 'how to give confidence to the forward members of an alliance in which nuclear power had for various reasons to be concentrated not in their hands but mostly in the hands of the rearmost member, on the far side of an ocean'.[2] Quinlan described this as an 'appallingly difficult dilemma' for which there was 'no inherently perfect solution'. The fix that was devised, whereby US nuclear weapons would be stationed in Europe under dual-key arrangements, and a dedicated decision-making body (the NPG) would be set up to ensure consultation between members on all aspects of NATO nuclear policy, was always seen as an imperfect compromise, and some of the Alliance's most serious internal crises have been triggered by the challenges involved in making that system work. But as far as Quinlan was concerned there was no alternative; the imperfect system had to work to protect Western Europe from another major war and from the brutalities of totalitarianism. For that reason above all others, NATO members had to be fully integrated into NPG decision-making so none of them could wash their hands of it. It was a shared burden and a shared responsibility – politically, strategically and morally.

More than any other factor, it was Quinlan's acknowledgement and acceptance of this responsibility that shaped his thinking on nuclear strategy and doctrine, and particularly his contributions to the NATO deliberations from 1977–79 over whether to deploy long-range theatre nuclear forces in Western Europe. The discussion and letters that follow focus on the part Quinlan played in those deliberations, beginning with a brief history of the events surrounding them and the role of the HLG, and expanding to explore Quinlan's take on the strategic rationale for NATO TNF deployment and his quiet participation in domestic debates over the logic and morality of that decision. Quinlan's response to the SDI is also included in this discussion, as it shows his deep suspicion of proposals that threatened to undermine NATO deterrence and to undo the sophisticated planning work of the HLG.

A brief history of the NATO LRTNF decision

The history of the 1979 NATO dual-track decision is beginning to be pieced together, thanks to the release of official documents.[3] In 1976, the Soviet Union deployed a new mobile intermediate range missile, known as the SS-20 *Saber*, which altered the European security environment in favour of the

Warsaw Pact. As a result of the deployment of the new missiles, which were mobile, accurate, equipped with multiple warheads and targeted on Western Europe, some NATO members – West Germany in particular – were concerned that they lacked the capacity to respond to a Soviet ground offensive. West German officials saw the increase in Warsaw Pact capabilities as undermining 'perceptions about the credibility of the NATO deterrent', and argued that this made West Germany especially vulnerable.[4] But at the same time, they believed the deployment of new NATO LRTNF in West Germany would not necessarily solve the problem – the missiles had to be deployed in other NATO European countries too to prevent West Germany becoming a target, and should be tied to arms control negotiations. British officials believed this to be an overreaction but were, nevertheless, concerned about the negative impact on West German confidence and on NATO solidarity.[5]

In October 1977, the NPG began meeting to discuss how the West should respond, and set up the high level group (HLG) dedicated to the task. The HLG consisted of senior defence ministry personnel from the NATO states, and became the think tank of the NPG, its activities conducted out of the public eye. Although the group was chaired by the US assistant secretary of defence for international security policy, Michael Quinlan played a central role in the work of the group, setting the agenda, providing briefing materials, and applying his mastery of nuclear doctrine and strategy to the discussions. He played a key role in ensuring US planners were fully aware of European concerns, and the implications for NATO if the US failed to understand and respond to the West German insecurities. Declassified CIA documents from the period show how persuasive these arguments were, as US intelligence officials became convinced that if the issue was not resolved successfully, 'Alliance cohesion could be shaken' and 'confidence in US leadership could suffer a significant decline' with 'the greatest danger [that] the FRG could begin to question the reliability of the US and NATO as the basis of its security'.[6]

After two years of studies and discussions, the HLG decided upon a 'dual track' approach to respond to Soviet superiority in TNF. On the one hand, NATO would deploy a new class of land-based nuclear missiles in Europe, known as long-range theatre nuclear forces, consisting of 464 ground-launched cruise missiles (GLCMs) and 108 *Pershing* II ballistic missiles. Although some defence officials were originally sceptical about this move, Quinlan provided an intellectually coherent argument to support the modernisation plan: NATO needed the capability to strike the Soviet Union with systems based on land in Western Europe, because they filled a gap in the escalation spectrum and would help convey to the Soviets a sense of risk from any aggression on the continent.[7] Because both the cruise and *Pershing* missiles could reach Soviet territory, they would deny the Soviets 'a sanctuary' from which to launch attacks on NATO with their LRTNF. *Pershing* II offered a counter-force capability because it could strike 'time-critical targets' while the GLCMs could 'attack a wider range of targets'. Once they were deployed, there would be no weak links in the NATO spectrum of military options.[8] The HLG plan was to deploy the *Pershing* IIs in West Germany, replacing deployments of *Pershing* I from the 1960s, with the GLCMs to be deployed in West Germany, Belgium, the Netherlands and the UK. This widespread basing of the new missiles was an attempt to ensure NATO cohesion through risk-sharing – a necessary step to address West German insecurities.[9]

The second part of the dual-track decision was an arms-control commitment. To appease public opinion in Western Europe and the US, which was concerned about nuclear arms racing, and to blunt Soviet efforts to exploit these public sensitivities via infiltration of the peace movement, the HLG recommended combining the LRTNF decision with an arms-control initiative aimed at removing the entire class of intermediate-range missiles that they were about to deploy. Thus the dual track approach helped NATO 'sell' the package to the public and at the same time, if negotiations succeeded, shift the nuclear balance in Europe back in NATO's favour.

Some members of the HLG, including Quinlan, had reservations about the arms-control element of the dual-track arrangement, concerned that it 'would not provide a justification for the deployment [of the new LRTNF missiles] but an excuse not to go ahead with them'.[10] According to British officials, it made more sense to explore arms-control possibilities only after NATO had established its total modernisation requirements. Moreover, removal of LRTNF could benefit the Soviet Union due to its superior conventional strength, leaving Europe more vulnerable. In the HLG, British officials were the most openly sceptical about the arms-control element of the dual-track approach, while West German officials were most enthusiastic.[11] In the end, a consensus emerged in the group on the strategic advantage of using arms-control negotiations to buy time for the deployment of modernised LRTNF and to make the move more acceptable to European publics. As far as the British were concerned, this was acceptable. As Quinlan later admitted, despite his reservations he came to regard the dual-track approach as a reasonable short-term fix – he did not believe the Soviets would agree to the total elimination of the intermediate-range nuclear forces anyway. The 'zero option' (the complete elimination of the entire class of nuclear weapons) had been raised by the Dutch and West Germans in the HLG as the best solution to the SS-20 dilemma, but it appears that at the time the British did not think it was feasible or take it seriously.[12] Throughout the discussions, a representative on the HLG had been sharing sensitive US intelligence that had identified new construction at Soviet SS-20 bases and new, more widely dispersed Soviet missile deployments, so from the perspective of British defence officials, the priority was to close the gap in NATO long-range capabilities as quickly as possible while maintaining NATO cohesion.[13]

In December 1979, NATO ministers formally adopted the INF decision. As soon as the decision was taken, the Kremlin launched a campaign to mobilise Western public opposition against it. At a meeting of the World Peace Council on 18 December 1979, the head of the International Department of the Communist Party of the Soviet Union (CPSU) told representatives from the Western anti-nuclear movement that 1980 must be 'a year of mass action against the imperialistic arms race' under the slogans 'Act Now: Eliminate the danger of the new US missiles!' and 'Atomic death is a threat to all of us – no atomic missiles for Europe!'[14] The strategy was to mobilise domestic protest by portraying the LRTNF decision as an imminent threat to all mankind. Four years later, in the midst of mounting public opposition, much of it secretly supported by the CPSU, cruise and *Pershing* II missiles were deployed in Europe – the first time NATO had used doctrine to determine a weapons system selection and the first time NATO members had reached agreement on the types and numbers of a new weapon before deployment. Michael Quinlan had played a significant role in this decision-making process. He viewed the new missiles not just as a response to the Soviet SS-20 missiles, but as filling an important gap in NATO's land-based long-range nuclear capabilities, taking over some of the tasks of dual-capable aircraft and thereby augmenting NATO's conventional capabilities at the same time. They would also serve an important political purpose, communicating to the Soviets the potential costs of aggression and hopefully persuading the leadership, at a critical stage in a conventional war, to reconsider its goals and terminate hostilities. But critics argued that the deployment left Europe more vulnerable. Most were concerned that the modernisation plan represented a general change in NATO nuclear doctrine from a defensive to a war-fighting posture, which made all-out nuclear war more likely. Others argued that the planned deployment was highly destabilising for a number of more specific reasons which were sometimes confused and even conflicting: a) the long range and accuracy of the NATO missiles and the short flight time of *Pershing* II would give NATO a first strike capability, which might tempt the Soviets to launch their own surprise attack before NATO got the upper hand; and/or b) the deployment would be destabilising because the new missiles would be vulnerable to a Soviet first strike and therefore the countries that agreed to base them on their territory would become easy targets. The Soviet propaganda machine exploited these fears and sensitivities in the hope that it would be able to shatter NATO solidarity.

The November 1983 deployment of the GLCMs and *Pershing* II missiles occurred at a time of escalating East–West tensions and one of the most volatile periods in the history of the Cold War. In March that year, US President Ronald Reagan had proposed the SDI – a massive research effort 'to restore the possibility of true defense', which the press nicknamed 'Star Wars' after the science fiction movie. The Cold War historian and former aide and adviser to John F. Kennedy, Roger Hilsman, described the concept in a way that helps explain why it was given that name:[15]

" The idea was to develop a defense system based largely in space that would prevent missiles from reaching the US homeland. Soviet launching sites would be monitored by spy satellites, and the instant they started to count down for a launch they would be attacked by lasers from other satellites or by other weapons based in space. A second line of defense would attack in mid-flight any missiles that got through the first line of defense. Satellites would carry nonnuclear weapons such as chemical lasers or particle beams. To this defense would be added x-ray lasers, launched from either submarines or bases on the ground and triggered by nuclear explosions in space. A final defense would be ground-based lasers attacking incoming missiles during the last stages of their flight, as they descended to their targets. **??**

As Quinlan argued at the time, the idea was misconceived on numerous technical and strategic levels, but during 1983 it was its political impact that was most disturbing. Reagan's SDI announcement came just a few months after the death of Soviet leader Leonid Brezhnev and the appointment of his successor Yurii V. Andropov – the former head of the KGB who was paranoid about the looming threat of nuclear war. Andropov saw the SDI proposal as 'proof' that the US was 'devising one option after another in search of best ways of unleashing nuclear war in the hope of winning it'; pursuing every possible measure to give the West unchallengeable military superiority.[16] In response, he stepped up Soviet monitoring of the West under an intelligence operation known by the Russian acronym VRYaN (which stood for 'surprise nuclear missile attack') and in September concluded that an 'outrageous military psychosis in the United States' was pushing the world to the brink of nuclear war.[17]

Deployment of the GLCMs and *Pershing* II missiles took place against the backdrop of this rising rhetoric, and on the heels of a large-scale Western military exercise called *Able Archer*, which included a simulation of procedures for the release of nuclear weapons in case of an all-out nuclear war. The latter was apparently misinterpreted by Soviet intelligence analysts as NATO preparations for an actual attack on the Soviet Union, and – according to some reports – a scare on the scale of the Cuban Missile Crisis was narrowly averted due to the failure of KGB analysts to pass information on to senior levels in the Politburo and defence ministry.[18]

Russian scholars have argued that the war scare triggered by *Able Archer* was overblown, and that much of the escalation in tensions during 1983 was deliberately engineered by senior figures in the Politburo, who believed they could turn Western tensions over LRTNF deployment and the SDI proposals to the advantage of the Soviet Union: they could create war scares to exploit cracks in NATO solidarity, and to intensify the European public backlash against the stationing of GLCM and *Pershing* II missiles on their territory.[19] Not enough information exists to determine which interpretation is more accurate (or whether they are both true, which is also possible), but it is clear that the LRTNF modernisation decision, in the context of Reagan–Andropov leadership and the SDI announcement, created dramatic and unanticipated dangers. It is also now known that, during the entire episode, the Thatcher government was being briefed on Soviet nuclear paranoia by the Soviet double agent Oleg Gordievsky, and was feeding information to US officials, including Reagan, urging the US to tone down its anti-Soviet rhetoric.[20] Official UK support for deployment of modernised LRTNF appears to have been unwavering, however – there, the concern seems to have centred on how the deployment was managed rather than on the logic of the decision itself.[21] Some senior MoD officials, on the other hand, were much more critical of the SDI proposals, as Quinlan's correspondence will reveal. It is clear that Quinlan did not foresee that US Star Wars proposals would contribute to the Soviet defeat in the Cold War arms race.

The rationale for the LRTNF decision

Although the original impetus in NATO for the LRTNF modernisation plan was provided by West German fears, Quinlan played a pivotal role within the HLG in building the intellectual case for the plan – a role that appears to have been significant in persuading an initially wary Carter administration to support it. The arguments he fed into the HLG can be found in a letter he wrote to Father Brendon Soane, in which he provided comments on a draft report of a Justice and Peace Committee meeting on the LRTNF decision, held in Brussels on 1 June 1982. In his letter of 12 July 1982, Quinlan provided the following rationale (which has been paraphrased for the sake of brevity) for upgrading NATO TNF capabilities:[22]

1) The decision was not 'just or even mainly a response to SS20 deployment'; it was an attempt to fill a gap in NATO sub-strategic deterrence. The rationale for the new systems was strategic: unlike the airfield-reliant LRTNF systems NATO had relied on up to that point, the new GLCMs and *Pershing* II missiles would be 'highly mobile' and therefore would be 'highly unfruitful targets for pre-emptive [Soviet] strike'.

2) By filling this gap with new and less vulnerable systems, the NATO nuclear deterrent would be more credible and thus more effective, reducing the risk of Soviet military aggression. The desire for deterrence stability was thus absolutely pivotal to the 1979 decision. As Quinlan put it: 'improved assurance of being able to hit the Soviet homeland warns the Russians that they cannot count on keeping the war limited and on their terms'.

3) In terms of the origins of the December 1979 decision, it was derived from the studies conducted by the NATO HLG. Contrary to 'flatly untrue' claims that the LRTNF modernisation plan 'was an American plan pushed upon reluctant European Governments', the Europeans (influenced by Quinlan's strategic arguments) were 'the main urgers of modernisation'.

4) The need to modernise NATO LRTNF was 'created primarily by the fact of a nuclear-armed USSR of repugnant totalitarian ideology'.

5) The modernisation plan would 'not change European reliance on the US, either up or down'; the comparable LRTNF that NATO had relied upon up to that point were already US-controlled (aside from the UK's aged *Vulcans*).

This basic rationale for the 1979 decision can be found scattered throughout Quinlan's correspondence, although rarely in the level of detail that he shared with Bob Beresford and Brendon Soane. The explanation of the modernisation plan that he gave to Andrew Edwards (a senior Treasury official) is much more typical. Asked for his comments on a text Edwards had written on nuclear deterrence, Quinlan informed him that: 'In pure strategic theory, the NATO LRTNF modernisation was not a response to the SS-20 … The real case is that NATO's strategy requires a capability at this level and that the existing means (F.111 and Vulcan) were obsolescent'.[23]

Not everyone in the UK defence establishment shared Quinlan's enthusiasm for the NATO LRTNF modernisation plan. Hockaday, who admittedly did not see eye to eye with Quinlan on a range of strategic issues, wrote to Quinlan on 4 January 1983 to explain why he viewed the 1979 decision as problematic, and why he had difficulty dealing with critics in public discussions on the issue. He found the 1979 decision difficult to defend:[24]

" I accept as plausible the Russian statements that they would regard an American missile on Russia as an American missile on Russia whether it was fired from the United States, from sea, or from Europe; and I infer from this that the probability of a large-scale Russian riposte against the United States is little different in any of the three cases. Against this background I have not yet met a satisfactory answer to the questions which I once put to you at the IISS: if the American nuclear guarantee to Europe is credible, what do new weapon systems in Europe add to deterrence? If it is not credible, how do they make it so?

I suspect that the case for the new TNF is more subjective, in the need which many Europeans feel in the face of the SS-20 (despite having lived in the shadow of SS-4 and SS-5 for twenty years) for a visible assurance of the link with the American strategic deterrent. But I tend to find in discussion periods that when, having dealt with the assertion that the cruise missile is a first-strike weapon and hence increases our vulnerability, I go on to deal with the assertion that it is being forced upon us by the United States in order to make possible a limited nuclear war confined to Europe, my references back to Helmut Schmidt and other expressions of European anxiety about SS-20 are met with 'Yes, but land-based cruise missiles are not what we wanted'. Is there a risk that the peasants will revolt against being told that the gentleman in Whitehall (or in the Palais Schaumberg) knows best how to soothe their worries? Perhaps the most convincing argument for the proposed TNF modernisation is that it offers the only serious prospect of getting the Russians to reduce their SS-20 deployment even if they do not go all the way to the zero option. I myself believe this to be true, but for at least the next twelve months it can only be assertion.

But more fundamentally the concentration of the debate upon TNF feeds the entirely understandable fears of a nuclear war in Europe. I believe that the risk of a nuclear war in Europe is negligible so long as both sides have a sufficiency of nuclear weapons of various categories (this is not necessarily a case for *Pershing* 2 and cruise missiles, for what do they add to SLBMs except in highly over-sophisticated targeting scenarios?).

[...] Although I was one of the midwives of 'flexible response' in 1967, when I think that it did make good sense, I believe that today the real followers of Ptolemy are those who tie themselves in knots constructing scenarios to the effect that if we used 'only a little one' there would be a substantial possibility (your own phrase...) that the Russians would conclude that their initial judgement had been mistaken and that for their own survival they must call off the aggression. Of course this is possible; nevertheless I worry about making 'a substantial possibility' a major plank of strategy, I worry too about your assertion that their vital interests would be less closely involved than ours – I believe that their hypothesis would be a different one. **"**

A number of scholars shared Hockaday's reservations over the 1979 decision, and in particular his belief that the deliberations of the HLG had been over-sophisticated to the point of absurdity in terms of trying to find an intellectually consistent strategic justification for what was essentially a political decision. In fact, more than ten years after the LRTNF decision had been made, the rationale for the deployment was still being debated among academics in the UK. In a letter to the *Times* in 1991, historian Michael Howard gave the following account:

❝ When the story of the TNF issue comes to be written it will bear a close resemblance to that of the ill-fated MLF.[25] Both originated in the exaggerated importance attached by the United States Government to the doubts expressed by a very small number of European specialists about the credibility of the American nuclear guarantee to Europe in the light of improvements in Soviet weapon technology, a concern which was quite wrongly believed to be widespread within the European defence community.[26] In an attempt to assuage these doubts the Pentagon came up with a technological solution for which there was no military requirement whatever but which would, they hoped, reassure those meticulous pedants who believed that, unless nuclear deterrence was precisely balanced at every level, it would no longer carry conviction. ❞

The domestic politics of the LRTNF decision

In the UK, as in the rest of Europe, the domestic political context of the LRTNF decision was fraught, and tensions escalated as deployment drew nearer in 1983. By that time, the Labour opposition had come out strongly in favour of unilateral nuclear disarmament (splitting the party in the process), and its leader, Michael Foot, and his shadow cabinet were keen to distance themselves from the nuclear policy discussions of the previous Callaghan government. In this new context of intense politicisation of the nuclear issue, with mounting public fear of all-out nuclear war, and growing support for the Campaign for Nuclear Disarmament (CND), there were strong constitutional pressures on Quinlan to withdraw from the nuclear debate. Not surprisingly, he tried to avoid making overtly political references in his correspondence, and so it is difficult to get a feel for the tense domestic and international debates over LRTNF deployment from his letters. However, a letter to Quinlan from journalist John Barry helps piece together the political context of the 1979 decision and the political tensions over deployment in 1983. Barry had written an article on the subject for the *Sunday Times*, and was seeking Quinlan's feedback on the accuracy of his draft.[27] In a note attached to the text, dated 17 January 1983, he explained that the purpose of the article was to 'set out, as factually as possible, how deeply Callaghan's people were involved in the *Pershing–Tomahawk* decision'. He added that: 'Clearly, it will cause something of a stir, since ... nobody has set it all down in quite this way before. So I need to be fireproof on fact.' Unfortunately, much of the text of the original document has faded with time, but the second part of the article remains intact, providing some interesting insights into the work of the HLG in the lead up to the 1979 decision, and the role of the Callaghan government in the decisions taken by the NATO NPG.

> **Draft of *Sunday Times* article on *Pershing–Tomahawk* decision**
>
> It is not necessary to trace in detail the HLG work. What matters here is Labour ministers' knowledge and approval of its various phases. As a matter of routine, summaries of the HLG progress would be sent up to the defence and foreign secretaries. It may also be taken that [Defence Secretary] Fred Mulley was far too canny, far too aware of Labour sensitivities in all matters nuclear to have done anything significant without clearing it with the Prime Minister. So did this mean that the British team on the

HLG were under orders to block any modernisation? On the contrary, the British played a key role in overcoming American efforts to block it.

Surprisingly quickly – by their third meeting at Los Alamos in January 1978, the HLG concluded that NATO did, in principle, need new and longer-range weapons, though what sort and how many remained to be defined. When word of this reached the White House in the person of David Aaron, Carter's assistant national security advisor, he was aghast.

Aaron was by no means convinced of the doctrinal or political arguments for new weapons. Besides, like many in the Washington defence and foreign affairs community, Aaron bore the battle scars of Kennedy's ill-fated attempt in the early 1960s to launch a NATO multilateral nuclear force. The bloodshed that caused in NATO convinced a whole generation of U.S. policymakers how hard NATO found it to make any nuclear decision. So Aaron foresaw real trouble over this Los Alamos consensus – quite apart from questioning its intellectual justification.

That was why, when the HLG next met, at Brussels in March, to translate the Los Alamos conclusion into a document for ministers, the American team had been joined by a member of Carter's National Security Council, answering directly to Aaron and with orders to emasculate that consensus. He failed. Politely but implacably, the British team on the HLG led the counter-attack. This was what the HLG had concluded: this was what should go to ministers. And it did.

NATO defence ministers – Mulley among them – took note of the HLG's conclusion at a Nuclear Planning Group meeting in Freidrickshaven [sic] in April 1978, and authorised the HLG to start work on the next phase: a detailed study of deployment options. This meeting alone makes nonsense of the claim, since made privately by some of the Labour ministers involved, that the HLG was purely an expert group whose work committed governments to nothing. That is technically true but, after Freidrickshaven, political nonsense. The time to argue against the whole idea of new missiles was then. But, on the contrary, Mulley spoke in favour of the HLG consensus at that meeting; it was the Americans who, in the corridors, were muttering reservations.

What happened next was that the Carter administration changed its mind. Following that NPG meeting, a mammoth inter-agency study got under way in Washington on the issue of NATO nuclear modernisation. By mid-July it was completed; and by mid-August President Carter had decided the US would after all support new deployments. (And as part of the study, Washington had gone a long way towards defining the types and numbers of new weapons that might be sensible). But Carter's advisors were determined to see that the fiasco of the neutron bomb[28] – when the Alliance leaders quite failed to grasp each others' concerns – should not be repeated. This time, the US would clear each step of the way in private bilateral talks with other NATO governments before seeking general NATO approval.

So, in the first days of October 1978, Carter's national security advisor, Zbigniew Brzezinski, flew to Britain for a secret meeting with Callaghan. The Labour Party conference was on, so Brzezinski had to go up to Blackpool. There he relayed Carter's decision, and the US view of how the matter should be handled. Callaghan agreed; and he agreed too with the idea Brzezinski floated of a private summit of key western leaders to thrash out the issue. That meeting, it was settled later, would be on Guadeloupe, in the French West Indies, in January 1979.

In the meantime, through the dying months of 1978, the High Level Group resumed work: its task now being to refine and recommend what numbers and types of long-range weapons should be deployed. The basic options paper was American – it was an edited version or a chapter of the inter-agency study – and it offered five possible systems: a new and long-range Pershing missile; ground-launched cruise missiles; sea-launched cruise missiles; the FB–111H aircraft; or an entirely new medium-range ballistic missile codenamed Longbow. The paper also offered a graduated scale of deployments, from fewer than 200 new weapons to well over 1,000. At the first meeting of the resumed HLG in October, delegates began to settle on 200–600 as the right sort of total, with a bias towards 600.

For the Labour Government, however, the crucial decision came as part of Mr. Callaghan's preparations for Guadeloupe. Though economic issues were also on the agenda, the summit was primarily to discuss the nuclear question. Carter wanted Alliance support for SALT-2 [the second round of the Strategic Arms Limitation Talks between the US and the USSR], which was running into trouble back home. And of course, he wanted political accord on the NATO programme. For his part, Mr Callaghan wanted to raise with President Carter the question of a successor to Britain's aging Polaris fleet. Rather than handle preparations for Guadeloupe through the usual Cabinet committee system, Mr Callaghan chose to do it by means of 'briefings' to a selected handful of senior ministers. Those he chose to involve were Foreign Secretary David Owen, Defence Secretary Fred Mulley, Chancellor Denis Healey and Employment Secretary Michael Foot –

whom the Prime Minister appears to have involved because he was the senior spokesman in Cabinet for the anti-nuclear faction. The conclusion this small group reached was that NATO should seek to defuse the SS-20 threat by means of arms control talks with the Soviets; that these should be in the next round of SALT, SALT–3; but that, if a deal could not be done, Britain would agree to the deployment of new weapons.

(Actually, the official advice reaching ministers was skeptical in the extreme about the prospects for arms control. For the Russians unilaterally to abandon the SS-20 would be contrary to the whole arms-control philosophy. Nor were Callaghan and his ministers more sanguine. But Schmidt was saying that an arms-control appeal would ease his political problems; and Callaghan, as well as wanting to help his good friend Helmut, thought the same would be true in the Labour Cabinet and Party).

Precisely what was said at Guadeloupe will never be settled, for the bureaucratic reason that no agreed record was ever compiled. The four leaders – Carter, Callaghan, Schmidt and President Giscard of France – came with only one adviser apiece. In Callaghan's case it was Cabinet Secretary Sir John Hunt. No notes were taken during the sessions, which were held mostly in a sort of Club Mediterranean beach bar, so the advisors had to write individual minutes afterwards by frantically comparing recollections. And some of the most important conversations were never recorded at all. The key exchange between Carter and Callaghan, for example came on a walk together along the beach. But that was the point: Guadeloupe was meant to be very, very private.

Nevertheless, the outline of what was said can be pieced together. Carter told his allies that he personally supported the new nuclear deployments and wished to press ahead with them; that it should be done quickly; that the US would take the lead in navigating the decisions through NATO but would require a consensus among European leaders that the programme was needed. The Germans had already made it clear in the High Level Group that they did not want to be the only country to house these new systems and Carter said he supported that. Carter also said he thought the problem should simultaneously be tackled through an arms-control approach: this, he thought, should be done in the context of SALT. In his view, the two tracks – deployment and arms control – should run parallel.

In reply, Carter did not get what he had wanted, which was an immediate declaration of support from the three Europeans. Giscard was the most supportive while making it clear that of course, there was no question of France, as an independent military power, deploying these weapons herself. Schmidt was the most worried and talked a lot about arms control. Callaghan tried to steer a middle path, keeping a certain solidarity with Schmidt yet also letting Carter know, in the course of the summit, of his own decision in favour.

The leaders did actually discuss possible deployment options, though some of their ideas were slightly weird. But what was formally agreed was that Carter would send an emissary to them in Europe with specific deployment proposals. Which is why David Aaron found himself spending long hours in mid-air over the Atlantic through the first months of 1979. And the preferred option that he brought with him from Washington was for a mix of *Pershing* and cruise missiles, with a total at the upper end of the 200–600 range. The *Pershings* would be based in Germany; the cruise missiles would be scattered through the rest of Europe. It was always clear that Britain would be one of the bases. Privately, Labour ministers – with the exception of David Owen – thought cruise missiles were a load of junk; and could never understand why Schmidt was so keen on them. But the logic, political and strategic, of basing the new systems widely throughout Europe was powerful; and for technical reasons, cruise missiles admirably met the requirement imposed by dispersal. So cruise it was.

Formally, the High Level Group had the task of coming up with a final proposal, though in reality of course its function was now rather overtaken by Aaron's missions direct to NATO leaders. Duly, by the spring of 1979, the HLG too had come up with a *Pershing*/cruise missile mix, totaling in all something near 600 systems. At a climactic meeting of the Nuclear Planning Group in late April 1979 – this one held on the US Air Force base at Homestead in Florida – NATO defence ministers accepted in principle the recommendation.

Callaghan had been dubious about Mulley going to that meeting. It was only days before the [1979] election, which Callaghan had accepted he was going to lose; and he did not think it was sensible to pretend Mulley could speak for his successor. But Mulley was proud of what had been achieved; and wanted to go; so Callaghan agreed. The final act of the Labour Government was to agree to the setting up of a new 'Special Group', to consider what NATO might offer in the arms-control package that would be prof-fered at the same time as the deployment decision. Before the Government would agree to this, however, ministers insisted that the rest of NATO realise that Britain's *Polaris* submarine would under no circumstances be part of that arms-control package.

It is unclear whether Quinlan commented on Barry's text – Barry himself cannot remember, and there is nothing in the files to suggest that he did (or to confirm whether he agreed to Barry's request for a private meeting in Quinlan's office the following week). For that reason, it is impossible to gauge whether Quinlan considered Barry's account of events accurate – either in terms of the role played by the HLG, or the extent to which the Callaghan government had played a role in the 1979 LRTNF decision-making process before formal assent was given under the Thatcher government. But newly released US documents (and other accounts in the scholarly literature) indicate that Barry's analysis was sound.

Countering UK opposition to the LRTNF decision

Quinlan advised the Thatcher government to be cautious in its presentation of the NATO LRTNF decision to the British public. Just as he encouraged politicians to argue the case for *Trident* on the basis of the need for a credible 'second centre of decision' (avoiding the more populist Gaullist justification for Britain's independent strategic deterrent), he urged the conservative leadership not to present the LRTNF decision as a response to Soviet SS-20 deployment. He believed the tit-for-tat rationale could be exploited by anti-nuclear activists who were arguing that East and West were engaged in a dangerous and limitless arms race. Instead, he tried to convince the Thatcher government to present the LRTNF decision as a logical step in long-term NATO efforts to generate deterrence stability. However, his correspondence reveals some frustration that his advice on how to present this was often ignored. In his 7 January 1983 letter to Edwards, he lamented that '(to my regret and against my advice!), politicians have increasingly taken the soft but risky option' of presenting the LRTNF decision as primarily a response to the SS-20.

The lack of understanding in political circles of a subject as complex and esoteric as NATO doctrine made it even more difficult to stop the public debate from becoming mired in confusion, exaggeration and misunderstanding. Whatever the rights and wrongs of the 1979 decision in terms of its strategic and political imperatives and the wider issue of the morality of deterrence, the fact was that in the early 1980s, many scholars, politicians, defence commentators, peace activists and church leaders in the West were drawing disturbing conclusions about the intentions of the NATO TNF modernisation plan. Many believed it represented a doctrinal shift in NATO towards an aggressive, war-fighting doctrine, which risked triggering a nuclear confrontation in Europe. While the latter might have been true in the context of the heated Reagan–Andropov rhetoric that dominated superpower relations in 1983, claims that the 1979 decision was part of a NATO plan to achieve escalation dominance were false, and as far as Quinlan was concerned, were dangerous nonsense. Even though he had left the MoD by the time the debate reached its climax in the long lead up to the deployment of the GLCMs and *Pershing* II missiles, Quinlan was committed to correcting the false analysis that was being put about by influential and respected commentators in the UK, US and mainland Europe, some of whom were more willing to accept Soviet interpretations of the 1979 decision than the explanations offered by Western officials. Quinlan's correspondence reveals that he found this exasperating and, at times (when he thought the author ought to know better), his normally careful and measured use of language is tinged with irritation and even anger.

This is all evident in a letter Quinlan wrote to Tom Burns, editor of the Catholic weekly, *The Tablet*, on 28 July 1981. The journal had recently run an article by Ed Doherty, entitled 'Nuclear War in Europe?' which had been written in response to unease among European academics and church leaders over the 1979 LRTNF modernisation plan. That unease had been clearly expressed during a public debate on the issue at the University of Groningen in April, which was co-sponsored by the University and by the US Center for Defense Information, and which a number of senior defence officials attended. The core argument presented in the Doherty article was that the stationing of GLCMs and *Pershing* II missiles in Europe was part of a new nuclear war-fighting doctrine, which would bring the continent one step closer to a nuclear holocaust. Quinlan responded to the article by providing *The Tablet* with a detailed, 45-paragraph critique, preceded by the following letter:[29]

> **"** I promised to tell you why I did not think well of the piece by Ed Doherty (whom as it happens I know and find personally quite agreeable). Herewith a point-by-point commentary. I apologise for what must seem undue asperity here and there – please put it down to haste. I probably have not picked up every point, but perhaps there is enough to explain my general view. No blame to any non-expert who did not pick up the weaknesses – on the face of things one might have felt entitled to assume that Ed was well-informed and accurate. **"**

A number of the points raised in Quinlan's critique highlight his mounting frustration at the inaccurate and one-sided nature of much of the commentary on the LRTNF debate and discussions over nuclear deterrence in general. A few of the most interesting comments are presented below:

> **"** 1. The suggestion, presented as fact, of a 'new doctrine of warfighting' is rubbish. Distinctions between deterrence and warfighting are misconceived … the

distinction between using weapons in war and using them for deterrence is bogus – the two are inseparable … 'Nuclear war planners' are nuclear deterrers.

2. The implication that people who station LRTNF will be targets for (Soviet) IRBMs whereas people who do not station them will not be has no basis in fact or logic. The converse might be true – consider Hiroshima/Nagasaki. NATO's new LRTNF will not be static targets easily vulnerable to pre-emptive strike.

3. [Doherty's claim that the Soviet leadership initiated the arms-control element of the dual-track decision] is inadequate to the point of being misleading. NATO's December 1979 decision was essentially two-track [from the start] – modernise and negotiate. Brezhnev originally, said 'If you modernise, I won't negotiate'. When NATO made clear that it was not prepared to do business on this basis, Brezhnev finally [conceded].

4. 'By no means all of whom can be regarded as pacifists' captures the balance of the conference more accurately than, I suspect, Mr. Doherty realises. The weighting was heavily anti-nuclear … I do not believe there was a 'good balance'. [Doherty's] choice of words [dividing the conference participants] into two groups: a) 'technically qualified specialists' and b) 'ethically and politically motivated peace activists'] is interesting. I regard myself, if you like, as an 'ethically and politically motivated peace activist'; but this, you may be sure, is not what Mr. Doherty means.

5. Escalation is not a tidy, uniquely pre-determined process. There is no basis for a statement, as though it were fact, that [use of] NATO's (relatively few) MRBMs would be the next step [in a nuclear escala-

tion] after 'tactical' weapons – of which MRBMs are indeed, by some definitions, a sub-category.

6. [Those who argue that 'a nuclear war in Europe would be a catastrophe unparalleled in the history of our civilization'] are claiming a degree of certainty no-one can possibly possess. If he confined himself to saying that the chances of limiting nuclear war are at best precarious, I would have no difficulty in agreeing.

7. [Despite Doherty's claim that the Vatican 'strongly condemned the use of weapons of mass destruction'] it did no such sweeping thing. It condemned, in effect, indiscriminate attack on cities qua cities – a much more limited matter. It is worth noting that Vatican II stressed multilateral and (explicitly) not unilateral disarmament.

8. [In response to the unilateralists' argument that the horror of life under communism – for example, life in present day Poland – would be preferable to life in a post-holocaust world where the living would envy the dead] firstly, we have no assurance that what we would get is the condition of today's Poland (disagreeable though that is). We might get the condition of Cambodia, or the 1930s Ukraine. Secondly, we are surely entitled to plan to have neither of the ['red or dead'] options [offered in Doherty's analysis]. **"**

Doherty ended his article with the sentence: 'One hopes that the irritation the conference produced among NATO and Pentagon officials will lead them to take more seriously the viewpoints expressed there'. To which Quinlan responded: 'If there was irritation as described may it have been because of the loaded character of the conference and the superficiality of much of the analysis?'

Doherty's analysis of the reasons for the anti-nuclear sentiment at the 1981 Groningen conference was understandably irritating for Quinlan and anyone else who had been involved in the deliberations of the HLG and NPG, but despite its flaws and factual inaccuracies, it did reflect the thinking of many anti-nuclear activists, who were convinced that the new missiles were components of a disarming first strike capability being prepared by the West. An exchange of letters between Quinlan and Dan Martin, editor of *Southwark Justice and Peace News* (a religious publication associated with the Southwark Archdiocesan and Peace Office) reveal how deep rooted this belief was. An article Martin had published in the December 1983 issue of the journal (to coincide with the deployment of GLCMs and *Pershing* II missiles in Europe) caught Quinlan's eye because it included extracts from an interview with an American bishop, who had mounted a campaign to encourage employees of the US atomic weapons establishment to resign on ethical grounds. The bishop concerned had even set up a fund to provide financial support for workers who followed his advice. Martin discussed the interview in a piece he called 'Faith and First Strike', informing his readers that if they wanted to receive further information about the dangers of first strike, they should contact his office. After reading the piece, Quinlan wrote to Martin, requested that he stop spreading misinformation about NATO doctrine, and included some literature that he hoped would make Martin realise that his claims were both mistaken and misleading. Martin sent him the following response, dated 29 February 1984:[30]

“ Your suggestion that I 'desist from the untruth' is received, as I am sure it was given, in the spirit of dialogue. I can assure you though that I have spent more than '5 minutes' looking at the facts. The statements made in the MoD leaflet are in disagreement with many of the books I have read by such people as Robert Aldridge, Paul Rodgers, Peter Pringle, etc.

In short, I would like not to believe what I have read about a 'disarming first-strike capability being prepared by the West' but I would need more than an A5 leaflet to change my mind. Any suggestions you have along this line I will try to follow up.

Finally, though you say we see things differently on this matter, I do not think a discussion between us would end in argument or be unfruitful. I'm sure there is much I can learn from you. 🔟🔟

Quinlan replied a few days later, with a more detailed explanation of the logical flaws in the first strike thesis:[31]

🔠🔠 I assure you I use the word 'untruth' in the strict sense, to mean simply a statement that is not true – that is, not in accordance with the facts. I neither intend nor regard it as carrying any implication about motivation or good faith, save perhaps in the special case (not applying here) of someone who must plainly be taken as fully aware of the true facts.

You are entitled to know why I maintain so firmly that you are mistaken on fact. So let me explain. I was head of the British delegation on the NATO group which developed the proposals approved by NATO Ministers in December 1979 for the deployment (failing an arms control settlement) of *Pershing* II and GLCM. I attended every minute of every meeting of that group throughout the relevant two years of work, and I saw all the papers. At no stage whatever, throughout the process, did any delegation suggest that what we should have been, or could have been, or were about was acquiring a capability for a disarming first strike. All of us knew perfectly well that that is not NATO's policy; that it is in any event an unattainable objective; and that the classes of weapons we were concerned with would be unsuited for any realistic approximation towards it.

You will be aware also, I imagine, that Ministers of all the participating NATO Governments have often indicated in public, collectively and severally, that the modernisation plan (like all other Western nuclear weapons programmes) is neither directed to nor capable of a disarming first strike.

You do not have to take simply on trust the veracity of the above. Consider these facts, all on public record:

a. The NATO plan, if carried to full completion in 1988, will provide 572 new missiles – 464 GLCM, 108 *Pershing* II (the latter directly replacing 108 *Pershing* I of shorter range, and the whole deployment being conducted within an overall net reduction of 35% in NATO's holding of warheads in Europe).

b. *Pershing* II from the FRG cannot reach beyond Moscow (if that far), and the GLCMs from most of the planned NATO bases not much if any further (precise reach depends on where the point of launch is and how much fuel is used up on evasive routing).

c. Most of the already-existing longer-range Soviet land-based missiles – including the vast majority of their 1,398 ICBMs (over 5,000 warheads), and many of their over-300 SS-20s (around 1,000 warheads) – are thus quite out of reach of the planned NATO missiles, as well as many times too numerous anyway for them to 'take out'.

d. The SS-20s are moreover mobile. Even were they all within range, NATO simply would not know for sure where to aim its missiles. (Satellite photography, I can assure you, does not solve this problem).

e. Quite aside from the huge, largely out-of-range and part-mobile land-based Soviet ICBM/IRBM/MRBM forces, the Soviet Union has nearly 1,000 ballistic missiles (about 1,800 warheads) in submarines; about these, when at sea, the new NATO missiles (or any other Western missiles) can do nothing.

f. If NATO had really wanted a disarming-first-strike capability, it is very odd that it should have opted for a force mix over 80% composed of GLCMs which take hours to reach their targets and, though at present hard to shoot down, are by no means as hard as the *Pershing* IIs.

The figures I have used above come from the 1982/83 edition of the IISS *Military Balance*. I have not the 1983/84 version immediately to hand, but the picture of the Soviet inventory will not have changed materially downwards; nor does it seem in the least likely, on present deployment momentum and experience, to have done so by the time the NATO force is complete in 1988. (The number of sea-based warheads indeed will almost certainly have risen greatly).

Consider also the facts of the arms control negotiations. The US have constantly (and under Carter, not only Reagan) indicated willingness to accept zero deployment, or many fewer than 572, if the Russians will accept parity. (The Russian bottom line, through all the shifts of detail, has unwaveringly been 'NATO no GLCM/*Pershing* II, USSR some SS-20s'). No doubt the elements of the bargain are debatable and neither side is faultless; but my point here is that a US willingness to cut planned numbers of its own missiles, in return for a Russian cut in missiles which are untargetable anyway, hardly suggests a determination to reach a disarming-first-strike capability, unless you assume that the US arms-control posture is totally insincere.

I no longer have time to follow the literature (which is enormously copious) as closely as I used to; I have not read the works of any of the writers you mention, and cannot therefore judge with any confidence whether they reflect a balanced reading-list on these hard matters. I do however know a good proportion of the main strategic studies specialists in this country, and a fair sprinkling of those in continental Europe and the US. Those of my acquaintance are by no means an 'establishment' consensus; several of them for example do not accept the case (undoubtedly complex, difficult and debatable) for the new NATO missile force. But I believe not one of them would take seriously the claim you make about the force's intended purpose; they understand too well facts like those I have set out above.

No doubt there is room for discussion about the precise significance of this or that element of what I have said. But when it is taken in the round, I submit that the view which you assert in your lead-in to [your article on 'Faith and First Strike'] can continue to be maintained in so unqualified a manner only if one is prepared to impute sustained mendacity on a massive scale … to US, UK and other NATO Ministers and officials, with matching gullibility on the part of the mainstream of Western strategic studies thought and criticism. I am aware that some people in (for example) part of CND's wide spectrum, and groups of left-wing political orientation, are indeed prepared to make just those imputations. You have, as a private individual, a citizen's right to be among their number. But I should be surprised – and frankly – a little disconcerted, given that I take you to be in some sense on the diocesan staff and with a particular duty of balance and objectivity in matters on which Catholics differ in good faith – if you do indeed maintain such a position; and in that event I confess I would be interested to know why. **"**

Martin appears to have been impressed with Quinlan's knowledge and his detailed critique of the first-strike case, although he does not seem to have been completely convinced by his arguments. He responded with a short letter on 26 April 1984:[32]

" For some time I have been meaning to write you a long letter to explain why I hold the position I do concerning the 'disarming first-strike capability being prepared by the West', but, time and other work considerations worked against me. However, I will respond briefly with a few thoughts. When I used the word 'West' I refer to more than to NATO. Also, I said 'capability' not intention; you seem to use those two words interchangeably. I said Pershings and Cruise are 'components of a disarming…'; I realise that they do not of themselves possess such capability. From my read, I gather that anti-submarine warfare on the part of the West is much more advanced than you suggest. Finally, in addition to the authors I mentioned before to you I will add Frank

Barnaby and Sir Martin Ryle. I hope to respond later in greater detail to these points and the others you raised in your 5 March letter. **"**

Quinlan was disturbed that a church organisation had aligned so publicly with the CND position on NATO nuclear posture – to the extent that on 3 April 1984 he wrote to Archbishop Michael Bowen about the situation:[33]

" I am writing to express concern about an aspect of the operations of the Diocese's Justice and Peace Office. In brief, it seems to me that the Office is actively promoting in respect of nuclear weapons a particular political line controversial as between Catholics and so not appropriate to carry any seal, whether apparent or real, of Diocesan support.

Over the last few months I have had telephone and written contact with Mr. Dan Martin, the Diocese's Field Worker in these matters. I have found him open and courteous. It is clear from our contacts and from the material he has sent me both that he is of what I may call, in shorthand, the CND view; and that he judges it right from the Office to promulgate this view and to further protest action in support of it. I shall not lengthen this letter with a recital of evidence in support of this assessment of the Office's line; I can do so if you wish, but it can scarcely be in doubt – the leaflet enclosed herewith (which came as part of the Office's standard pack) is a clear illustration of active promotion.

I do not doubt Mr. Martin's good faith, nor question his right as a private individual to hold and advance whatever political views he sees fit. But the CND view is a matter of vivid political controversy, and many

Catholics (including, I believe, a number of the bishops) reject it after just as much conscientious thought and with as much moral conviction as its proponents can claim. Bodies like Pax Christi are of course free to take sides as their members see fit. But your diocese is the diocese of us all, not a voluntary organisation or a pressure group. It seems to me, and to other Diocesan parishioners whom I have consulted, seriously out of place that this particular line – or any other committed political line on the subject, for I am not at all urging the simple substitution of different one – should be pursued from the Diocesan Office, or in any way with the aid of diocesan resources. The incorporation of a brief disclaimer at the end of a Newsletter in no way removes the difficulty, any more than it would if the preceding substance were publishing (say) specific Conservative, Labour or Alliance views on disputed questions of social policy about which individuals held strong moral views.

To forestall any misunderstanding let me make my own position clear. I am a Civil Servant who used to work in the Ministry of Defence on nuclear policy issues, under both Labour and Conservative Governments. My interest in and knowledge of the subject naturally originated there. However, I left that Ministry nearly three years ago; for all I know I may never return there; my continuing personal interest is in no way requested, briefed, instructed or guided from there; and in the particular matter with which this letter is concerned I have had no dealings of any kind with Government contacts.

I am sending a copy of this Letter to Mr Martin. He is welcome to show you the correspondence which he and I have had. **"**

Quinlan's letter to Archbishop Bowen followed two weeks after he had written to former Cabinet Secretary John Hunt on the same subject. He wrote the letter, dated 20 March 1984, seeking his advice (as a fellow senior civil servant, Catholic, and advocate of nuclear weapons) on what should be done about Dan Martin's anti-nuclear activism:[34]

> **"** I should be grateful if, when we see one another next week, I could take your mind on a worry I have about the operations of the Southwark Justice and Peace Office.
>
> In essence, this office is operating – from Clergy House – as an active branch of CND in respect of nuclear issues. I have not the least reason to doubt the good faith of the individuals concerned, but this seems to me seriously objectionable.
>
> The background is briefly as follows. A Mr. Dan Martin, who seems to head the operation, rang me some time ago to ask me to appear with Bruce Kent on a platform to discuss nuclear issues. I said I couldn't, and at my suggestion he successfully tried Fr Gerry Hughes. We fell into correspondence thereafter. He sent me some of his literature; I complained to him of an assertion that GLCM and Pershing were part of a Western plan for a 'disarming first strike capability'; he maintained his view; I sent him further and better particulars – copy herewith. (No reply as yet.) Following paragraph 10 of my letter I received yesterday a pack of papers of which I enclose the relevant bits. This leaves, to my mind, no doubt that the office is not merely of CND views but in positive promotion of CND activities.
>
> I do not need to spell out why this seems to me wrong (and I would say the same if the Office were similarly slanted to, say, the viewpoint of the British Atlantic

Committee, which many Catholics would endorse with no less moral conviction).

I would very much value your opinion about this. Does it matter? If so, what might best be done? I am very ready to write to the archbishop though that carries the slight disadvantage that if the issue thereafter comes to argument the 'opposition' might try to score debating points about my supposed allegiances. **"**

It is unclear whether John Hunt responded to Quinlan's concerns, but the correspondence files do include a response from Archbishop Bowen, dated 9 April 1984, in which he thanked Quinlan for his letter, explained that he appreciated the point Quinlan was making, and sought his permission to circulate the letter about Dan Martin's anti-nuclear activities to members of the Justice and Peace Group management team.

First strike and Star Wars: 'The Pentagon on the warpath'

Concerns over the NATO LRTNF plan sparked the biggest peace protests in Europe since the Second World War. Although public opposition to the plan was not as intense in the US, it was nonetheless widespread among US scholars, church leaders and peace activists, many of whom shared the concerns of European commentators who believed NATO had shifted to a more aggressive nuclear posture. At the time, the work of the writer and campaigner Robert C. Aldridge was attracting the attention of the US media and Western peace movement. A former missile engineer who had resigned from his job for ethical reasons and become a fierce Pentagon critic, Aldridge argued that the *Pershing* II missiles, which could carry advanced maneuvering warheads, were the most accurate long-range weapons ever produced. In his 1983 book on the subject, which he gave the title *First Strike,*[35] he argued that the decision to deploy *Pershing* missiles to West

Germany was part of a US drive to acquire 'a genocidal capacity' to launch a nuclear attack on the Soviet Union so devastating that it would be unable to respond and its entire society would collapse. Although some interpreted this to mean that the US was planning for nuclear Armageddon, Aldridge argued that the US intention was not actually to use the weapons in a military strike, but rather to employ them as an instrument of foreign policy to intimidate the Soviets. But in his view, this was an irresponsibly risky strategy – he feared that the Soviet Union could launch a pre-emptive nuclear attack on West Germany to avoid falling victim to a US first strike.

Aldridge's book (along with a series of his earlier publications on the subject) had a significant impact on the peace movement in the UK. It prompted Dan Martin, after three years of silence, to resume his correspondence with Quinlan: he sent him a copy of *First Strike* and put him in touch with Aldridge. The subsequent exchange of letters between Quinlan and Aldridge exposes the huge chasm in their attitudes to nuclear weapons and in their general views of the world. Quinlan, as he explained in a letter to Martin, regarded Aldridge as having a 'conspiracy view of history, whereby data and statements are typically chosen and assessed (for acceptance or rejection) primarily according to whether or not they bear out a basic thesis which the writer is pre-disposed to accept'.[36] He admitted that 'Mr. Aldridge might from his standpoint have counterbalancing criticism to voice on my own (scantier) writings; none of us who have addressed the subject at all can claim pure neutrality about it'. Martin appears to have forwarded Quinlan's letter to Aldridge, who responded with the following letter, dated 30 April 1987:[37]

> **❝** It is somewhat difficult knowing exactly how to commence. I don't wish to adopt an adversarial position

and neither do I presume to convert your sincere beliefs. I understand that Mr Martin has furnished you with my book entitled *First Strike* (which is somewhat dated now) so you know something about my interpretation of current military programs. Therefore, I believe it best to simply explain how I feel and why I came to feel that way.

During World War II, I was an artilleryman and saw combat in the Philippines so I am not uninformed about war and military matters. Since then I became an aeronautical engineer and worked on submarine-launched ballistic missiles for Lockheed. I was the cognizant design engineer for underwater-launch and surface-launch testing of the *Polaris* missiles which are now in British submarines. Later I transferred to reentry systems and was deeply involved in developing the MIRVed warheads on *Poseidon* missiles. At the beginning of the *Trident* Program I had concept design responsibility for the Mark-500 maneuvering reentry vehicle which was an offshoot of the Antelope program, as was the British *Chevaline*. It was on this assignment that I recognised something was wrong with the deterrent policy in which I then believed so strongly.

That is a brief resume of my background. Possibly the chief factor in bringing about my present feelings was being challenged to question established policies. The process was painful during the late 1960s when it became obvious that the objectives of my country in Vietnam were not what I had always envisioned. Since then there have been numerous occasions, now well known, in which my government has not been candid with its citizens. I could name much more deception in military programs but will not go into that at this time. I'll simply say that it is now very difficult for me to accept at face value anything announced by official sources. That may seem harsh but it is the result of my experience.

My approach since resigning from Lockheed in 1973 has been to analyze military programs and technological objectives from an engineering viewpoint to determine their integrated capabilities. Results from this analysis convinces me that the United States will achieve a first strike capability sometime in the 1990s if the various programs are successful. Of course the Soviets are also striving to match US efforts but they lack some key technologies such as computerisation, sensors, submarine detection and more. It would take them much longer to attain a first strike capability.

I had the privilege of giving testimony before, and providing consultation to, the committee that drafted the American bishops' Pastoral entitled 'The Challenge of Peace: God's Promise and Our Response'. I feel that I was instrumental in helping the bishops understand one key point – that the United States has two types of policies. There is on the one hand an 'action' policy which would be followed under given circumstances and, on the other hand, an 'announced' policy which [US Secretary of State for Arms Control] Paul Nitze described as geared for political and psychological effects. Within the past few years I seem to notice that the term 'policy' refers to announced policy whereas what is called an 'option' or 'capability' seems to reflect the action policy. Thus the US can claim it has no first strike policy or launch-on-warning policy. But it can have those options. When John Tower (recent chairman of the Tower Commission investigating the Iran–Contra controversy) was chairman of the Senate Armed Services Committee he stated that the

United States should not have a first strike policy but it should have a first strike capability.

I have outlined the basic elements of a first strike capability in my book. US allies, including NATO seem to be contributing. For instance, Norway, Britain, France, Japan, Australia and New Zealand contribute greatly to ASW [anti-submarine warfare] detection and shadowing. France has recently signed an agreement with the US to share ocean surveillance satellite data – information critical to feed into ASW computers to predict sound paths. And, yes, I believe Pershing 2s and GLCMs (all under US control) play a vital role in the first strike scenario.

The 108 *Pershing* 2s would serve as decapitators. You must know that all the first echelon command and control facilities for the Soviet government and its military forces are within a 50-mile radius of Moscow. These could be reached by Pershing 2s in 12–14 minutes. Decapitation of the Soviet leadership could be the key to a successful first strike.

Also, as you must know, fratricide[38] is a little understood phenomenon. Cruise missiles approaching low and slow could possibly penetrate beneath a cloud of dust and debris which would be lethal to ballistic warheads coming down at high speed from outer space, and destroy Soviet missiles while they are also held down by the fratricide environment. It wouldn't be just the GLCMs in Europe but also 758 nuclear-tipped sea-launched cruise missiles and thousands of air-launched cruise missiles. **"**

Quinlan's in-tray was too full to send a detailed response, but he did make two points by way of reply on 11 May 1987:[39]

66 a. DoD motivations quite apart, I shall be interested to hear how you come to the view (if I understand you rightly) that Western ASW will by the mid-90s have attained an effective capability for large-scale pre-emptive strike on the huge Soviet SSBN [ship submersible ballistic nuclear submarine] force. This is an opinion widely different from any knowledgeable-seeming one that reaches me.

b. As you can readily ascertain from enquiries around suitable Washington corridors, I personally played (for good or ill) a major part in the shaping of the 1979 NATO decision on INF; and accordingly *I know* what the formative history of that decision was in the NATO-context. Frankly, you and I will have difficulty in constructive communication if you are not prepared to accept what I report in that regard. **99**

Aldridge appears to have been surprised at Quinlan's reaction. He wrote back that he was 'puzzled as to why you think that [I am not prepared to accept your reporting on the history of the Intermediate-range Nuclear Forces (INF) decision from a NATO perspective]. I reviewed my last letter and the only thing which seems to foster such an impression was my statement about having difficulty accepting official announcements. I was referring to press releases and other information reflecting the posture of the US administration. I certainly do not dismiss the opinions of conscientious people within that administration.'[40]

Quinlan agreed to meet Aldridge on 14 July 1987, when the latter was visiting London. No further correspondence between the two took place thereafter (with the exception of a letter Aldridge sent Quinlan on 3 December 1987, congratulating him in his appointment as PUS at the MoD and expressing his tremendous relief 'that a man of Christian conscience is in that position'). However, a few days after his meeting with

Aldridge, Quinlan sent Martin his impressions of how the meeting went:[41]

> **❝** I read [the copy of *First Strike* that you sent me] with much interest, but mixed reactions. I have no difficulty in agreeing that a good many things which are or have been done in the arms field seem unnecessary, wasteful and even positively undesirable for other reasons, though my list of such things would probably be shorter and less deeply-etched than Mr Aldridge's. But I am not even remotely persuaded either that the cumulative armoury is, or is likely to become, anywhere within reach of a real-life first-strike capability, or that there is a sustained, comprehensive and mendaciously-concealed drive to build up such a capability. I have the impression, from the talk Mr Aldridge and I had on Tuesday, that he might himself now no longer press this latter proposition with the vigour and conviction which the book as published seems to imply. However, I do not wish to put words in his mouth – the fact that he did not stress this theme may perhaps have been due to a courteous preference to look for aspects of the issues on which we might be more likely to find common ground. I enjoyed and valued the chance to meet him; it was a pleasant encounter, and we identified a good deal that we would agree about in respect of the general directions in which practical policy ought to move. Many thanks to you for arranging our meeting. **❞**

Many critics of NATO and US nuclear doctrine seem to have viewed the LRTNF deployment in the context of Reagan's SDI initiative: taken together, it is easy to see why some believed the US was pursuing a nuclear war-fighting, nuclear war-winning capability, despite official pronouncements. Reagan's March 1983 'Star Wars' speech, which set out a vision for the creation of a shield to protect the US and its allies from incoming missiles, was seen as evidence that the US was no longer interested in stable deterrence; it was seeking the capability to decapitate the Soviet Union (hence the deployment of *Pershing* IIs to West Germany), and to wipe out the Soviets' ability to retaliate (hence the pursuit of an ambitious missile defence system). While Quinlan spent a lot of time trying to counter the arguments of those who drew these conclusions, and made no secret of the fact he had been a major player in the 1979 LRTNF decision, his correspondence reveals that he had severe reservations about the wisdom of SDI, which he saw as entirely separate from – and potentially deeply damaging to – NATO's deterrent. In the US, the SDI proposal was being presented by the Pentagon as a vision that offered new hope for ending the 'permanent nightmare' whereby the West had 'to rely on strategic forces that can revenge a missile attack but not defend against it, on weapons that can destroy cities but not protect them, on forces forever poised to avenge but never to save lives'.[42] Quinlan, however, saw it in a very different light, as did many in the UK defence establishment. On reading Reagan's speech, Quinlan immediately wrote to David McGiffert (US assistant secretary of defense during the Carter administration) with the following comment:[43]

> **"** I see in my newspapers this morning that the President has sought to give a great crusading impetus to ABM development. I don't know how that will go down on your side of the water; but speaking privately as now an irresponsible amateur I think it both fundamentally misconceived in strategic reality, and likely to cause a great deal of political trouble – of which we have enough

already – over here in Europe. I hope I am wrong, but I doubt it. **"**

McGiffert replied with a two-sentence letter, agreeing on the dangers of the president's vision and sending Quinlan newspaper clippings from the US, including highly critical analyses of the proposal by William Perry[44] (who called it 'an expensive technological risk') and Harold Brown[45] (who argued that the SDI research should be 'carried out in a spirit of skepticism sorely missing in the president's speech').[46]

Quinlan and Hockaday, who disagreed on a host of nuclear issues and were always ready to debate their points of difference, were of one mind where SDI was concerned. Both were involved in CCADD (a Christian forum for expert debate on defence and security issues, which is still active in the UK today) and discussed their views on Reagan's proposals in the context of a speech that Hockaday was preparing for a CCADD meeting on the subject. Hockaday sent his speech, which probed various aspects of Reagan's proposal (from the feasibility of the technology to the strategic, political and cost implications) to Quinlan for comment. Quinlan's growing concern about the impact of Star Wars on deterrence stability is evident in a note he sent Hockaday on 16 July 1985:[47]

" As widely interpreted, President Reagan's 'Star Wars' speech looked forward to a situation in which the technical development of highly effective means of defence against nuclear attack would mean that the safety of nations could rest on physically assured invulnerability rather than deterrence by prospect of counter-strike.

This is open to objection on several counts:

a. It sets an aim whose prospects of attainability are extremely poor. Given the enormous destructive power of nuclear weapons, a satisfactory physical defence system would have to have a very high probability of near-total impenetrability – in face of an enemy with (say) 10,000 warheads available, even a 1% failure rate in interception could mean enormous loss of life and property. Few if any scientists of repute would rate highly the chance of achieving such near-perfect defence by way of any technical avenue even remotely in sight. The Soviet Union has the ability, and would certainly have the will, to devote enormous high-quality effort to ensuring that Western defences did not achieve impermeability. And the defence has to be impermeable not just against long-range fixed ICBMs of relatively predictable trajectory but against aircraft; cruise missiles; and ballistic missiles launched (e.g. from submarines) from unexpected directions, on low trajectories and with short flight times.

b. The cost of even trying seriously for impermeability would be colossal, and might displace important other expenditures in or beyond the defence field.

c. The attempt would certainly cause much East–West political friction – the Soviet Union would view it with apprehension and deep suspicion.

d. The attempt would probably fuel an arms race in offensive weapons, as the Soviet Union sought to main-tain its ability to strike effectively (that is, in effect to defeat defences by numerical saturation).

e. This last point would also be catastrophic for endeav-ours towards arms control of offensive weapons. Moreover, the attempt would destroy the ABM Treaty of 1972, one of the few solid achievements in the nuclear arms control field. It might also indirectly damage the 1967 [sic] Non-Proliferation Treaty, since it would be seen or claimed as a deliberate flouting of Article VI's promise that the nuclear powers would scale down their competition.

f. The effect on the viability of the relatively small British and French nuclear forces of an ABM Treaty breakdown and a resultant superpower free-for-all in defensive systems could be very damaging and costly.

There have been some qualifying suggestions that a more modest objective might be sought – the provision of defences to improve the ability of Western retaliatory systems like fixed ICBMs to survive attempted first strike. That would be a less unreal objective, but several of the above difficulties would still apply in very substantial degree. The Soviet Union would still be apprehensive of how far the attempt might be extended – and arms control prospects would still be gravely damaged. There are other and less harmful ways (such as more emphasis on underwater systems) of guarding against the remote risk of attempts at disarming first strike.

The underlying truth in all this is that the 'Star Wars' aspiration is a sort of technological utopianism. The pervasive and permanent reality under which we all live is that science has put in man's hands – probably irrevocably – virtually infinite destructive power. No technical 'fix' will grant us escape; our only realistic hope lies in ensuring that we maintain, in an absolutely unmistakable manner, awareness on all sides that we have reached the reductio ad absurdum of warfare, and that the initiation of major war can never again be a rational option. Sustaining this at least cost is essentially a task for political skills, not technical ones. **"**

In addition to sending Hockaday this note, Quinlan also sent some feedback on his CCADD paper, urging him to expand and make more of some of his points:[48]

> ❝ I would be inclined to make more of the point (that is, if you agree with it) that the whole SDI enterprise is a search for a technological fix for the problems of deterrence. I regard it as a sort of blinkered utopianism.
>
> […] I would be disposed to make more than you do of the relative probabilities in the situation … Suppose that we face a choice between a first-best and a second-best solution; that the first-best solution has a 5% chance of achievement; and that the second-best solution has a 95% chance of achievement. But then suppose also that pursuing the first-best solution seriously damages the chance, should it fail, of subsequently securing the second-best solution, or makes the cost and timescale of securing it much worse? Pursuing the first-best solution, even if it cannot be proven to be absolutely out of reach, may then be positively the wrong thing to do. One may argue about the precise values to be assigned to SDI and 'current' deterrence in this simple model, but I believe it is one of the necessary ways to look at the situation. More concretely, I believe that the pursuit of the Reagan dream will run clean against the pursuit of still greater stability, reduced friction and lower cost in 'current' deterrence, and that the quest for the very doubtfully attainable will gravely damage the quest for the realistically attainable. It is almost certainly a blind alley. ❞

This exchange between Quinlan and Hockaday, in which they shared their serious misgivings about the potential impact of SDI, sheds a very interesting light on a batch of seemingly unrelated letters that date from around the same time. Quinlan was always keen to correct what he regarded as mostly well-intentioned but inaccurate and potentially damaging interpretations of UK, NATO and US nuclear doctrine, for fear that they could undermine deterrence stability (by feeding the arguments of the unilateralists, undermining NATO solidarity, or generating misperceptions on the part of the Warsaw Pact countries). Much of the time, he was able to provide information to counter the arguments of those who took 'the conspiracy view of history', and where such information was not immediately available, he sought it out. There are many examples in Quinlan's correspondence of him using his official US and European connections to conduct research that would strengthen the counter-arguments he was making in response to the UK peace movement. But there is one batch of letters that is doubly interesting: firstly, because he went to such lengths to obtain the information to counter a CND claim that was potentially damaging to deterrence stability, and secondly, because he appears to have been genuinely worried that the CND claim might actually be true.

Quinlan had read a letter that Bruce Kent (who at the time was general secretary of the CND) had sent to *The Tablet*, and which the editor had published in the 7 July 1984 issue. The letter, which was a response to an article defending the concept of nuclear deterrence, had sought to expose dangerous developments in US DoD thinking about the uses of nuclear weapons. Quinlan found one sentence in Kent's letter particularly troubling: '[Mr. Caspar Weinberger, US secretary of defense] urges "preparation for winning an extended nuclear war against the Soviet Union and for waging war effectively from outer space"' (a quotation Kent claimed he had acquired from an official Pentagon policy document – the Defense Department Fiscal Report of 1984–88). The letter prompted Quinlan to research the origins of the phrase, in the hope that he would be able to expose it as misleading or fraudulent, and he wrote in this capacity to a number of people, including Richard Perle (US assistant secretary of defense whom he had earlier served with on the NATO HLG) to ask for assistance in tracking down the document. He explained to Perle that Kent had 'made damaging play' with the quotation, and that he was:[49]

> **"** therefore anxious to probe [its] authenticity – not least because it would be salutary, even with a limited readership, to put [Kent] down publicly if this is after all a plain example of misrepresentation … I seek therefore to know whether the Secretary has in fact used these or closely similar words in any official document. Could you or someone on your staff help me with this? **"**

When he did not receive a response from Perle (the letter seems to have gone astray and did not reach him), Quinlan sent a similar request to Moray Stewart, NATO assistant secretary-general for defence planning and policy:[50]

> **"** In a letter in *The Tablet* of 7 July last – photocopy herewith – Bruce attributed to Weinberger, from a document he called (oddly) Defence Department Fiscal 1984–88, the urging of 'preparations for winning an extended nuclear war against the Soviet Union and for waging war effectively from outer space'. These were, in the context of Bruce's letter, damaging words; and since, though I have not known him consciously tell specific untruths, I have found his use of evidence pretty cavalier, I was reluctant to take it at face value. Enquiry of John Blelloch, and by him of the US Embassy, provided no authentication of the quotation; and I then wrote to Bruce. He

replied urbanely, citing the editorial of *Jane's Aircraft* as his source (though he had, characteristically, neither acknowledged how indirect his evidence was nor reproduced in his use of it *Jane's* attribution of it to unspecified 'reports', which carried a cautionary implication). I then wrote to the editor of Jane's. He replied that he believed the quotation to be exact and said it was copied from a quotation in a leading US newspaper, 'probably … the Washington Post or New York Times'. Finding this unsatisfactory, I wrote at about the beginning of September to Richard Perle. I heard no more.

The time for pinning Bruce publicly to the wall on this, if the quotation does after all prove bogus, has probably gone by; but I wouldn't mind sending him (and John Taylor, the *Jane's* man) a tart letter should the facts indeed so turn out; he will without doubt have put the material into CND's standard anthology. **"**

Stewart sent Quinlan a handwritten response, promising to look into the origins of the quote (which he described as 'wildly improbable'), and then followed up with senior officials in the US Air Force, one of whom provided the following information in a letter dated 13 February 1985:[51]

" [Our] staff were unable to find the statement which Monsignor Kent attributes to the Secretary of Defense. It appears to be based, at least in part, on inaccurate media reporting of US military strategy.

Kent's quote seems to be based on Richard Halloran's May–June 1984 articles in the New York Times which misconstrued and selectively quoted the classified DoD Defense Guidance FY 1984–1988 (published 22 March 1982).

The statement which Kent attributes to the secretary is inconsistent with the US strategy of deterrence, which is based on an understanding that nuclear war cannot be 'won' in the classic military sense. In his Annual Report to the Congress for FY 1984–1988 (and in subsequent reports), Secretary Weinberger stated (p. 51): 'We, for our part, are under no illusions about the dangers of a nuclear war between the major powers; we believe that neither side could win such a war'. Both the Secretary and the President have repeated this belief on numerous occasions in public speeches and testimony. **”**

In his subsequent letter to Quinlan, Stewart reinforced the point that US official sources all asserted 'nuclear wars are not winnable wars' and added that it would be very unlikely that anyone in the senior US leadership would make 'references to waging war from outer space'.[52] The paper trail ended with Stewart's letter, suggesting that Quinlan was reassured by the information he provided, both as evidence that senior figures in the Pentagon had not gone completely beyond the pale in their nuclear policy planning, and as confirmation that CND claims about US nuclear war-winning plans could continue to be truthfully and forcefully countered by the UK establishment.

This episode confirms a certain nervousness that appears beneath the surface in much of Quinlan's correspondence. On one hand, he believed that the defence and security needs of the UK and Western Europe were best served through NATO; by cultivating and sustaining the US strategic commitment to its alliance partners. The majority of his thinking on the logic of deterrence and his policy-planning decisions within the HLG need to be understood in this context. But at the same time, it is clear that Quinlan believed the UK should be prepared for a breakdown of NATO solidarity and/or a failure by the US to stand by its pledges when the chips were down. Concerns over the potential for decoupling or other ill-conceived strategic decisions by the US government led Quinlan and the UK defence establishment to maintain a plan B, in case plan A (NATO deterrence) failed. That back-up plan was the UK independent deterrent.

The UK and *Trident*

The UK's independent nuclear deterrent has featured more prominently in the headlines, especially since the financial crash of 2008, as scholars, practitioners and journalists have debated whether the huge economic and political costs of maintaining it can be justified on strategic grounds. There are various options for change, but underlying the debate is a deep-seated concern among those with the ultimate responsibility for UK national defence that it is important to err on the side of caution and avoid taking steps that would irreversibly weaken the UK deterrent and be regretted down the line. The reality is thus that, despite probing questions about the nature of contemporary threats, from WMD terrorism to cyber attacks, and the irrelevance of *Trident* in this context, belief in its value remains strong among key decision-makers, if only as an insurance policy against possible future threats. The UK's logic for retention (which can be found in numerous official statements on the subject, including the MoD's February 2010 document 'The Future Character of Conflict' and the 2006 White Paper) can be summarised in two sentences: If the UK hadn't already developed an independent nuclear deterrent when it faced an overwhelming threat during the Cold War, it would not opt to develop one now. However, an independent nuclear deterrent was acquired, and at great cost, and so the UK should continue to invest in it in case it needs it again in future (including to provide options in situations in which the US and France cannot be relied upon).[53]

This was Quinlan's line of reasoning right up to the end of his life, when he began to have some doubts. Even long after the fall of the Soviet Union, while he acknowledged the important goal of nuclear disarmament, he never advocated unilateralism. He had played an important part in the decision to acquire *Trident*, and he never had any doubt that it had been the right decision at the time. Whether it should be retained indefinitely was more open to question, as he felt the political costs of nuclear status were steadily increasing and that eventually nuclear possession could become unsustainable. However, on balance, he still favoured replacing *Trident*.

A brief history of the *Trident* decision[54]

At the time Quinlan was appointed to the post of deputy under-secretary for policy (DUS(P)) at the MoD, a secret decision to indigenously develop a successor to *Polaris*, taken under the Edward Heath government in 1973, was under pressure due to defence cuts and spiraling costs. Prime Minister James Callaghan and a handful of ministers decided to continue with the upgrade programme, known as *Chevaline*, despite these pressures. The decision was underpinned by the strategic necessity, according to established wisdom among defence officials, for Britain's independent nuclear arsenal to be able to destroy the Soviet capital, Moscow. This was considered the key factor determining the credibility of the British unilateral nuclear deterrent and become known as 'the Moscow Criterion'. Official documents obtained by the nuclear historian Brian Burnell reveal that Quinlan played a role in these discussions (although unfortunately, Quinlan's correspondence files contain very little material from the period before 1979).[55]

In 1978, Callaghan set up a Ministerial Nuclear Policy Group and commissioned an official Steering Group on Nuclear Matters to discuss the future of the UK's independent nuclear deterrent. The steering group commissioned a Nuclear Matters Working Party to produce a two-part report: the first part, chaired by the senior diplomat, Sir Anthony Duff, would explore the political-military requirements; the second part, chaired by Professor Sir Ronald Mason, chief scientific adviser to the Ministry of Defence, would focus on technical options. Various procurement options were under consideration: cruise missiles, *Trident* or the development of an indigenous SLBM programme with a multiple independently-targetable re-entry vehicle (MIRV) capability. The possibility of co-designing a *Polaris* successor system with the French was dismissed on the basis that it would only be attractive as a last resort (if the US was unwilling to supply *Trident* or if it placed restrictions on the supply that undermined the independence of the system).

As policy director at the MoD, Quinlan had a significant influence on the report, which became known as the Duff–Mason Report.[56] He favoured replacing *Polaris* with *Trident* I missiles. The longer-range, more capable *Trident* II system was apparently discounted at this stage because the US was not expected to decide whether to proceed with the system until 1982 or 1983. At the same time, a decision was taken to keep in step with developments in the *Trident* system in order to prevent the need for a unique mid-life upgrade of the British *Trident* force (to prevent a repeat of the difficult and expensive *Chevaline* upgrade of *Polaris*). To Quinlan, the need to ensure the credibility of the deterrent was more important than ever in the late 1970s, due to the development of strategic nuclear parity between the superpowers, and a much stronger and more versatile Soviet non-nuclear capability than before (wielded with growing adventurism, as highlighted by the 1979 Soviet intervention in Afghanistan).

The *Trident* proposal was supported by Callaghan but strongly opposed by the foreign secretary, David Owen, who was part of the Ministerial Nuclear Policy Group. Owen argued in favour of a cruise-missile system that he believed would have been cheaper than *Trident*, but which had strategic limitations.[57] Callaghan took the decision not to seek cabinet approval for the *Trident* decision until after the general election that was pending. Most of the cabinet was not aware of the discussion that had been taking place. One of the important conclusions reached in the Duff–Mason report was that the Moscow Criterion no longer needed to be given the degree of priority that it had in the past. Although being able to hold Moscow at risk was still seen as important for deterrence, various other large Soviet cities were also high value targets.

Before the election, Callaghan met privately with US President Jimmy Carter to discuss the *Trident* option. At a meeting on the sidelines of a NATO Summit in Guadaloupe, Carter gave a commitment that, subject to Congressional approval, the US would supply *Trident* missiles to the UK if the cabinet requested them. The Labour party manifesto promised a full and informed debate on the issue before any decision on *Polaris'* replacement would be taken (suggesting, somewhat misleadingly, that it was still very much an open question and that unilateral disarmament was a possibility), whereas the Conservative manifesto hinted strongly that it would have no qualms about replacing *Polaris* to ensure 'the continuing effectiveness of Britain's nuclear deterrent'. The Conservatives won the election, and Margaret Thatcher, the new prime minister, immediately convened a select cabinet committee to examine the nuclear issue. Unknown to parliament or the rest of cabinet, the committee, known as MISC 7, was given the Duff–Mason report by Callaghan and opted for *Trident* – specifically for the *Trident* I missile.

The new defence secretary, Francis Pym, announced the secret *Chevaline* programme to parliament for the first time on 24 January 1980, explaining that its costs had spiralled far beyond the original estimates. He explained that the modernisation programme was deemed necessary because 'the Soviet Union has continued to upgrade its ABM capabilities, and we have needed to respond to that so that we can maintain the deterrence assurance of our force'.[58] Later the same year, Thatcher announced to her cabinet and to parliament that she and the other members of MISC 7 had decided to procure the *Trident* I missile from the United States. Following the announcement, the government published a paper to justify the *Trident* decision. This special memorandum, which was drafted by Quinlan and entitled 'The Future United Kingdom Strategic Nuclear Deterrent Force', set out the rationale for the UK independent deterrent.[59] It was to serve as a 'second centre of decision-making' – a signal to the Soviet leadership that if they believed at some point in a conflict that the US would be unwilling to resort to nuclear use to defend Europe, British nuclear weapons could still inflict such a punishing blow that the penalty for Soviet aggression would be too high.[60]

In the document, Quinlan used the phrase 'key aspects of Soviet state power' to describe the target of Britain's independent nuclear deterrent – a phrase that deliberately avoided specific reference to Moscow or to other Soviet cities while at the same time not exempting them. The new *Trident* system, with its greater accuracy, would for the first time allow the UK to be more discriminate in the choice of nuclear targets, with the potential for fewer non-combatant deaths and thus, in the opinion of Quinlan and others, making Britain's national deterrent 'more ethical' than it had been in the past. It would still, however, have to be capable of posing a massive deterrent threat, independent of US nuclear forces, in order to serve the second-centre role.

The following year, in response to Reagan's decision to modernise US nuclear forces, the Thatcher government reopened the discussion on *Trident*. Caspar Weinberger (the new US defense secretary) had briefed her on the US decision to accelerate the development of its advanced *Trident* II missile system, which would mean it would likely meet the UK time-frame for replacing *Chevaline*. On October 1981, Reagan made a formal offer to supply the *Trident* II to the British government, leading Thatcher and her MISC 7 group to decide in favour of the *Trident* II missile system. Thatcher later explained the rationale for this decision in her memoirs, writing: 'we were now faced with a new situation. If we were still to go ahead with *Trident* I we risked spending huge sums on a system that would be outdated and increasingly difficult to maintain as the Americans went over to *Trident* II'.[61] A discussion also took place at the same time on the number of submarines that would be required. The Treasury's preference was for three, which it argued could satisfy the UK's deterrence objectives at minimum cost. The MoD contended that relying on three submarines would open gaps in the British national deterrent, 'allow[ing] no margin for unseen contingencies', while four submarines would allow the UK to make a greater contribution to NATO and would make it possible for the UK to maintain one subma-rine on station at all times (continuous-at-sea-deterrence, or CASD).[62] The Royal Navy and the Chiefs of Staff wanted five submarines, as this would mean two boats could be on patrol at all times.[63] In the end, the final decision on a fourth boat was kept open for discussion but – mainly for cost reasons – a plan for a fifth was deemed unlikely to gain support.[64]

The full cabinet was briefed on the MISC 7 discussions in early 1982 and concurred with the decision on the *Trident* II missile. In a speech published in the *Times*, Secretary of State for Defence John Nott re-emphasised the 'second centre of decision' rationale that had been set out by Quinlan in 1980 as justification for the decision in favour of *Trident* II, stating that:[65]

> **"** while the United Kingdom has every confidence in the American strategic guarantee, it is possible that at some time in the future, under circumstances that were different from those prevailing now, a Soviet leadership might calculate ... that it could risk or threaten a nuclear attack on Europe without involving the strategic forces of the United States. If the Soviets were ever tempted to make such a horrendous miscalculation, the existence of an immensely powerful nuclear force (Britain's) would be an enormous complicating factor and a powerful argument for Soviet caution. **"**

The strategic rationale for *Trident*

The rationale for the UK's national nuclear deterrent has always been a controversial issue. Some, including Quinlan, have always stressed the official 'second centre of decision' argument noted above. Others have stressed a 'Gaullist justification' or, in other words, a symbolic role in maintaining British strategic and political independence and prestige.[66] But despite the obvious appeal of the Gaullist justification for the British public and for the UK's political leaders, Quinlan was always wary of it, concerned that nuclear justifications based on prestige arguments made little sense (given the UK's technological dependence on the US) and, furthermore, could have some very negative consequences: they could send the 'wrong message' to other states seeking to enhance their prestige and status, acting as a proliferation driver; and they could undermine the fragile ethical case that he constantly made for nuclear possession. This helps explain his unease when in the early 1980s, the Thatcher government and even some senior officials in the MoD and FCO emphasised the simpler and more populist Gaullist justification for procuring *Trident*. At the time, Quinlan had been transferred to the Treasury and then to Employment and thus was not in a position to easily steer the debate. His letters from the period show that there was significant confusion and disagreement over second-centre arguments in government (including in the cabinet and at senior levels in the MoD) and more generally among defence thinkers. Quinlan's letter to Dr Keith Middlemas, dated 24 April 1985, presents the main strategic argument against the Gaullist justification for the UK's national deterrent:[67]

> **❝** I have a fairly basic point here, perhaps reflecting a real divergence of judgement between us. There are (simplifying slightly) two different cases for UK independent nuclear capability. One is the 'second-centre' case, developed in Francis Pym's Commons speech of (if memory serves) 24 January 1980; the other is the Gaullist one, towards which John Nott inclined. Your discussion seems couched essentially in terms of the latter. I happen myself to prefer the former, and I suggest it should at least be mentioned. I cannot now recall whether we discussed the point or whether I gave you any of my jottings on it; but I suspect that in logic, if we really mean the Gaullist case, we ought to have gone (as the French have, paying the price) for independence of procurement, not just of operation. **❞**

An earlier letter that Quinlan wrote to Hockaday, dated 11 January 1983, explains the case against the Gaullist rationale in more depth and exposes some of the divisions among senior civil servants on this issue. It is also revealing in that it clearly shows Quinlan's desire to keep the UK nuclear debate grounded in sound and consistent reasoning and his efforts to facilitate this, even after he had been transferred out of the MoD. At the same time, there are hints at some frustration, and a definite sense of resignation that, due to civil service protocols and the demands of his new role at Employment, he would not be able to steer the debate as easily as he could when he was policy director. The letter provides feedback on an article former MoD colleague and Anglican, Hockaday, had written on nuclear deterrence:[68]

> **❝** Very many thanks for your letter of 4 January (and in particular your kind good wishes for my new occupation). As always, I enjoyed and valued what you say on the nuclear issues, and agreed with most but not quite all of it! What follows mostly does not waste space on recapitulating the agreement, but offers a few supplementary comments and one or two points of disagreement.
>
> As you imply, it is not easy to keep the debate in Britain tidy and on the best ground. *Trident* and GLCMs are the specifics of current decision, and can hardly be avoided; but the arguments about them operate at several levels. I agree that the most basic and most important of these, at the heart of most CND-type opposition, concerns the whole business of Western deterrence and peace-with-freedom; and that the more this can be brought out, the better. People like the authors of 'The Church and the Bomb' attempt a half-way stance not really defensible in their own ethical logic, and this needs to be rubbed in.
>
> On *Trident*, I share your view that the prime question is whether money spent on this will provide a

better increment to total Western deterrence than the same amount spent elsewhere in defence. We differ on the answer to this question ... I do incidentally feel – as perhaps you would – some private regret that over the course of 1982 the Government's defence of *Trident* shifted from 'second-centre' towards Gaullism. I regard the latter as presentationally more awkward (partly for the non-proliferation reason you touch upon) in the long run, whatever its short-term domestic appeal and apparent simplicity; and also as, genuinely, the less important substantive reason.

On GLCMs, I think you rather underrate the technical arguments – especially in relation to Soviet perception of military capability, which obviously matters – for having these as well as SLBMs. But I accept that this is not the main point. That point, in deterrence terms, is not (with respect) how the Russians would react to use, but what estimate they would form, before the event, of the likelihood of use; and I believe there may be a difference here between GLCMs and SLBMs, for reasons both technical and political. Indeed one might argue that the very fact that the Russians have been trying ... to align US perceptions about GLCMs and SLBMs show that they suspect those perceptions are significantly different. More generally, I think your presentation of the matter does not sufficiently recognise that the LRTNF plan is genuinely a modernisation of an existing category of capability (F.III/ *Vulcan*), and that to forgo it would be a real change in force structure.

Beyond all this, of course, there lies the now inescapable fact that vast political western capital has been invested in the modernisation programme (not so much by deliberate choice as by the inevitable consequence of having to fight off unilateralist opposition); and that accordingly to abandon it without a major arms-control offset would be deeply damaging.

In passing, a comment – probably unnecessary – on your reference to the cross-examinations about LRTNF you undergo at meetings. The main answer to those who attack the plan as preparing the way for limited nuclear war in Europe is not that European Governments themselves wanted it (true though that is) but that if the Americans really wanted to improve the chances of a superpower-sanctuary option, the very last thing they would then contemplate would be the deployment in Western Europe of new Russia-reaching missiles.

You will not be surprised that I continue to regard your compartmentalisation of deterrence ('primary' and other) as misconceived; I do not agree that nuclear weapons deter only other nuclear weapons. I regard this presentation of Western deterrence as neither realistic nor desirable. I find it hard to believe that the Soviet calculation of the consequences of conventional aggression ever would or should ignore (or hitherto have ignored) the possibility that they might thereby trigger a nuclear contest. Yet this seems to me the implication of what you say.

The above comment is relevant also to your view that we are in a de-facto 'no first use' situation. By chance, I had just commented on this in a separate correspondence, as you will now have seen – copy of the relevant passage herewith for Mr Blaker.

I am sorry if I have been unfair to Mike Carver. I have not read his book, and doubt whether I shall quickly find time to do so; but the bits you quote do indeed sound sensible. He nevertheless continues, as your P.S. notes, to espouse 'no first use' and to operate, orally and in writing, with a concept of rationality which fundamentally fails to understand or think through what nuclear weapons have done to the whole of major East–West warfare, not just its nuclear component. I am bound, in sheepish candour, to say that I think this last point may apply equally to some of what you yourself say; it is not at all clear to me what concept you have, differing from mine, of what the use of non-strategic weapons would actually be for. Why have any gradation at all in weapon systems, on your theory?

Apologies that this rather hasty reply is so disjointed; but if I don't get it off quickly I may vanish indefinitely beneath the Employment paperwork. Rather reluctantly – though Mr Blaker, to whom I am sending a copy of this letter and of my [Royal College of Defence Studies] script, may be reassured! – I feel bound to lay off this field, at least for the foreseeable future and unless occasionally there are special private things which it might be hard for anyone else to do, for example in the RC context. **"**

Targeting

While the strategic rationale for the UK independent nuclear deterrent was clearly stated in the 1980 Defense Open Government Document (DOGD) 80/23 and in official statements on the 'second centre of decision', information on British targeting plans for *Polaris* and *Trident* has always been fuzzy. For obvious reasons, the circle of decision-makers involved in targeting has been kept extremely small, and few of the highly classified details of the plans have leaked out to those outside the inner circle of the MoD and Joint Intelligence Committee (JIC). What is known is that plans were drawn up on the assumption that the UK needed the capacity to pose a massive deterrent threat to the Soviet Union, independent of US nuclear forces, but given there was no way of calculating how much destruction would suffice to deter Soviet decision-makers (or to serve the purpose of war termination), capability and targeting issues were always very controversial. Disagreements hinged on what type and scale of damage Soviet leaders might think likely to leave them critically handicapped after a nuclear strike by the UK (based on the assumption that the US was still relatively unscathed). Recently declassified documents from the period reveal the extent of these disagreements and the pivotal role that Quinlan played in the top secret Whitehall deliberations.[69] One document in particular – a memo written by Quinlan on 18 December 1978 in response to an internal paper by David Owen (who was foreign secretary at that time) – is particularly revealing.[70] Owen had argued that *Trident* was unnecessary: Britain's nuclear options could be scaled back on the basis that the threat of 'a million Soviet dead' would be more than adequate to deter an attack by the USSR. But Quinlan disagreed; in his opinion, an effective deterrent required the capability to kill up to ten million Soviets.[71] Other declassified documents from the same year reveal that MoD officials had calculated that Britain needed to maintain the option to conduct ground-burst nuclear strikes against the Soviets in order to subject 55–60% of the target city to a radiation dose sufficient to cause rapid debilitation followed by death for most people in the area, and to contaminate water, food, air and both damaged and undamaged buildings.[72]

Some nuclear strategists and at least one former permanent secretary of the MoD (Frank Cooper, Quinlan's predecessor) acknowledge that nuclear targeting has never been a British strong point. On the one hand, as we have seen, internal MoD assessments deemed the strategic deterrent needed to be able to inflict massive damage (up to 10 million dead), and this calculation influenced the decision to procure *Trident*. On the other hand, from 1980 onwards, once the Trident decision had been taken, British officials publicly claimed that the UK deterrent did not rest on threatening massive loss of life among the Soviet population at large but was concerned with posing a potential threat to key aspects of Soviet state power.[73] Although it is true that *Trident* opened up new possibilities for more accurate targeting (a point stressed by Quinlan), the phrase 'key aspects of Soviet state power' could arguably be seen as misleading given official UK assessments of the Soviet 'threshold of horror' and the fact that the targets held at risk by the UK deterrent were located close to major population centres.[74] This discrepancy was the subject of a significant portion of Quinlan's private correspondence, although he did not often address it in a way that was clear and frank. There are, however, some letters exchanged between Quinlan and his correspondents that are revealing. A letter from Frank Cooper (Quinlan's boss when he was DUS(P), whom Quinlan greatly admired) is particularly interesting. Quinlan had forwarded Cooper a paper by Lawrence Freedman on British nuclear strategy, which Freedman had sent Quinlan for his comments.[75] Quinlan had then forwarded the paper to Cooper, asking for his comments on Freedman's discussion of British nuclear targeting. The letter, dated 19 January 1987, provides some insight into the different attitudes among MoD officials to the British independent deterrent:[76]

> ❝ As you well know targeting has never been a British strong-point … The central criterion has always been the capacity to inflict on an aggressor an unacceptable degree of damage. In a national context we have taken this to be measured by cities and people. In an international

context we have fallen into line with [NATO Supreme Headquarters Allied Powers Europe] and US targeting plans where account has been taken of weapons availability, geography, etc. etc.

We kept national heads well down in terms of discussion of targets and, of course, the more they are discussed the more we move away from the concept of 'dissuasion'. This coupled with the apparent process of Americanising the British deterrent and our inability to take national pride in it has done much harm. **"**

When corresponding with those outside the MoD inner circle, Quinlan was almost always at pains to explain that he was unable to disclose any details on targeting, however frustrating that might be for his correspondents. In a letter to war veteran and charity worker, Leonard Cheshire dated 31 May 1983, Quinlan stated that: 'On targeting, there is as yet no official UK statement of the kind you seek. I hope before long there will be; but at present all there is on the record is the reference to "key aspects of Soviet State power"'. Cheshire may have been willing to accept this vagueness (there is nothing in his letters to suggest otherwise), but other correspondents were not. One of the most outspoken critics on the lack of transparency over targeting was Brian Midgley, politics professor at the University of Aberdeen. He felt strongly that Quinlan ought not to publicly engage in debates over the UK's nuclear deterrent if he was unable to back up his arguments over the morality of nuclear use with facts and evidence on targeting.[77]

Quinlan seems to have felt conflicted about the official secrecy over the UK's targeting strategy.[78] He understood that much of the debate over nuclear ethics hinged on targeting, and whether nuclear weapons could be used in a way that was both proportionate and discriminate (thus fulfilling Just

War criteria). He believed they could be, and he felt a duty to communicate this to those troubled by the moral dilemmas of nuclear deterrence. As far as he was concerned, speculation over targeting was unhelpful, because talk of city-busting strategies in which civilian populations were deliberately targeted provoked horror inside and outside the church, as did references to 'the Moscow Criterion' (the strategic necessity for the UK independent deterrent to be able to destroy Moscow), which dominated public discussion of British targeting policy. Quinlan's reference to 'key aspects of Soviet state power' in his letter to Cheshire was an attempt to distance himself (and the MoD) from what could be regarded as morally indefensible, indiscriminate targeting policies, without revealing too much in the process. In his letters he presented this nuanced language, which could in theory embrace a range of targets from hitting a large city to hitting a missile silo, as an important development in targeting transparency and ethics.[79] He clearly hoped that it would influence those who were so appalled by the inevitably catastrophic consequences of nuclear use that they questioned the whole basis of nuclear deterrence.

In the article he sent Quinlan, Freedman dismissed this more ethically driven national targeting strategy as unrealistic and as something of a fudge – a flaw in UK official nuclear strategy that some of Quinlan's correspondents noted.[80] Freedman's point was that even targeting key aspects of Soviet state power (rather than a deliberate 'city-busting' plan) still required the targeting of military command-and-control centres, which were 'concentrated in many cities and certainly Moscow', and thus unlikely to reduce significantly the human consequences of nuclear use. The UK had no choice but to rely on NATO's broader range of dual-key capabilities for more discriminate sub-strategic nuclear use, and thus any claims that *Trident* would provide the UK with a more 'ethical' independent nuclear deterrent were highly dubious. Peter Hodgson, to whom Quinlan had also sent Freedman's paper, commented in his reply to Quinlan that he thought Freedman's conclusions on the targeting fudge '[weren't] far out', adding more weight to the contention that, at least from 1980 until the end of the Cold War, a gap existed between official British nuclear doctrine and strategic reality.

It may be more accurate to suggest that Quinlan had a much more nuanced interpretation in mind when he used the phrase 'key aspects of Soviet state power'. In his eyes, the phrase reflected a UK desire to keep its targeting options open, and to adopt a more discriminate targeting plan, if the conditions arose, rather than a commitment to move away from city-busting altogether. Such a 'flexible' doctrine would not necessarily lead to fewer civilian casualties in the event of a nuclear strike, but the intention not to deliberately seek maximum deaths from a nuclear attack was key. This, in his view, did not suggest that targeting cities and populations was necessarily wrong in all circumstances. A letter from Quinlan to Richard Harries at King's College London suggests that interpretation was indeed what Quinlan intended – that despite his preference for discriminate targeting, Quinlan was not prepared to rule out targeting cities and population centres with nuclear weapons. In the letter, dated 6 February 1986, he asked:[81]

> **❝** Can we be certain that we must *never* drop *any* nuclear weapon near *any* heavily-populated area, wholly irrespective of what the direct target was and of what contribution its destruction was reasonably expected to make to war-termination? That would be a little too rigid for me. **❞**

This seems to confirm Midgley's assertion that in reality, despite the use of nuanced language, little had changed in UK targeting policy. In his letter of 7 November 1980, he made the point that:[82]

66 Certainly, I am not reassured about the UK targeting policy by paragraph 10 of the *Trident* memorandum [1980 Open Government Document on *Trident* (OGD 80/23)]. Paragraph 10 is followed by paragraph 11 which would indicate (though in rather general terms) that no really fundamental change in targeting policy has taken place since I transferred from my work on *Blue Streak* [a British intermediate-range ballistic missile designed in 1955]. 99

Opposition to the *Trident* decision

Though the majority inside and outside government supported the *Trident* decision, there was some strident opposition to it in political circles, among civil servants, and in the public at large. Neville Mott, physics professor at the University of Cambridge, was deeply troubled by it. He found it difficult to understand the logic of the decision, given that any use of *Trident* by the UK against the Soviets would amount to national suicide. He explained this in an undated letter, which Quinlan noted in his own handwriting that he had received on 15 March 1986:[83]

66 I had not seen the MoD paper of July 1980. You gave us a very vivid picture of flexible response – the shot across the bows, then the more serious attack (power stations, command centres, but not deliberately cities). Where does *Trident* fit in? Is it for the second stage? I admit the need for strategic weapons assigned to NATO; otherwise tactical weapons can be trumped (I do not know if any US *Tridents* will be – or are – assigned to NATO).

But I cannot imagine a situation in which the Russians had not used nukes, in which the US was not backing us, and in which we would fire this whole armoury of *Trident* – courting the destruction of the UK within a few hours. *Trident* – UK or American-owned, seems to me a necessary part of NATO, but as a response to nuclear attack only, first use being limited to tactical and IRBM.

The [1980 White Paper] argues that the British *Trident* introduces additional uncertainty and so adds to deterrence. Of course I understand that – provided we have real plans to commit national suicide in certain circumstances, hopefully very improbable.

Of course, whether one advocates flexible response or no-first-use, we are planning in certain circumstances to kill many million Russians in circumstances where we are already destroyed and it can't do any good ... I had wondered whether Catholics, who believe Jesus is God (I had thought), would find this difficult. But perhaps not. **"**

Quinlan replied to Mott on 2 June 1986 with the following note:[84]

" I agree that *Trident* is, on its own, a poor instrument for flexible response. For that reason it seems to me important that we should retain some lower-level UK nuclear options, as we have for decades past (though public debate, it seems to me, rarely notices this). We have 'tactical' weapons of varying yield which we can deliver from several types of aircraft, notably Tornado.

You speak of *Trident* use as equivalent to national suicide. I believe that that is rather too simple, and claims too much knowledge of, or inexorability in, the adversary's response in all circumstances. But the point, right or wrong, is not unique to the UK; it applies in principle to every participant in nuclear exchange. Its significance for national policy therefore needs wary consideration.

The case of 'final retaliation' is indeed difficult, even though I do not think it has to take a revengeful form; this is one of the ethical (and practical) issues around deterrence which debate has not yet teased out adequately, so far as my observation goes. It is not clear to me that those who believe in the divinity of Christ (as Hugh Beach and I do) are faced with a special difficulty in this regard by the Sermon on the Mount, unless one takes it with a literal legalness which very few exegetes do, and which would pose acute difficulties for a far wider range of human activities than just nuclear deterrence. **"**

Hockaday had also expressed similar reservations over the *Trident* decision as a case of 'nuclear overkill' and an unwise allocation of limited funds that would be better spent on boosting the UK's conventional military capabilities. He explained his misgivings in a letter to Quinlan in January 1983 (although it is dated 4 January 1982, it appears that Hockaday had not yet adjusted to the recent year change):[85]

" I will not bore you with the arguments, all too familiar to you, which lead me to the view that Britain could with greater advantage spend ten billion pounds on her contribution to the primary Western deterrent than on something which can only be an ultimate deterrent against a nuclear threat to the British Isles, a threat which I see as fairly far down the line.

… I believe that putting nuclear deterrence in its proper perspective would not only make it easier to mobilise support among the well-intentioned but worried central mass (you will never reach those at the further extremity) but would also provide a better philosophical and political context for the struggles that our old department will face in getting adequate funds for our conventional forces. I do not regard this as a hopeless task. I do not believe that NATO's conventional inferiority is as great as we have talked ourselves into thinking (partly because I suspect that the Russians are not much bloody good either!). I believe that General Rogers is probably about right in his assessment of what we need to do to satisfy ourselves that we have a really adequate conventional deterrent. I do not regard it as impossible for Governments to carry through programmes of this order if they can support a proper resolution with a demonstration that this is about primary deterrence and is designed to reduce our dependence on nuclear weapons. Paradoxically popular concern about the nuclear deterrent could provide a more propitious climate than the apathy of past decades; and skilful presentation could also build on one of the lessons of the Falklands war, namely that people find it very much easier to identify with sailors and soldiers than with aircraft or missiles or nuclear weapons – Michael Howard brought this point out well when addressing the IISS international conference at Scheveningen last year. In the British case, of course, the Rogers target could be effectively met without additional funding if the resources earmarked for Trident were reallocated. **"**

Vocal opposition to the *Trident* decision was most strident among members of the political opposition parties. The Labour Party, under the leadership of Michael Foot, had come out strongly against *Trident* and in favour of unilateral nuclear disarmament, deeply dividing the party in the process and provoking the departure of David Owen and other senior Labour politicians to found the Social Democratic Party. Owen had served in the Callaghan cabinet as foreign secretary from 1977–79 and during that time had served on the Ministerial Nuclear Policy Group. He had opposed *Trident* from the start, arguing that Britain's defence needs would better served by procuring the much cheaper cruise-missile system. His public criticism of both the Conservative decision on *Trident* and his deep dismay over the Labour Party's swing to the left under Foot, attracted the interest of the British media and of Quinlan, who had been closely involved in the Labour government's deliberations over *Trident*. Quinlan's correspondence files contain a long transcript of an interview given by Owen to the journalist John Barry in October 1980.[86] Barry had sent the transcript to Quinlan with a note offering it for Quinlan's 'private interest and amusement' and also for comment.[87] According to Barry's note, Owen was willing for his comments to be 'on the record'. Towards the beginning of the interview, Owen explained that he was first involved in the UK nuclear programme when he was minister for the navy in 1968. Apparently, a mistake was made over his security clearance, and thanks to that he came to know a great deal about the deterrent. From that time forward, he took a keen interest in every detail of British nuclear decision-making. One of the striking points that Owen made in the interview was that the civil service, under the leadership of John Hunt, put pressure on the Labour government to come out in favour of *Trident*.[88] In his handwritten notes, Quinlan dismissed this claim as 'paranoid nonsense', but given the nature of nuclear decision-making in the UK, it is likely that there is a stronger basis for Owen's assertion than many senior officials have been willing to admit:[89]

" [In my opposition to *Chevaline*, which I wanted to cancel, and to *Trident*] I fought one of the most interesting internal battles that Whitehall has seen for some time.[90] It was basically between myself and Sir John Hunt. This was an intellectual battle, though it was all done through others. Hunt, undoubtedly – and perfectly legitimately – is a very clever man, and he wanted to get the Labour Government on board for Trident. He wanted continuity across political parties. And he had the ear of Callaghan, and he knew basically he had a patriot in him. He knew too that Callaghan had a very close working relationship with Carter; and this was the time, he felt, to try and tie up the deal. Unfortunately, he had not reckoned with having a new Foreign Secretary who in no way was going to go down this route; and that really is the history of the debate. It surfaced over *Chevaline*, because *Chevaline* was being justified on strategic grounds as being necessary to take out Moscow. I refused point blank to accept ever that *Chevaline* was justified on strategic grounds. And I constructed the argument entirely on the level: you have spent this vast sum of money (at this stage it was £700m, and rising every six months) – I am quite prepared to seriously consider cancelling *Chevaline* … because it's just a waste of money.

… [and so] the Moscow criterion was never endorsed while I was Foreign Secretary. It was kicked into touch and it then merged into the *Trident* debate. But the *Chevaline* decision was never made – and the minutes are quite clear on this – on the basis that … well I never got them actually to say that the Moscow Criterion was dead, but we never endorsed it. And so Hunt was never able to use [the argument] in the subsequent *Trident* debate that ministers had already made the decision that they think the Moscow Criterion must be satisfied. And of course he was totally absolutely in favour of it. But I was equally serious … And I am a bitter opponent of this idea of a departmental view. There isn't as far as I am concerned a departmental view: I pick up the problems for the FCO and I pick up the accolades. They knew this was my view.

What happened was that once Hunt saw that he had severe opposition from me, he got Jim to accept that what it would be right to do would be to have an internal paper which would put the options down for decisions by the incoming government … I thought this was unconstitutional … But on this particular thing, a specific decision was taken that ministers would not involve themselves in the assessment; and the assessment would be made independently. So Duff was 'our man', so to speak. Now Michael Palliser [permanent under-secretary at the FCO] was not an absolutely fervent addict of the idea that the deterrent had to be maintained at all costs and to the end of time. They were broadly, at the FCO, in favour of it. But they were not zealots on this, thank goodness. So they went off to do this study. Then it became apparent that there were pressures building up to make this decision earlier. And anyhow the decision to do the study was taken, I suppose, in 1978, early 1978 and that was on the basis that we would have the election in 1978. When we didn't have an election in 1978, funny, funny, funny, we now suddenly find that this bloody study is up and although you could say that it didn't make a decision it was absolutely angled to a continuation of *Trident* … They never looked at the serious alternative option, which was to put cruise missiles on hunter-killer submarines. This whole argument about dedicated platforms,

I mean to listen to them ... The MoD has always had a life of its own; and take someone like [Victor] Macklen [former director of weapons development at the Atomic Weapons Establishment] – absolutely dedicated, very able; extremely splendid chap but like many of them: they have got their [departmental] view.

... At Guadeloupe Jim went further than he was entitled to go, in terms of ministerial responsibility.[91] At the time Jim said that he wanted to raise with Carter some of [the nuclear] options privately. He did get ministerial authorisation, but again it was a rather small, informal group; and Jim said he would make it absolutely clear to the president that no decision had been taken or would be taken; I think however that at Guadeloupe Jim probably made it abundantly clear – now exactly what wording he used I do not know – I am pretty sure he made it clear, as he was perfectly entitled to do, by saying: Look if I become PM again I'm going to go for *Trident*. Because that was Jim's view at that stage. He knew damned well that he wouldn't get me on board for it: I was pushing very hard for the cruise missile option ... I knew I wouldn't be FS any longer; there was no bitterness and ill-feeling ... all four of us got on very well on all this: all four were committed to the idea of the nuclear deterrent, no unilateralists there at all; it was entirely an argument of [which system and] how much it was all going to cost. **🗩🗩**

Mounting cost concerns

Concerns over the cost-effectiveness of *Trident* became a hot political issue in the 1987 general election. The belief that *Trident* represented overkill was still widely held, as Peter Hodgson's[92] December 1986 letter to Quinlan reveals.[93] At the time, there were discussions among defence experts and officials over the future of UK nuclear policy, especially in the event of a change of government following the general election that was due to be called in 1987–88. There were questions over how the next government (if not Conservative) would reconfigure UK defence policy, due to Labour's record on nuclear issues while in opposition; growing international momentum for arms control and disarmament; and doubts over how a hung parliament would handle the nuclear issue (particularly given David Owen's arguments in favour of pursuing more cost-effective Anglo-French nuclear cooperation). In 1986, polls showed support for the Labour Party and Conservatives was closely matched, with the SDP–Liberal Alliance trailing them but still with a significant portion of the vote. A hung parliament looked like a distinct possibility.

Hodgson, who was very much in favour of scaling back *Trident*, wrote to leading Social Democrat, Bill Rodgers, warning him of the reasons for the MoD's traditional scepticism of Anglo-French proposals, and then wrote to Quinlan to brief him on Rodgers's response, and to ask for Quinlan's help in providing material on which the SDP and Liberals could build their case in favour of cuts. He wanted two things from Quinlan, who the letter suggests was sympathetic to the 'overkill' arguments and favoured reducing *Trident* to three submarines. In his letter, dated 19 October 1986, Hodgson wrote:[94]

> **"**As I mentioned I sent Bill Rodgers a few cautionary words about the Anglo-French line which D. Owen has been floating. He replied last week showing some ignorance, but commendable suspicion, of the subject. Then he added:
>
> 'I have believed since 1980, and it is the joint policy of the Social Democratic Party and the Liberals, that

Trident is too expensive and represents overkill. There is no problem in continuing *Polaris* to the end of its life but is there another alternative to *Polaris/Trident* after that? I am sure that the problems we have had with the Liberals would be solved were Britain to retain its own strategic nuclear weapons but at roughly no greater cost or capability than hitherto. I have to confess that I do not know at the moment how this can be done'.

He ends by asking if I can let him have any thoughts on the subject which he could discuss with the others (notably David Owen and in due course the Libs) concerned.

I have in mind to reply with two papers:

a) The passage above goes near to asking the wrong question in that the world has moved on from 1980 and the Tories have since spent quite a lot of money and committed even more. That money is now irrelevant.

b) It could well be said that 4x16 *Trident* represents overkill but the Alliance could cut the bill by going for 3x12 (i.e. Quinlan) or even 3x8 (given that 3 is enough to maintain 1 boat on station).

c) On this basis the opportunity cost of a modified *Trident* solution is a great deal less than [£]11 billion.

d) The arguments for going for such a solution are [your W2 paper of Feb 1982].

Obviously, you won't want to be involved, so my first question concerns W2. Would perhaps the best course be for me to paraphrase your paper unrecognisably? Even if I produced as I should an inferior version, it would still greatly improve the SDP's thinking.

The other point on which I'd like to consult is: do you know where I might look for publicly available information on *Trident* expenditure to date? I shall be looking at recent White Papers at the IISS tomorrow, but if you have come across any informed article on the subject and can give me a reference I'd be most grateful.

I hope this is not embarrassing or too much of a nuisance. **"**

It is unclear whether Quinlan forwarded the materials that Hodgson requested, but further correspondence shows that Hodgson drafted a cost/capability assessment on the future of the UK national deterrent for the Liberal–SDP Alliance, on which Quinlan provided feedback. The final document, which took into account Quinlan's comments, argued that, should the alliance win the election or join a coalition government, they should 'not rule out the possibility of modifying [*Trident*] rather than cancelling it'. In the event, the Liberal–SDP Alliance appears to have ignored Hodgson's advice; their 1987 election manifesto promised to 'maintain, with whatever necessary modernisation, our minimum nuclear deterrent until it can be negotiated away, as part of a global arms negotiation process', but it also committed the Liberal–SDP Alliance to cancelling *Trident* 'because of its excessive number of warheads and megatonnage, high cost and continued dependence on US technology'.[95] The alliance's short-term solution to the UK's deterrence needs was to assign the UK's minimum deterrent to NATO and to look to Europe to meet the UK's procurement and strategic questions; a position Quinlan would not have supported.

Like Hodgson, Quinlan was very concerned about the changing cost–benefit ratio of *Trident*. As far as he was concerned, the benefits of maintaining a national deterrent still outweighed the costs, but it was always important to him to ensure that the UK's deterrence needs could be met with the minimum possible expenditure. Despite having been out of the MoD for

most of the decade, Quinlan was still in the loop when it came
to discussions on the future of *Trident*. His letter of 30 March
1987 to Blelloch reveals he was still privy to key MoD documents and offered advice on drafting the Strategic Defence
Estimates. He was concerned that, if a decision was taken to
cut back *Trident*, the language used to justify four boats in the
official estimates would not be a hostage to fortune:[96]

> ❝ You and I have gossiped from time to time about the
> scale of *Trident* provision, especially warheads. Against
> that background, could I offer, on a private and amateur
> basis, two suggestions about the wording of the *Trident*
> essay at the end of Chapter 4 of the draft [Statement on
> the Defence Estimates]?
>
> Firstly, might you consider dropping the final
> sentence of paragraph 10? Quite aside from the consider-
> ations that it may box you in, and that it appears to claim
> a precision of assessment of which I for one would be
> skeptical, it is arguably defective in logic to characterise
> as a 'minimum' something described in 'no more than'
> and 'up to' terms. (I leave aside, by the way, the Owen
> criticism of the '2 times' arithmetic.)
>
> Second point – a good deal more difficult, I recognise.
> Do you have to be quite so flat-footed on boat numbers
> as the second sentence of paragraph 9 now is? Could
> you perhaps say 'As with *Polaris*, four boats provide a
> guarantee of one on patrol at all times'? Those would
> be easier words than the present text to swallow if, for
> whatever reason, one ever wanted to think about three.
>
> Please forgive this intrusion. ❞

Questions over the future of *Trident* began to feature more
prominently during Quinlan's time as MoD PUS. Critics argued

British nuclear doctrine had become outdated, unnecessarily perpetuating bi-polar tensions and putting international relations on a permanently adversarial footing with no chance of change. An interesting perspective was provided by Alastair Mackie, the former air commodore and nuclear bomber pilot, who wrote to Quinlan along these lines on 30 November 1988, urging him to rethink his position on deterrence doctrine:[97]

> [Your Ampleforth lecture which you sent me] is, if I may say so, eloquent, sincere, and superficially convincing (I hope I don't demean it by comparing it in those respects to Pym's – was it really his – apologia for the nuclear deterrent in Defence Open Government Document 80/23). But what it doesn't do is look below and beyond deterrence theory: why, that is, the Soviet Union appeared, and arguably still appears, to threaten us. That omission arises from the idea that the clash is East v. West; it isn't. It's between the Euro/Asian heartland, landlord the Soviet Union, on the one hand; and on the other the continents and islands surrounding the heartland, landlord the USA. That and her history are why the Soviet Union is so aggressive. Redeeming the resulting situation must start by alleviating the counter-aggression. We will never do it by continuing to 'deter', i.e. to threaten. If we do, the system, as you put it, of adversarial deterrence, will have to be simply accepted as mankind's path to peace – which it could never be. I don't think that's what God had in mind when he left nuclear weapons around. He might just possibly have done that as part of a final effort to induce us not to suck everything dry, to show one modicum of restraint.
>
> End of counter-lecture. No reply needed.

Others were less sceptical about the Cold War rationale for *Trident*, but increasingly worried about the proliferation of nuclear weapons and the implications of the UK's national deterrent for non-proliferation and international stability. A letter dated 17 August 1987 from Elizabeth Llewellyn-Smith (a senior official in the Department of Trade and Industry) sets out some of these concerns:[98]

> " [...] thank you for taking the trouble to send me your papers on deterrence. I delayed only because I thought I would read them properly first and consider them. They are very interesting, especially the recent paper on the Management of East–West Security.
>
> As between East–West I find your argument persuasive. But I was pleased to see that you began by telling the Ampleforth [school]boys that the arguments are hard. It is surprising to me that so many people on both sides will not recognise there is a case to answer on the other.
>
> My own position, which is not the outcome of rigorous thought, is pretty near the one you castigate as 'morally unsustainable'. That is to say, I think that it is morally justifiable to own, refine and plan to use nuclear weapons (or any weapons for that matter) for the purpose of deterrence. But I find it virtually impossible to envisage circumstances in which using them would be legitimate – or even prudent. If you use them first there is the risk of escalation. If they are used against you on any significant scale I cannot see how retaliation could produce a situation which would be better than the alternative.
>
> However, there are so many imponderables that I suppose it may be reasonable to proceed on the assump-

tion that all options should be kept open. The ignorant layman can only hope that the command and control systems would be adequate to allow for intelligent thought should the time come.

It seems to me that the biggest danger lies in proliferation. Your papers deal with regimes which are basically cautious and rational. Many are not, cf the Gulf now.

Your main conclusion must be right – that the crucial thing is for statesmen to prevent war and improve political relationships! After their failure to do so throughout recorded history one cannot feel confident that this is realistic for the rest of time. **"**

It is clear from Quinlan's correspondence at the time that he recognised these concerns, but he did not fully share them. On balance, he continued to believe in the wide margins of deterrence stability and to regard nuclear weapons as a necessary tool for preventing major conflict between the great powers. The wide gulf between the pro- and anti-nuclear camps was thus becoming more pronounced than ever, as though their members inhabited separate universes.

Post-Cold-War debates on *Trident*

With the collapse of the Soviet Union, the key role for the UK's nuclear deterrent had disappeared, sparking a nationwide debate on what the future would hold and whether and how nuclear deterrence should be extended into the new era. The key question, as expounded by strategic studies scholar Beatrice Heuser, was whether nuclear deterrence 'could be harnessed to a new stabilising world order, one that protects peace and checks aggression, or will it in future be the cover under which rogue regimes can conduct limited wars?'[99] Quinlan, newly released from the restrictions of his civil service career, jumped into the debate feet first, leading discussions on the nuclear future at Ditchley and IISS. As Quinlan pointed out to John Keegan at the *Daily Telegraph*, Britain's role in the world needed to be reassessed, and in the light of that reassessment, new thinking on nuclear strategy and doctrine was needed. He was frank about the tendency of most career civil servants, due to the nature of their job, to need prodding from the academic community to force them to think outside the box and even admitted to having been somewhat stuck himself in what he described as 'obvious-adversary patterns of thinking'. Harnessing the efforts of scholars and practitioners to break out of the Cold War box thus became his number one priority:[100]

> ❝ I have been a fan, in a general way, of outside involvement in defence policy cogitation since the early [19]60s, when I was secretary to an unusual Air Ministry committee[101] (the brainchild of the then permanent secretary, with memories of Tizard[102]) which comprised eminent scientists – Zuckerman, Hawthorne, Lighthill and the like[103] – invited to address themselves to such general strategic or similar matters as the future of UK nuclear forces, air defence, limited war, military use of space and so on. Very good education for me, and I like to think they helped in some degree to improve the quality of thinking among the staffs. But the problem both then and later (when Neil Cameron, heading the Defence Policy Staff in which I served in the late 60s, awoke my interest in the IISS, King's and all that) was to prove and measure the contribution.
>
> My own belief – but this is, I admit, what I want to believe – is that they do tend to make the in-house staffs think harder and more clearly, and expose assumptions and judgements more explicitly, than would happen

otherwise. I cannot however readily recall any particular case where an academic study, or the intervention of a particular academic, plainly modified policy. (In fairness, that would be a hard test to apply). [The] MoD does occasionally commission specific pieces of work, but usually for the enrichment of understanding rather than the receipt of concrete recommendations.

I recognise the point you make about the difficulty people have – inside [the] MoD as well as outside – in breaking away from Cold War obvious-adversary patterns of thinking; I am myself, I suspect, a prime exhibit, given how much of my intellectual capital was invested in the metaphysics of bi-polar deterrence. My current impression (mostly from King's and thereabouts) is that the British academic world is by now not doing too badly in shifting its ground – it does at least, to my perception, accept the need for a shift, which is the beginning of wisdom. I remember that you had misgivings about the Centre for Defence Studies people, but some of their output seems to me quite decent. They're certainly quicker on their feet than a good many in the bureaucracy, both military and civilian.

At risk of stating what is both obvious and perhaps irrelevant to your immediate purpose, I note that one of the important functions of the defence academic community has been to help communicate wider understanding of defence to the public at large – the sort of thing that [Michael] Howard, [Laurence] Martin and [Lawrence] Freedman (and you yourself) have done well – in addition to the cumulative effect of their normal teaching output. I think this matters a great deal, and of course it cannot be done just from within the bureaucracy. It was a large part of my own motivation in pushing the [King's

Centre for Defence Studies] idea.

Between you, me and the gatepost, I suspect that the biggest current handicap to the modernisation of defence policy in Britain is the reluctance of a tired Government, faced with a small majority and a rampant Right, to grasp any more institutional and industrial nettles, when excision rather than all-round shrinkage is the real need. **"**

Quinlan's letter, dated 11 October 1993, was prompted by two notes John Keegan had sent him about the role of outside involvement in defence policymaking. Keegan, having read an article exploring the policy influence of research centres such as the IISS and the CDS in the journal *Army Quarterly*,[104] was keen to sound out Quinlan (who he saw as the instigator of many of the MoD's outside links into academia and particularly to King's) before writing something on the subject. Keegan's view was that academics in these centres were 'still pointing in the wrong direction, following the MoD of the Cold War', and failing to 're-align themselves'.[105] It's clear from Quinlan's response that he did not share Keegan's concerns, believing the Conservative government and what he referred to as 'the rampant Right' as the source of the backward-looking defence thinking Keegan had noted.[106]

At around the same time Quinlan and Keegan were corresponding on this issue, Quinlan was continuing to maintain his close links with the MoD, and to feed his own perspectives on the future of the UK's deterrence strategy and doctrine into departmental policy discussions. A letter dated 4 November 1992 from Nick Witney, who at the time was serving as the MoD director of nuclear policy and security, shows that his input was appreciated and widely circulated among defence officials. The letter highlights Quinlan's belief in a continuing role for UK nuclear weapons to support US defence commitments and extended deterrence relationships, and – perhaps more significantly in terms of current debates over the future of Trident – hints at MoD concerns that the UK may not always be able to rely on the US nuclear deterrent:[107]

> " Many thanks for sending me your paper on 'The Future of Nuclear Weapons', in its All Souls seminar version; I have taken the liberty of giving it a certain distribution within MoD. I find the degree of congruence with the sort of things [Defence Secretary] Mr [Malcolm] Rifkind said at the Joxe colloquium[108] on 30 September reassuring!
>
> I was interested in the passage about the duty of support owed by partner countries to the US in bearing the nuclear task. As you say, there is a question of political onus here – which makes me wonder whether the argument that, in relation to deterrence outside the East/West context, no one need ever doubt the credibility of the US deterrent, tells quite the whole story. Certainly, when I tried the line on a US official recently he was quick to say that, if any future coalition needed to threaten nuclear action against any future Saddam, he would urge the US President to ensure that the other western nuclear powers were fully involved. Uncomfortable, but one can see the point. "

Quinlan continued to maintain his close MoD links and influence over nuclear policy throughout his retirement, including during the review of British nuclear policy that took place under the Labour government in 2005–06. It was clear by that time that, despite over a decade immersing himself in scholarly debates about the need to rethink deterrence and consider the potential for moving towards a disarmed world, on balance he supported the view that the UK's independent nuclear deterrent should be maintained. However, he was more concerned than ever that *Trident* should represent value for money. A letter dated 18 June 2006 from Quinlan to Patrick Turner, who was policy director at the MoD, explored how to reduce costs in a *Trident* replacement. It suggested replacing only three boats instead of four and cooperating with France to share the burden:[109]

> **❝** You have been very patient in listening to my ancient and amateur views on the 'renewal' question, and I am very grateful for your unofficial help in my avoiding factual solecisms in my imminent article in Chatham House's *International Affairs* – copy of final text herewith. But I venture now to set down such thoughts as I have on the 'three boats' issue, and on a possible interaction with France. I fully recognise that I am probably quite out of tune with the Department's thinking; and I seek no reply.
>
> I recognise that four boats give virtually total assurance of always having one at sea even if there is some unforeseen technical mishap and even while there is one boat in long refit. My doubts concern whether that degree of assurance is, in post-Cold-War days, worth all the costs of a fourth boat (though of course I do not know what those costs amount to). The three/four comparison would need to assess – as again I cannot – exactly what the capability/probability/risk is with three. For example, I do not know for just how much of the time, with new boat design – or indeed even with the *Vanguards* – one boat has to be in refit; I assume, perhaps mistakenly, that it is not all the time as in *Resolution*-class[110] days.
>
> But the case for having a boat always at sea used to centre, in my long-ago DUS(P) days, on the argu-

ment (paras. 13–15 of DOGD 80/23) that in the Cold War setting we must maintain this ultimate level of insurance against the admittedly-remote hypothesis of super-power bolt from the blue. That hypothesis has surely evaporated. Can we not now assume, for any realistic scenario, that we would have some warning – some period of rising tension – during which we could bring at least one boat to at-sea readiness even if none was already there? I am familiar with the argument – I remember hearing ex-CND Robin Cook[111] solemnly urge it on Cardinal Basil Hume! – that sailing a boat at such a time might be an undesirably temperature-raising act. But I question whether that consideration – about which anyway I am skeptical (even if we didn't positively want to send a signal, SSBNs would surely be coming and going often enough for movement to be unremarkable) – can be anywhere near worth the cost of a boat.

Now my 'European' point, related to the above though by no means an inseparable condition of it. I suspect that the French, despite current brave protes-tations, are going to find their nuclear-weapon-force provision under growing politico-financial pressure. One option for them would be to go in the next genera-tion for three boats, on much the same reasoning as that sketched above. If they and we were fussed about the 'boat at sea' point, might it be possible to ease it by attempting some coordination with them on refit timings so that (assuming that I am right in supposing that neither country now needs or will in the future need to have always one boat in refit) the periods when there were only two in the operational cycle did not coincide, or were reduced. None of this would imply any dilution or pooling of national control; but it would, at least by implication, recognise that circumstances must be very remote in which either country got itself in to a nuclear-level confrontation in which neither the other nor the United States was involved.

All this is distinct again from the question whether there could be any procurement collaboration, carrier-style, in the building of new SSBNs. I know that missile fits would remain entirely different; but would it really be out of the question, or of no financial attraction, to look positively (in a spirit of 'what could we do?' rather than 'why we would rather not') for aspects that might be common – hull, propulsion, tactical weapons fit, or whatever? I have the impression that the French [nuclear-powered ballistic missile submarine] long-term replacement timetable might be found to fit by no means ill at the end of our own likely build time-table. **"**

As it happened, the December 2006 White Paper deferred the decision on the number of boats, as it became clear not enough information was available on the submarine design to be able to answer the questions posed by Quinlan in his letter. The relevant text in the review document stated that:

" Currently we require a fleet of four submarines to maintain one continuously on patrol and retaining this posture is essential to assure the invulnerability of the deterrent. We will investigate fully whether there is scope to make sufficiently radical changes to the design of the new submarines, and their operating, manning, training and support arrangements, to enable us to maintain these continuous deterrent patrols with a fleet of only three submarines. A final decision on whether we require three or four submarines will be taken when we know more about their detailed design.[112] **"**

No decision was taken in the 2010 Strategic Defence and Security Rreview (SDSR) either, but it did announce that detailed design work on the new class of submarines was about to begin to determine whether continuous-at-sea-deterrence (CASD)[113] would require 'four submarines or only three' and that a decision can be expected around 2016.[114] In November 2010 Prime Minister David Cameron also announced that the UK and France had signed a burden-sharing treaty that will allow the two countries to share nuclear-testing facilities at Aldermaston, England and Valduc in France. The agreement rules out the more advanced sharing arrangements that some had proposed, and Cameron made his views very clear by stating at the time of the announcement that the UK 'will always retain an independent nuclear deterrent',[115] but the new arrangements do appear to reflect a shift in MoD thinking on burden-sharing that may have partly been influenced by Quinlan.

Cameron's certainty that Britain will always maintain an independent nuclear deterrent would not have sat well with Quinlan, who, despite his support for *Trident* replacement, developed a more acute appreciation of the political costs of nuclear weapons towards the end of his life. Quinlan began to regard the nuclear future as an open book: he was in no way ready to reject nuclear deterrence or embrace unilateral disarmament, but his position on indefinite nuclear retention had begun to shift. As the last part of this book will show, although Quinlan continued to believe in the fundamental strategic logic of nuclear deterrence and to doubt whether it would be possible to ensure security and stability in a world without nuclear weapons, in his final years he became convinced of the need to work in good faith towards that goal.

PART THREE

Arms control and disarmament

Quinlan's beliefs on nuclear arms control and disarmament were cautious, sceptical and at times even dismissive during his time in the civil service. But his ideas began to change after his retirement from the MoD in 1992. The collapse of the Soviet Union had a powerful impact on his thinking: the West no longer faced what Quinlan referred to as a brutal, atheistic, totalitarian superpower, which meant much of the context for his arguments about the logic and morality of nuclear deterrence had suddenly changed. In the Cold War context, nuclear elimination appeared foolhardy if not impossible; in the new context, it still seemed a risky and unlikely prospect, but nuclear reductions became desirable, and the idea of multilateral disarmament and even abolition became a more serious subject for debate. Had Quinlan stayed at the MoD after the Cold War had ended, his attention would no doubt have turned increasingly to disarmament challenges anyway. But the timing of Quinlan's retirement just as the Cold War ended facilitated this process: suddenly, he was free from his official responsibilities; released from some of the tight constitutional restrictions on his ability to publish and engage in public debate; and able to turn his mind from the day-to-day practicalities of defending the nation to more conceptual questions about the future. At Ditchley Park, King's College London and the IISS, he threw himself into policy debates about the post-Cold War international system and the various costs and benefits of a nuclear-armed future. Reading through Quinlan's letters from the period, it seems as though the seeds of nuclear disarmament had suddenly found the right conditions to germinate: changes in the international system provided the sunshine, and intellectual freedom the rain. The result was not a sudden flowering of disarmament optimism or advocacy but a steady growth of interest in disarmament possibilities.

This was a significant development in Quinlan's thinking. Many of his letters from the Cold War period reveal that he viewed nuclear disarmament as a dangerous enterprise, to be treated with extreme caution. While the Soviet Union remained a serious threat, he believed the obstacles to a peaceful, disarmed world were immense and rashly underestimated by disarmament advocates. This helps explain why, throughout his civil service career, he devoted so much of his energy to countering the ideas of disarmament advocates, and to questioning the logic and consequences of US–Soviet arms-control initiatives.

This part of the book covers Quinlan's correspondence on these issues: the first half explores his thinking on US–Soviet arms-control negotiations as well as his contributions to UK debates on multilateral arms control and proposals for enhancing strategic stability; the second charts his contributions to disarmament debates. Much of the discussion focuses on Quinlan's correspondence while he was in the civil service, when he held complex beliefs about the role of arms control in Cold War crisis stability and mostly dismissive attitudes to nuclear disarmament. The concluding pages chart Quinlan's post-retirement thinking on nuclear issues, when he became more interested in nuclear disarmament. Although much of his private correspondence from this period occurred via e-mail (most of which, unfortunately, it has not been possible to acquire), he began to publish more material and give more media interviews after his retirement, so insight into his thinking is still readily available. His output shows that right up until his death in 2009, Quinlan remained uncertain about the plausibility and desirability of a disarmed world and the conditions under which nuclear abolition might be possible. But he had begun to probe some interesting questions, and in doing so, overturned some of his own disarmament resistance and contributed to nuclear debates that are still centre stage today.

Arms control and non-proliferation

Quinlan regarded arms-control negotiations as artificial and awkward, and strongly opposed involving the UK in a process that he believed would be of no strategic advantage. Although (at least within cautious limits) he supported international efforts to curtail US–Soviet arms-race dynamics, he believed that the UK could not afford to reduce the roles and numbers of its own nuclear weapons if its anti-Soviet deterrent was to remain credible.[1] But this wariness, which was widely shared by the British defence establishment at the time, did not lead Quinlan to detach himself from Cold War arms control and disarmament negotiations; far from it. His letters show that he played important direct and indirect roles in responding to US–Soviet bilateral arms-control initiatives. His main concern was to ensure that arms-control momentum did not undermine the integrity of UK or NATO deterrence – a task that depended on clearly communicating British and European interests to Washington (and later, Moscow). Through his participation in the negotiations for the Intermediate-range Nuclear Forces

(INF) treaty (as they affected the UK), and the drafting of Margaret Thatcher's 1982 speech to the United Nations, one can follow his developing attitude to multilateral arms control during the last decade of the Cold War and his thoughts on improving Cold War crisis stability.

The UK and the INF negotiations: a brief history

The final decade of the Cold War was a dynamic period in the history of arms control. One development was of particular significance to Quinlan's correspondence: the success of the US–USSR arms-control negotiations over the elimination of intermediate nuclear forces, which led to the entry into force of the INF Treaty in June 1991. This initiative had originated in the dual-track decision of 1979, when the HLG and NPG had attached an arms-control proposal to the decision to deploy LRTNF in Western Europe. The move was mostly symbolic – intended to ease the growing fears of European publics, who were worried that Cold War arms-racing dynamics were increasing the prospect of nuclear war. But two years later, the Reagan administration, with strong support from the West German government and public opinion in Europe, made the dual-track decision a central plank of its arms-control policy.[2] To a large extent, this strategy appears to have been a game of bluff: when Reagan proposed the 'zero option' (the removal of all long-range theatre nuclear forces from Europe) at the start of the INF negotiations in 1981, few seriously thought the Soviets would agree to his proposal. They did, however, hope it would take the sting out of the tail of the European peace movement. Thus, while British defence officials, including Quinlan, were uneasy about the strategic implications of abandoning LRTNF, they did not challenge Reagan's commitment because they were not convinced it would come to anything.[3] But it did. In 1986, Mikhail Gorbachev offered to eliminate all

SS-20s in Europe, and from that point onwards, he refused to accept anything other than the zero option. (In fact, he went further, proposing to include a ban on all shorter-range range missiles as well, known as the 'double zero option'). When the INF treaty was eventually signed in December 1987, it banned all cruise and ground-launched nuclear missiles with a range of 500–5,500km and their launchers, and included rigorous verification procedures that the US had insisted upon.

Quinlan was not entirely happy about this outcome, which made him more cautious about arms control, increasing his conviction that officials should be careful to avoid situations where public pressure is allowed to dictate arms-control initiatives that have serious strategic implications. It was better for the US and its NATO partners to be cautious and not to promise too much. Quinlan's response as PUS of the MoD was to authorise steps to prepare for a possible weakening of US commitment to the defence of Western Europe: the 1989 Defence White Paper made it clear that the UK had no intention of entering the Strategic Arms Reduction Treaty (START) process and that disarmament was not a long-term goal of British security policy; the decision to procure a successor of the UK's ageing non-strategic WE-177 gravity bombs also made it clear that, as long as the Soviet Union was considered a serious threat, the UK intended to maintain a sub-strategic nuclear capability as well as its strategic deterrent. It is easy to see why some commentators believed these decisions put the UK out of step with the US and Soviet Union, whose leaders were launching major arms-control initiatives and making visionary speeches about the long-term goal of nuclear disarmament. For the UK though, talk of disarmament and arms control rang alarm bells over the erosion of US extended deterrence, and it was only after the Cold War was over that British defence officials felt the time was ripe to (quietly and independently) trim and restructure UK nuclear forces to fit the strategic realities of the post-Cold War world.

Supporting arms control: a British balancing act

Quinlan's correspondence shows that during his civil service career, senior officials often relied on his understanding of the strategic implications of arms control and disarmament – even when he was at the Treasury and the Ministry for Employment. In 1982, for example, he was asked to draft Margaret Thatcher's speech to the United Nations Special Session on Disarmament. His logical arguments were also in demand on a more day-to-day basis: FCO officials sometimes called on him to help draft advice to ministers on how to explain policies that were unpopular with key sections of the British electorate (such as UK government opposition to the CTBT in 1991). More often, his advice was sought in a semi-official capacity to assist in FCO public information efforts. A letter from Michael Pakenham (Head of the FCO Arms Control and Disarmament Department in the early 1980s) makes this relationship clear: he wrote to thank Quinlan for some materials he had sent him, which unfortunately had reached him a day after he had given a talk to CCADD on the arms control scene in Washington. 'I could certainly have used your wisdom to bolster my grip on the subject!' he explained. 'I should like to say how useful I found [your papers] for our own work here, and particularly for adaptation to our public information effort. I hope you won't mind if we trade occasionally on your ideas – without attribution of course'.[4]

This reliance on Quinlan is hardly surprising given his mastery of strategic issues (although one can question whether Quinlan was ever a good source of information on the non-proliferation regime as a whole[5]). It cannot have been easy for Britain's political leaders and senior officials to manage the

UK's complex balancing act on arms control: publicly, they declared their support for arms-control initiatives, and in fact were genuinely supportive of any US–Soviet nuclear-force reductions that they judged would not weaken NATO deterrence. But at the same time, they wanted to avoid involving the UK arsenal in any nuclear arms-control process. The official justification for this approach was that it was practical for the superpowers to lead the way in nuclear cuts given that they had by far the largest arsenals; it made sense that the UK would join a multilateral process at some later, unspecified date. But this was not the full story. Quinlan summed up the reasons for Britain's resistance to multilateral nuclear arms control in a letter to John Roper, MP, dated 5 January 1983:[6]

> **❝** I have never yet seen any explanation in cool practical terms of why it is likely to be to Britain's advantage, or in the West's, for us to get involved in START. We believe our strategic force is already at a minimum viable level; what then have we available to bargain with? Experience in other arms-control negotiation warns clearly enough that the minor third can be very uncomfortably squeezed. Other than an ephemeral feeling of importance, what could we hope to gain? The fact that the USSR would doubtless like to have our head on the block is hardly a reason for us to put it there. **❞**

This strategic reality created a continual public-relations headache for British officials. They spent much of their time trying to counter the efforts of the Soviet propaganda machine, which used British refusal to engage in multilateral nuclear arms control as an opportunity to fuel public dissent in the UK. Presenting British policy in a positive light and in a way that minimised Soviet opportunities to exploit it as a weakness was a challenge; one that Quinlan was able and willing to help with – including during his time 'in exile' from the MoD, when he had no official responsibility for defence and security matters.

Insight into the role Quinlan played in shaping UK arms control and disarmament diplomacy can be found in Thatcher's June 1982 speech to the UN Special Session on Disarmament, which Quinlan helped to draft. He left a note in his file, written in 1998, explaining how he became involved in the speech-writing process when he was at the Treasury:[7]

> ❝ The history of this exercise, as touching me, was I believe as follows. Mrs Thatcher was due to make a major speech at the UN Special Session on disarmament in June 1982. She thought poorly of the draft submitted by the FCO (not then in her good books, in the wake of the Falklands episode[8]) and asked Hugh Thomas of the Centre for Policy Studies to try his hand. She did not think much of that version either. At a meeting of Ministers soon thereafter (I believe the 'Falklands' Committee[9], but I am not sure) she apparently bemoaned the fact that the deadline was approaching and she had no decent draft to work on. John Nott, it seems, said something to the effect that Michael Quinlan was now in the Treasury and probably under-employed, and might usefully be put to work on this task. (Mrs Thatcher knew me as a drafter on nuclear weapon issues, and in this respect at least had a good opinion of my work). I was accordingly summoned to a meeting at No. 10 with the PM, [assistant under-secretary of state] David Gilmore, and [private secretary to the prime minister] John Coles, and produced a draft in the light of the discussion. There were, I think but am not sure, more than one such meetings and more than one draft.

I was not involved in the later stages of the exercise. **"**

Quinlan kept numerous drafts of the speech in his files, including the original FCO draft that Thatcher was so dismissive of, and the redraft by Hugh Thomas that she didn't like much better. He also kept a number of his own drafts, including one he submitted to Thatcher (via John Coles) on 15 June 1982, which he described as a 'very rough first shot'. In many ways, this first draft is the most interesting one, as it is the most unvarnished insight into Quinlan's thinking on arms control and disarmament. It begins with a list of bullet points, which he may have jotted down during his initial meeting at No. 10 Downing Street, and then expands to five pages of close-typed prose, replete with crossings out and handwritten scribbles:[10]

1. Defend our values.
2. Every country has the right and duty to defend itself.
3. The purpose of disarmament is not to weaken these objectives, but to ensure that they are achieved at the lowest possible cost.
4. History shows that war is caused not by the strong attacking the strong – but by the strong constantly probing for weak points. Weakness leads to war.
5. Bismarck 'Do I want war? Of course not, I want victory'.
6. Those who use force in internal affairs are the most ready to use it internationally.
7. Disarmers have concentrated on nuclear weapons. But the last 25 years have shown that these weapons have carried out their proper function of deterrence.
8. There have been 140 conflicts since 1945. All fought with conventional weapons.

9. Destabilisation in a hitherto stable area can be caused by one state suddenly acquiring new arms.

10. Importance of verification.

11. Myth that arms race inevitably leads to war.

Draft speech begins:[11]

Mr President:

This is the first time that I have had the opportunity to address the General Assembly. I account it a privilege to do so, and to do so under your Presidency.

But what makes the occasion most special to me is the subject – the subject of peace. The leaders who have come here, as I have, carry in this matter an especial duty; not just to our own countries' interest but to the common interest of all, in the most vital matter of all. We are collectively the trustees of our generation. I shall try to speak now in that spirit; I shall not be concerned to score national debating points.

Our generation faces a very special responsibility because of what the march of modern technology has done to the weapons of war. We are all conscious of that most vividly in respect of nuclear weapons. Mankind now has – and can never lose, never forget – the knowledge of how to blow itself up, and we have to live, as our forebears did not, with that irreversible fact, and to manage its implications.

In its own terrible way, however, that fact also carries a special opportunity. For part of what it means is that the initiation of war among the major nuclear powers is simply not a rational option. Given what these appalling armouries can do, recourse to war between these powers can never be a sane way of setting about the regulation or resolution of differences. The history of the past thirty seven years displays a deepening recognition of that by every participant. In circumstances often tense and difficult, deterrence has been stable; it has kept the peace between East and West; and that is an achievement beyond price, one which we must not for the future relinquish or endanger.

I believe nevertheless that we can sustain that vast achievement at much lower levels of these awful armouries and at much lower costs, if we have the will, the vision and the flexibility to agree to do so. These are major goals, and I shall have more to say later on the ways towards them. But let us throughout have the wisdom and the honesty to recognise that to attempt or pretend to dismantle the deterrent system wholesale – above all to do one-sidedly[12] – might be a course of reckless danger, and danger for the whole world. I do not want to make world war seem a rational option again; it cannot be, and it must not for a moment be allowed to appear so.

I have spoken so far of nuclear weapons. These were a special concern of the 1978 Special Session; they must manifestly remain so for us. But I am uneasy that they may sometimes mask the appalling facts about what we sometimes call, in the over-cosy jargon of the strategic theorists, conventional weapons and conventional war; and I venture to hope that this Session may focus renewed and sharper concern upon these. Let us consider just a few facts. Since the disaster of Nagasaki nuclear weapons have not been used at all. But there have been something like one hundred and forty non-nuclear armed conflicts, and in those conflicts perhaps up to ten million people have died. This very week we watch the tragedy in the Lebanon; and I naturally have vividly in my own mind the many hundreds of men – brave young men from my country and from Argentina – cut down in the South Atlantic by the impersonal killing-power of modern armaments. Nuclear war is indeed a terrible threat; but conventional war is a terrible reality. We must seek to do something about the dangers of conventional war, and its burdens. Those burdens, let us remember, are far greater than those of nuclear weapons. If we deplore, as I certainly do, the amount spent on military preparations in a world where so many go hungry and so much else needs to be done, our criticism and our action should turn above all to conventional forces, which absorb far the greatest proportion – over ninety per cent – of military spending world-wide.

We are all of us involved in this – virtually all of us have conventional forces. I am personally convinced that we need a deeper and wider effort throughout the non-nuclear field, looking at weapons and manpower and deployments to see what we can do together to lighten the risks and the burdens and the fears.

But in a sense, Mr President, I have still not come to the root of the matter. For the fundamental risk to peace is not the existence of weapons, whether nuclear or other, of particular types or in particular numbers or places. It is, above all, the existence of political willingness to initiate recourse to force, to the use of arms. It is here, and not in 'arms races', whether real or imaginary, that the springs of war lie. I mentioned a moment ago a hundred and forty conflicts since 1945. Few if any of those can plausibly be traced to an arms race. No informed historian can imagine that the World War of 1939 to 1945 was caused by any kind of arms race. On the contrary, it sprung most clearly and tellingly from the belief of a tyrant that his neighbours lacked the means or the will to resist him effectively – from weakness in deterrence. A formidable countryman of that tyrant, seventy years earlier, is quoted as saying 'Do I want war? Of course not – I want victory'. Hitler believed he could have victory without war, or with not very much or very difficult war. The cost of disproving that belief was immense; the cost of preventing him from forming it in the first place would have been infinitely less. The lesson is that disarmament and good intentions on their own do not guarantee peace; in the wrong circumstances they may even damage it.

It can be not merely a mistake of analysis but an evasion of responsibility to suppose that we deal with the problem of war, and the duty of peace, primarily by focusing upon weapons. These are more often symptoms than causes.

We are entitled, every one of us, to live in peace with our own values and way of life; not to have the doctrines, the institutions or the control of other countries forced upon us, not to be compelled to choose between peace and freedom. We are entitled to be protected from external aggression – if necessary through our own efforts, if possible (and preferably) through a just international system. The efforts of political leaders for peace, both through this great organisation and in other ways, need to be directed first and foremost to removing the conditions that lead to conflict – injustice between and within nations, mistrust and secrecy, the denial of human rights – and to strengthening the methods and mechanisms for resolving conflict without war. We have to work at this urgently; but we must also do so realistically, without illusion.

Mr President, I have explained why in general I do not believe that armaments cause wars or that action on them alone will prevent wars. But I have said all this not in any way to decry disarmament and arms control but to give them their real value, to set them in their true context. It has in my view been a frequent and serious disservice to their cause to attribute to them potentialities which they cannot make good; excessive claims and demands have too often been not an aid to practical action, but a substitute for it. Disarmament measures cannot, in any realistic framework, remove the possibility of war. But the limitation and reduction of armaments can still do a great deal. It can reduce the economic burden of military preparation legitimate for self defence; it can ease political friction and the fears this may heighten; it can moderate the scale or inhumanity of conflict; it can sometimes seal off or limit the destructive exploitation of advancing science. To do these things and to do them in a way that is balanced, visible and dependable, is to do a very great deal; and we must seize every opportunity and indeed make new opportunities. I should now like to turn briefly to some specific issues in this direction.

In the nuclear field, the hopes of the world lie above all with the direct dialogue between the United States and the Soviet Union, which have by far the largest arsenals. As I implied earlier, I believe that provided reasonable balance is not lost these arsenals could both be greatly reduced without any danger to peace. This is where decisive action, not just deceleration or standstill is needed; and I therefore welcome the radical proposals made by the United States for eliminating intermediate-range systems and substantially cutting the strategic armouries. The negotiations must surely have the urgent support and goodwill of us all.[13]

I am deeply worried about chemical weapons. When the world community in 1972 decided to ban biological weapons – a matter in which I am proud that Britain played a major initiating role – we all looked forward to successful action on chemical weapons. It has not happened; indeed, many of us have been greatly disquieted by persistent reports that these weapons have actually been used. The Committee on Disarmament needs to give renewed and special impetus – and Britain has sought recently to contribute to this – to arriving at a convention banning development and possession; and the reports I have just referred to underline how vital it is that such a ban should be truly verifiable if it is not to be simply a source of danger, instability and suspicion.

I spoke earlier about the huge weight of conventional forces. The biggest concentration and confrontation of such forces anywhere in the world lies in Europe, my own continent. Something needs to be done about this, to reduce the burden without creating imbalance or insecurity. This must be possible if both sides truly want it, and the Western participants in the long negotiations in Vienna have recently made an important fresh proposal. Britain would also like to see a conference take place soon to agree quickly on mandatory confidence-building and security-building measures in Europe. This would be a powerful complement to action on numbers at Vienna.

There are several other efforts in progress to which Britain gives its full support like the valuable project under the Secretary-General's auspices for much greater openness about military spending, and the work on the relationship between disarmament and development. I shall not catalogue all this work in detail now; my country will demonstrate its support by the breadth and quality of our practical participation.

I have no reason to be ashamed of Britain's record over the years in the disarmament and arms-control field – I believe it stands up well to comparison. But I cannot be complacent; Britain and everyone else needs to do more. And the way in which we need, all of us, to do it is not by speeches, still less by propaganda postures, but by patient, realistic, relevant work, step by step in difficult and complex matters. Frankly, I am not very interested in disarmament theory or rhetoric; I am interested in disarmament action, because that is what people want. It will be a long business, and an unspectacular one; but there is no short cut and no sensible alternative.

I should like to finish what I have to say, Mr. President, by reverting to the central theme of peace. There is, I believe, a real prospect that we can keep the option of all-out global war, of nuclear war, simply obsolete and unreal; and I believe we can do it at less cost than today if we have the wisdom to agree on the measures to that end. We cannot yet, I fear, make all sorts of war obsolete; I doubt whether our generation can realistically expect to achieve in full the goal which Pope John Paul proposed during a visit to my country only last month, when he said 'War should belong to the tragic past, to history; it should find no place on humanity's agenda for the future'. But we can less and less afford to regard that objective as wholly unattainable, or just a pious theoretical aspiration. We have to make it a central political goal, genuinely shared by all, to be pursued by concrete practical action directed to removing real causes and risks. All of us can help, in large ways or small. Disarmament and arms control are important among the instruments

available to us. I hope and expect that this session will
make a distinctive contribution to exploiting them more
fully. I pledge my own country to play its part.

The content of a letter sent by Quinlan to John Coles on 17
June 1982 indicates that discussions between Thatcher and
Quinlan continued after she had read the first draft. She asked
him to unearth quotes by Aleksandr Solzhenitsyn and Andrei
Sakharov (Nobel Prize-winning Russian political philosophers
who criticised communism) and to add them to a revised draft
of the speech. Quinlan dutifully did some research (with the
help of the Soviet section at the FCO), only to discover that
Solzhenitsyn's analysis of the evils of Communism was partly
underpinned by the argument that arms racing leads inexo-
rably to war (which was not a message Quinlan wanted to
endorse – it clearly challenged his own belief that the weapons
themselves were not the problem).[14] So Solzhenitsyn was
abandoned, and instead Quinlan built some text around the
arguments of Sakharov, who argued that the militarisation
of the Soviet economy was placing a chronic burden on the
people of the Soviet Union, encroaching on their democratic
rights and freedoms.[15]

The text of the speech that Thatcher actually made to the
UN Special Session is very close to the original draft penned
by Quinlan.[16] David Gilmore wrote to him shortly after she had
delivered it, explaining how it had been received in New York:[17]

❝ I attach a copy of the prime minister's famous speech
to the United Nations Second Special Session on
Disarmament. You will be amused to compare it with
earlier versions.

I think a good deal of Quinlan is left in the text,
although it has been pared down to some fairly bare

essentials. As you may know, I went with the prime minister to New York and Washington and we spent about 3 hours on the outward journey going over the text and making a mass of small amendments to it. Even when this was complete, the prime minister insisted on going through it once again, at midnight New York time, to iron out the last kinks. As you would imagine, it was a wearing process, but the prime minister was good humoured throughout and, I think, was persuaded that she had a good basic text on which to work.

The final text as uttered would not, I think, be the pride and joy of the professional disarmer. Nonetheless, it received, by United Nations standards, warm and enthusiastic applause. I watched from the back and noted that a large number of non-aligned countries appeared to be as enthusiastic as anyone. After the speech the prime minister received congratulations from the long line of delegates. I spoke to the American, German, French and Belgian Ambassadors, all of whom were, I think, quite genuine when they praised the simplicity, clarity and punch of the prime minister's speech. All in all then, a far better outcome than I would have anticipated 10 days ago. Indeed, the prime minister's popularity in New York (one television interviewer described her as 'an American folk hero') had a lot to do with it. 🖙

The enthusiastic response to Thatcher's speech provides an example of the UK's skilled management of a potentially awkward situation: it masked its multilateral nuclear arms-control allergy with declarations of support for the bilateral US–Soviet arms-control negotiations, including US proposals for eliminating intermediate-range forces, and with evidence of the UK's proactive efforts to address the threat posed by biological and chemical weapons. What was left out of the speech was just as important as what was included, however, and despite the positive response Thatcher received, she made no commitment to involve Britain in multilateral nuclear arms-control negotiations.

Although Quinlan rarely explained his own thoughts on arms control in his private correspondence, he did so in a letter to Lawrence Freedman, dated 25 September 1986. The previous day, during an event at Chatham House to launch his latest book, Freedman had touched upon the question of whether the UK and France should engage in the START process, appearing open to the idea. Quinlan was quick to dispel any illusions Freedman might have about the benefits of UK involvement in arms-control negotiations with the USSR. Instead, he proposed that if the UK did make cuts to its nuclear armouries (something he considered possible and desirable in future if the appropriate circumstances arose) it should be done independently of any external process:[18]

> **"** I much enjoyed and admired your talk at Chatham House yesterday, and am even more moved than I was already to look forward to reading the book.
>
> Had time (and perhaps also bureaucratic discretion) allowed, I should have liked to sound you out in question time about the idea, on which you touched, of UK nuclear capability as subject-matter for arms-control negotiation. It has long been standard rhetoric for every political party to recognise the idea as apt some day, and no doubt this has become so ritual and received that to speak in a contrary or sceptical sense would be thought odd, or bad form. But I am perplexed about what the case is by hard-headed standards of advantage and achievement, as distinct from what you termed 'atmospherics'.

What would be the substantive nature, and the point, of the bargain?

One presumably starts with some basic view about what independent UK capability is for – seat at the top table, second-centre, Gaullist last-ditchery, or whatever. If one believes, Carverwise,[19] that all these are bosh, no doubt it doesn't much matter what the trade is, since the goods on our side are effectively valueless. But if one doesn't fully share that view, I find it remarkably hard to see what it is that one could remotely hope to get from the Russians in negotiation that makes any material difference to the nature or strength of the case, in any version, for our capability. None of the cases, so far as I can see, is in the least sensitive – certainly within any degree of adjustment likely to be contemplated on the Soviet side – to variations in the size or composition of the Soviet nuclear armoury. We are of course interested – from the viewpoint of the scale, technical character and cost of our capability – in what strategic defences they have, but I find it hard to imagine that they would ever trade in that currency with us or the French; and even if they did, that still would not touch our case for being in the business at all. Yet at least some of our politicians imply that that basic issue would be on the table on our side.

It might of course be, in principle, that though proportionately modest Soviet reductions secured by UK negotiations did not touch the basic case, they would confer on us some other benefit powerful enough to make it worthwhile surrendering that case. But I have never seen any concrete suggestion of what such other advantage might be; nor can I think one up.

You will, I hope, recognise in all this that I do not regard our independent capability as of infinite value, to be held on to regardless of opportunity cost; nor (between ourselves) would I maintain that reductions in its prospective size and cost are unthinkable or in no circumstances worth attention. But if adjustments were to be made, I suspect – rather on the lines of the argument (with which I agree) you deployed about SRTNF – that they would be much best done unilaterally, with maximum éclat, rather than snarled up in all the awkwardnesses of a largely-artificial negotiation. I need not spell out what those awkwardnesses are, especially as between mismatched participants. **"**

The arms-control doubts set out by Quinlan reflect the dominant view of the British defence establishment, although they are rarely expressed as frankly as in Quinlan's letter to Freedman. As Quinlan implied, the usual policy was to make what were arguably hollow declarations of support for multilateral nuclear arms control, while taking every possible step to protect and maintain Britain's minimum deterrent, including using the US–UK special relationship to try to prevent bilateral superpower reductions from undermining British interests.

Even though the UK was able to resist being drawn into multilateral arms-control negotiations, there were times during the final years of the Cold War when British officials became very uncomfortable about the nature and pace of US–Soviet bilateral arms-control initiatives and their implications for the UK and NATO. On one hand, bold arms-control commitments and far-reaching nuclear reductions by the US and the USSR helped ease the concerns of disarmers who were worried about arms-racing dynamics and their impact on international stability; but on the other hand, they increased the domestic political pressure on the UK government to support initiatives that defence officials believed would undermine Britain's nuclear deterrent. Handling this situation created challenges for the FCO and the MoD, especially when the church became involved, as it did over the nuclear freeze and nuclear-weapon-free zone proposals of the mid-1980s.

UK opposition to key non-proliferation proposals

The nuclear freeze and the nuclear-weapon-free zone (NWFZ) proposals caused presentational difficulties for the British defence establishment, even though they were both easily dismissed on a strategic level. The creation of a nuclear-free zone in Europe would have left the UK and its NATO allies vulnerable to nuclear-weapons systems (such as the Soviet SS-20) based outside the zone but targeted on it.[20] Moreover, the mobility of many land-based nuclear missiles meant that they could be rapidly deployed back into a NWFZ at a time of tension, which officials argued would heighten the risk of war. Similarly, nuclear freeze proposals (whereby all nuclear-weapons states would agree to freeze the development of new nuclear weapons[21]) were considered dangerous because they would perpetuate Soviet superiority in a range of weapons, which many suspected was the motivation behind Gorbachev's support for the proposal.[22] But rejecting these proposals outright was considered unwise – it could backfire if it made the defence establishment appear unwilling to countenance arms-control initiatives that had the support of one or both superpowers. The official line was therefore neither to endorse nor reject the proposals, but instead to argue that they were complicated and quietly imply that they might be part of a Soviet propaganda campaign.[23]

Quinlan's correspondence includes a batch of letters on the 1985 freeze and nuclear-weapon-free zone campaigns, most of which involve the Catholic Church and Quinlan's contacts in the FCO. In April, John Hunt (who had been invited by

Bob Beresford to join the Peace and Justice Commission) had sought Quinlan's advice about a move by Bishop O'Brien (the commission chair) to publicly endorse the freeze and zone proposals. Quinlan responded with the following letter, dated 15 April 1985:[24]

“ We spoke about Bishop O'Brien's inclination to give full-scale endorsement to nuclear freeze and nuclear-weapon-free zones. I attach a couple of pieces (both slightly dated, I fear) from the FCO on these topics. For my own part – and assuming that the immediate aim is to secure a pause for reflection and recognition of complexity, rather than a conclusive rejection of the ideas – I would be disposed to stress these points:

Freeze
a. What does it mean?
Are we to halt research? development? testing? manufacture? deployment? And of what? – Launch platforms (submarine? aircraft? – many of these are dual-purpose)? delivery vehicles (various sorts of missiles, again potentially dual-purpose, Like SLCMs)? actual warheads? And how do we determine operative dates and conditions? – e.g. for a *Typhoon* submarine already on sea trials? Is one-for-one replacement allowed? If so, what are the measures of equivalence? There are large definition problems hereabouts and consequently enormous scope for argument between the parties. Any notion that this is a simple idea would be wholly wide of the mark.
b. How is it to be verified?
Lots of the things listed under a. above are wholly beyond our verification capabilities – notably the warheads themselves. An unverified agreement would

be a rich source of friction, suspicion and risk; and a very bad precedent.

c. What is the actual effect? In some key areas – notably INF – a freeze would reward those who led current areas of arms competition, by halting matters in a position of Soviet advantage. The fact, on which we might all agree, that both sides have more than enough weapons in numerical total does not prove that armouries are quantitatively and qualitatively adequate to ensure deterrence at every level of the complex military balance.

d. What precisely is the point?

I have never seen any persuasive argument that freeze will reduce the risk of war, which is surely our ultimate concern.

e. What will it do to prospects of reduction?

Harm them, in my view – both by diverting negotiating effort and by taking the heat off the Russians.

f. How long is it to last?

Any notion that 'freeze' is a quick short-term holding operation is quite false, given negotiating realities. But if it goes on for a long time, it stands not only to obstruct healthy pro-stability changes (like more reliance on SSBNs, moves to lower-yield warheads, and the like) but also to cause acute problems for those faced – as we will be – with real problems of obsolescence.

NWFZ

a. What exactly is the NWFZ idea trying to achieve? Less risk of war? In the real circumstances of Europe it might increase it, if the effect were to offer the Russians some sort of purported guarantee of an area in which aggression could be conducted immunely from nuclear risk. In fact, though, the attempt is unreal – every part of

Europe is covered by the range of Russia-based nuclear weapons. Whether we like it or not, nuclear weapons are an integral part of strategic reality in Europe.

What does it actually mean?

Hiroshima and Nagasaki were nuclear-free zones, until someone from outside delivered weapons there. Note, in passing, that NATO is well advanced in a 35% net reduction of US warheads deployed in Europe. Note also, more fundamentally, that what matters most about nuclear weapons, if ever used, is not where they start but where they arrive; what does NWFZ do about that?

These are rather disorganised jottings; and I am at your service if a word on the phone would be useful. But I hope they may suffice to show that both notions are complex and difficult. There is nothing approaching consensus that they are sound, and NATO Governments – not just our own and the US – have so far been disposed to reject them. Given all this, for the bishops suddenly to leap in with an endorsement (unbacked, moreover, by any substantial scrutiny in discussion) would be naive and even wild. **"**

In his direct correspondence with the church hierarchy, Quinlan was more guarded in his critique of the proposals – he did not reject them outright, but raised enough doubts and questions to encourage senior figures to think twice about throwing their weight behind them.[25] An exchange between Quinlan and Michael Bowen, the archbishop of Southwark, shows the success of this measured approach. The archbishop had sought Quinlan's advice on whether he should accept an invitation to become a patron of the Freeze campaign, to which Quinlan supplied the following response (which, according to a subsequent letter from the archbishop,[26] persuaded him to hold back from accepting the invitation):[27]

66 Thank you for your letter dated 7 June about FREEZE. The organisation is new to me, and I have not been able to find out as yet whether it has, for example, any background such as might point to supping with a long spoon.

The idea itself, however, is a familiar one. Reasonable people disagree about it in good faith. Some US Catholic bishops have supported it, but I am not sure whether they have done so in any clear collective manner. It was an incidental issue in the US presidential election, in that Mr [Walter] Mondale [Democratic candidate in the 1984 US presidential election] favoured a version of it, qualified in a way FREEZE would be unlikely to agree with. NATO governments, including our own, have generally opposed it. So it is a matter of political controversy.

I had occasion earlier this year to jot down privately for Lord Hunt, who had been asked about the matter by Bishop James O'Brien, some of the reasons why 'Freeze' is not as straightforward as campaigning proponents would often have people suppose; and I enclose the relevant material. There are of course legitimate points to be made on the other side – my notes do not purport to be a comprehensive survey of the factors. Their purpose (and I have the impression, at second hand, that Bishop O'Brien may have been ready to accept that John Hunt's account of them legitimately achieved this) was simply to convey that the issue was genuinely complicated, debatable, and political rather than ethical, so that instant support from the Church's authorities was accordingly inappropriate. I venture to think that this remains right. (The letter to you [from Freeze], incidentally, is quite wide of the mark factually in implying that an unconstrained 'arms race' is in progress). **🗲🗲**

Shortly afterwards, in a letter to Bob Beresford dated 15 August 1985, Quinlan reasserted his reasons why he thought it would be wrong for the church to support Freeze, and why he believed Beresford should not dilute an information note he had drafted on the subject. Quinlan had received a copy of a letter that Paul Rogers (professor of peace studies at the University of Bradford) had sent to Beresford, in which he had asked him to tone down parts of the memo. Quinlan advised Beresford not to carry out Rogers's request on the basis that few people with 'real operational experience in the striking of dependable arms-control bargains with the USSR would regard the achievement of a comprehensive freeze … as [anything] other than an enormous and protracted under-taking far removed from a quick fix or a snappy holding operation'.[28] He ended with the comment: 'That, as I read your draft, is the key message of the relevant passage; and I do not think you should materially dilute it'.

UK strategic doubts over INF negotiations

British discomfort over the pace of bilateral arms control was evident during debates over the 'zero option' in INF negotiations. Quinlan, like much of the British defence establishment, was wary of the zero option due to concerns that it could punch a hole in the systems available to NATO in pursuit of flexible response. When he led the UK delegation in the HLG, he had agreed in principle to arms-control negotiations over long-range theatre nuclear forces for two reasons: firstly, because he believed it would ease public concerns that NATO deployment of *Pershing* II and GLCMs was fuelling a dangerous arms

race; and secondly, because he (in common with his US counterparts) did not believe the Soviets would take the bait. As it
turned out, the second assumption was wrong: not only did
the Soviets take the bait, they swam off with it, agreeing to
eliminate all cruise and ground-launched nuclear missiles with
a range of 500–5,500km and their launchers. The result was that
the UK felt exposed, fearing that an INF treaty could weaken
NATO nuclear strategy.

Quinlan's files contain a number of letters from John Killick,
sent to him during the final months of INF negotiations. Killick
(who served as British ambassador to NATO from 1975–79
and was appointed president of the British Atlantic Committee
(BAC)[29] in 1984) sent Quinlan a copy of a letter he had written
to David Mellor at the FCO, dated 22 June 1987, which set out
the reasons why he and other British defence thinkers were
concerned about the zero option:[30]

    ❝ You may note that I forbore to offer congratulations on
the job! As you plunge into the welter of complications
and acronyms that make up arms control, you may well
feel that commiserations would be more appropriate! It
is unfair of me to bother you so soon on one particular
subject, and I do so on a purely personal basis, and not
as president of [the British Atlantic Committee] BAC. It
is the so-called zero option. I expressed some serious
worries about this in correspondence with [Conservative
Party Chief Whip] Tim Renton last year … I signed off in
my letter of 8 September on the basis of what seemed like
a sound assumption – that the Soviet side would never
accept it.

    Now, as a result of the adroitness of Mr Gorbachev,
we seem to be in a right mess. I am not writing now in a
spirit of 'I told you so'. We are hoist with our own petard

and appear to have some kind of NATO-wide agreement on the basis for negotiation. It may still prove impossible to reach an acceptable agreement with Moscow, I feel sure we are not out of the woods with the Germans.

But the immediate problem for me is how to justify what is in prospect in terms of the maintenance, let alone the reinforcement, of deterrence. We are apparently removing two rungs in the ladder of escalation. Some dispute this on the grounds that there will remain other nuclear weapons systems to meet the requirement. But these are, so far as I know, either aircraft (whose doubtful penetration capability and requirement for other tasks were a major factor in considering modernisation of LRTNF ten years ago) or the *Poseidon* warheads allocated to [the NATO Supreme Allied Commander, Europe] SACEUR[31] (whose lack of visibility on the ground does nothing for European – particularly German – confidence, and which have the grave disadvantage of being, as seen from the Soviet end, part of the US strategic inventory). If there is in fact any logic in removing all INF weapons, what logic is left in defence of the retention of the remaining shorter range and battlefield weapons? They are in fact the very ones whose total removal might have made sense, in conjunction with conventional force improvements, as a means of raising the nuclear threshold.

Putting things the other way round, so far as I am concerned, and in default of convincing arguments to the contrary, an agreement on the lines now envisaged amounts to a significant lowering of the nuclear threshold, in that 'use 'em or lose 'em' will be the name of the game with what we have left. It goes without saying that I hardly expect a quick or comprehensive answer. But I do

> underline that the government – and indeed the Alliance
> – have a major problem. If people as well disposed (and
> as experienced as myself) – and I doubt if I am alone
> – can be so disturbed, there must be something wrong.
> And it is not a matter of writing me a letter telling me
> where I am mistaken, but of somebody making a clear
> and credible public statement of the merits of what is in
> prospect.
>
> At the end of the day, I of course accept that an
> agreement may be inevitable; the president (or Nancy
> [Reagan]?) seems set on it and the Alliance has painted
> itself into a corner. But that doesn't make it good
> news! **"**

Quinlan, who had been away from the MoD for so long at this point that he no longer considered himself a 'safe checking mechanism' for those seeking clarification on arms-control negotiations, nevertheless did engage with Killick on the issue. He appears to have been sympathetic to Killick's concerns, although he expressed them in his usual carefully calibrated language. This is clear from a letter he wrote to Bob Beresford, in response to an information note in which Beresford had stated that, with the exception of the United States, NATO members 'had difficulties' with the INF arms-control negotiations. In his response, dated 22 April 1987, Quinlan pointed out that the US' European partners, including the UK, were not opposed to the INF negotiations 'in principle' but that all were concerned that in practice: 'the detail does not damage the complex and interdependent structure of deterrence in the circumstances (inescapably asymmetrical) of Europe'.[32] He added that 'that is not, in principle, an unreasonable caution'.

Just as the INF negotiations were in their final stages, Quinlan was moved back from the Treasury to the MoD, to a very different world to the one he had left behind in 1981. In a letter to Quinlan dated 11 November 1987, Killick enthused that he was 'absolutely delighted' to see that Quinlan was going to 'get to the MoD after all' (during a meeting at Ditchley Park earlier that year, Quinlan had told him the prospects that he would be able to move back had looked bleak).[33] He added that it 'should have come much sooner!' and then posed a question that may well have been on Quinlan's mind too: 'I wonder how far you'll be able to get into 'policy' at MoD, without putting the nose of DUS(P) out of joint!' He explained that that was where he thought Quinlan's inclinations lay, but that he suspected that, in addition to the usual civil service protocols of not stepping on the toes of colleagues, Quinlan would probably have too much on his plate in the 'financial and programme fields' to spend much time on policy.

Maintaining strategic and non-strategic weapons 'in significant numbers'

Killick was probably right about the increasing demands on Quinlan's time, which would help explain the sudden decline in Quinlan's letters after 1987. Of course Quinlan was as interested in policy as ever when he went back to the MoD – just too busy to maintain the same extraordinary pace in his private correspondence. However, a speech that he gave to the Soviet General Staff in Moscow in November 1990 gives a fascinating insight into his thinking as the Cold War drew to an end. Despite the rapid improvement in East–West relations, Quinlan maintained his firm belief in nuclear deterrence and urged the Soviets to continue to view nuclear weapons as 'the keystone of an arch of freedom from war'. This meant rejecting disarmament as a non-starter for the foreseeable future and adopting a cautious approach to arms control. The following extracts are taken from his speech:[34]

" In both Britain and NATO circles I have worked extensively on nuclear aspects of security policy. And I now place my cards on the table. I wish to explain to you why my government holds a view which may well be uncongenial to many of you: the view that – except perhaps in a future too remote and uncertain for the prospect of it to shape policy today – the retention of nuclear weapons in smaller but still significant numbers on each side, at both strategic and non-strategic levels, will remain a prudent and positive element in the construction of a dependable international system for preserving peace among the countries of East and West.

[…] Security policy has by its very nature to be built upon caution and realism, not sentimentality and hope; and it would be foolish for us in the West to expect you, or for you to expect us, to act today as though that ideal condition of permanent trust and confidence had been completely established in the East–West context … History, and deep and long-standing differences in attitudes and systems, cannot be instantly forgotten and ignored, especially at times of great change and turbulence with much uncertainty still about the future outcome. The truth is now, and must be likely to remain so for at least decades to come, that neither you nor the West could be expected to be content with a situation in which the other had available to it low-cost or low-risk options for advancing its interests, at the expense of ours, by the use or threat of military force. Even after the changes and reductions now in prospect, you will still retain very large military forces. We understand why you do so; but you for your part must understand, against the historical background, why the smaller countries to the West of you judge it still necessary to organise a collective counterweight to those very large forces.

[…because of the advent of nuclear weapons] we are accordingly faced with a basic change that is certainly enormous, probably inevitable, and I suggest also irreversible. And if that perspective is right, it carries utterly radical consequences for our entire understanding of warfare, at least between great powers … Both East and West are now, for all human purposes, infinitely strong: and an all-out competition of strength between infinitely strong adversaries is of course logical nonsense … This is in one sense a terrible situation; but in another and very real sense it is a hopeful one. For it means there should be no rational incentive, in any circumstances at all, for anyone to start a war between nuclear powers. The practical task of strategy, in my view, is not to try to change these facts – it seems to me that they almost certainly cannot be securely and permanently changed – but to recognise them clearly and to exploit them positively, to construct the most effective possible system for what has so evidently become now not just a very desirable objective, as it would have been in the past, but an utterly essential one: the absolute prevention of war between great powers or alliances.

The fact is, surely, that we cannot abolish nuclear weapons while maintaining the option, the possibility, of major war; what we have to do is to exploit nuclear weapons so as to abolish war. That is, after all, to go to the heart of what we must want to do; what we are ultimately against is war itself, not the mere existence of particular instruments. So I do not pretend to see, nor to think that it would be realistically useful to work towards a future in which the processes of negotiated disarmament, within a system still of opposed nation-states with a historical propensity towards war, have removed nuclear weapons from the scene. We seek, instead, a structure in which the irreversible fact of nuclear weapons is the keystone of an arch of freedom from war, built – and this is after all what keystones essentially do – more dependably, more efficiently and more economically than would otherwise be possible ... We should look not to supersede the current nuclear-based system of war prevention and find some other military system, but to maintain and improve this one while the long process goes forward of building irreversibly peaceful political confidence.

... The nuclear armoury for war prevention must be of a type, and a size, that can hold at risk a wide diversity of military targets. This is not because the message can be transmitted only by attack on a large number of targets – that is neither necessary nor desirable – but because the circumstances of conflict could be so varied, and are so difficult to foresee in detail, that there needs to be a wide choice of options available. In addition, the technical military task of any military aggressor is made more difficult, and the basic aim of war prevention is therefore made more assured, if he has to recognise that every element of his military power, near or far, may be at risk to nuclear action if he persists. It is this concept – the concept of a wide range of different options –that is now and has been since the late 1960s, the essence of NATO's defensive strategic concept. It is not a strategy of predetermined first nuclear use, nor of attempting somehow to fight or neutralise the opposing nuclear armoury, nor of massive nuclear use, nor of a rigidly fixed sequence of actions in progressive escalation. On the contrary, it is precisely a strategy to provide political leaders with military choices of diverse kinds so that they can respond on a carefully limited scale yet in a way relevant to whatever the particular circumstances may be, not using more force than is needed for the purpose of ending the conflict. But if we are to have flexible choice, we must have a flexible armoury; not just a massive long-range strategic armoury, but one capable of swift reaction, of accuracy and of measured, controlled choice. **"**

Quinlan's belief in the need to maintain strategic and non-strategic weapons in significant numbers helps explain why the UK approach to arms control and disarmament remained extremely cautious, even as the Cold War was coming to an end, and why he took on what might seem an unusual task of explaining that caution to the Soviet General Staff. It also sheds some light on a batch of letters in Quinlan's files on the issue of nuclear testing, which were written at around the same time he gave his speech in Moscow. The letters all stem from an FCO memo on a Partial Test Ban Treaty (PTBT)[35] Amendment Conference (PTBTAC), which was due to be held in New York in January 1991, the aim of which was to convert the PTBT into a CTBT. The memo, which is dated 23 November 1990, confirms that UK doubts over whether a CTBT could be effectively verified (the official reason both the UK and US gave for their opposition to a CTBT at the time) were a secondary concern; the UK and US primary objection to a treaty was that it would prevent them from testing new nuclear warheads, and thus undermine deterrence credibility. The memo also provides some useful background material concerning the CTBT debate:[36]

" *Problem*

The PTBTAC takes place in New York next January to consider amendments to convert the PTBT into a

Comprehensive Test Ban Treaty by banning under-ground nuclear testing. Given our requirement for continued testing, and the inevitable unpopularity of our position, we should be grateful to have Ministerial endorsement of our approach to the Conference.

Recommendation

Our substantive position is set out in the attached speaking notes for use in Mr. Hogg's meeting with a delegation from 'Parliamentarians for Global Action'[37]... There are also important procedural issues concerning the PTBTAC to be considered now. I recommend: that we co-ordinate closely with the US on the detailed presentation of our case; that representation should be at official level; that we oppose moves to develop a mechanism to keep returning to the CTBT question, i.e. through annual conferences; that the Secretary of State minute to alert MISC 7 (on 11 December) to the conference.

MoD agree.

Background

Our main justification for testing is the need to ensure our weapons remain up-to-date and so provide the deterrence to which we and NATO are committed. MoD see no substitute for regular testing (in practice about every 14 months): testing is an integral element of the of the US/UK nuclear relationship, covered by the 1958 Agreement. Our tests are related to development of new weapons, not checking the existing stockpile, hence our cessation of tests in the late [19]60s/early [19]70s in the interim between *Polaris* and *Chevaline*. Development of the TASM warhead will mean continued testing for several years. Since 1962, all our tests have been conducted at the Nevada Test Site, most recently on 14 November.

We also argue that a CTBT would not stop development of new weapons delivery systems, and is irrelevant to practical arms-control measures such as the INF and START Treaties and the beginnings of SNF negotiations. The verification of a CTBT remains highly problematic (see below).

We have therefore discouraged as far as possible the conference from taking place at all. But the amendments are supported by a large number of Third World countries and we have had no alternative to fulfilling our responsibilities as a Depositary Power and convening the PTBTAC. As the amendments proposed for the Conference can be vetoed by any of the three Depositary Powers (UK, US and Soviet Union) our legal right to continue testing is not at stake.

UK Objectives

However, our position at the Conference is likely to be uncomfortable. The worst case is that we shall be in a minority of two with the US in opposing the amendments, and forced to use our veto. Even if we are not pushed to this extent, we anticipate considerable Parliamentary and press interest. But we see no scope for compromise.

Since we wish to continue testing, our primary objective is to emerge from the Conference with our right to do so firmly protected. Our veto, and that of the Americans, will ensure this. Our secondary objective should be to limit the damage caused by our isolation, principally by disputing and therefore weakening the political and intellectual linkage which some try to establish between a CTBT and the future of the Non-Proliferation Treaty (NPT). This will be less easy. Our third objective should be to prevent the establishment of a mechanism to continue to pursue a CTBT beyond the Conference in January. This may be impossible, in which case we and the Americans need to reconsider whether or not to participate in any lengthy follow-on. One option is to suggest referring the question back to the existing forum of the Conference on Disarmament which discusses the issue without a negotiating mandate.

NPT Linkage

A major risk is that some delegations may use the Depositary Powers' commitments to the NPT as a lever to try to force the passage of the CTB amendments. The NPT Review Conference in September failed to agree a Final Document as a result of Mexico's attempt to establish a too explicit linkage between the CTBT and the NPT. In the end, Mexico's Third World supporters would not stake the future of the NPT on the CTB issue and Mexico's intemperate stand has lost it some support. Nonetheless, reaffirmation of the NPT at the 1995 Review Conference may be connected to how far the nuclear powers have fulfilled their disarmament obligation under Article VI of that Treaty. Our stance on testing may have a bearing on this.

We reject any connection between the NPT and a CTBT despite previous British Governments' statements agreeing a linkage (at the NPT Conference last September, Mexico quoted from UK speeches delivered in 1967 in support of a CTBT as evidence of our alleged breach of faith). Our past support for a CTBT was largely a result of political circumstances: in the early 1960s our support for a CTB was a result of our having successfully tested a thermonuclear device, so establishing a technological parity with the US and Soviet Union. A test ban would have frozen such equality. Our support in the late 1960s and late 1970s reflected the policies of the Governments of the day.

Positions of Other Depositary Powers
Our tactics at the Conference will be influenced principally by the US with whom we will consult closely throughout.

US position: Washington have been strongly negative throughout about the PTBTAC. They share our views on the damage a CTBT would do to deterrence. The US has however accepted that further steps toward a CTB cannot be postponed indefinitely. The US has hinted that there may be a possibility of reducing the Threshold limit of nuclear tests under the 1974 Threshold Test Ban Treaty (which set a maximum test ceiling of 150kt). A lower threshold under the TTBT might head off criticism at the PTBTAC, but the Americans have also said they want to wait to see how the verification pressures of the TTBT work. More likely therefore is that the Americans will take a robust stance at the Conference, offering no compromise.

Soviet Position: The Soviet Union is publicly committed to a CTBT and are likely to line up with the Mexicans et al in January. They have, however, just broken their unilateral year-long moratorium with a test in Novaya Zemlya in the Arctic. At the Conference, the Russians may argue that the only way of allaying the public concern in the USSR and Nordic countries is to establish a CTBT.

Other positions are:
France/China: Not a party to the PTBT (or the NPT).
NATO: The Allies support US/UK arguments despite some strong reservations. They generally abstain when testing comes to a vote.

Verification
The difficulties of verifying a CTB and the dangers of a treaty which cannot be verified with total confidence to prevent cheating have been an important secondary UK objection to a treaty (until 1988 they were our primary objection). It remains the view of the government's seismic detection experts at [the UK Atomic Weapons Establishment laboratory, Blacknest] originally stated in their paper presented to the [Conference on Disarmament] at Geneva in 1985, that effective verification by seismic means is impossible, given the difficulty of identifying low-yield tests.

Despite Blacknest's continued confidence, our position is disputed by governments and NGOs. At the PTBT Preliminary Conference last June, the Soviet and Swedish delegations argued that satellite and radiation monitoring, allied to existing seismic capability, render verification possible. Moreover the official US group, Defence Advanced Research Project Agency, has succeeded in establishing a series of seismic monitoring stations in the Soviet Union. Nonetheless the US government [is] likely to support us in disagreeing with this view.

If our position on verification comes under severe pressure we may have to acknowledge the uncertainty surrounding the subject and refer the question back to the Ad Hoc Group of Scientific Experts at the Conference on Disarmament, going beyond purely seismic techniques. This would relieve the immediate pressure at the Conference but might lead to our arguments being refuted. Furthermore it might result in a continuing mechanism for exploring the merits of a CTB, beyond the control of the Depositary Powers. **"**

Quinlan became involved in trying to limit the fallout from the conference after the FCO's worst-case scenario did in fact transpire: only the UK and US voted against amending the PTBT. Crucially (and embarrassingly for the US and UK governments) key allies voted in favour of the amendment, including NATO partners Denmark, Greece, Iceland and Norway, as well as non-NATO allies Australia, New Zealand and Sweden. This outcome gave a boost to disarmament advocates in the UK, including the technical experts among them, who poured cold water on the government's claims that a CTBT could not be verified. Quinlan was subsequently contacted by John Hunt, who had recently joined the Committee for International Peace and Justice (at the invitation of Bob Beresford), and discovered that the bishops were preparing to send a letter in support of a CTBT to Foreign Secretary Douglas Hurd.[38] According to Hunt, the bishops' initiative had been triggered by Brian Wicker, who had circulated a paper by verification expert Patricia Lewis to committee members. The paper, which was strongly supportive of a CTBT, accused the UK and US governments of unnecessarily prolonging the arms race through their opposition to PTBT amendment, despite the fact that the Cold War was over. Hunt asked Quinlan's advice on how to handle the situation. The following extracts are taken from Quinlan's reply to Hunt, dated 1 August 1991:

" In my view, the path is, in overwhelming probability, to be found in tackling the political causes of war rather than trying to seal off particular instruments for its conduct.

As [the military historian and co-founder of IISS] Michael Howard approvingly noted in a piece some time ago of which I am fairly sure Bob Beresford has a copy, the continuance of nuclear testing has helped us move to more accurate and less destructive weapons. I would add, also, to better safety design; and, indirectly, to lower numbers (because smaller warheads lead to missile systems more assured of penetrating defences and/or with longer range and so better target coverage). If one is going to have a nuclear armoury at all, these are not trivial considerations.

There is no ground for supposing that the proliferation danger, whether large or small, turns on the CTBT question, though various non-nuclear nations have found it a handy occasional instrument for twisting the nuclear ones' tails politically. A CTBT – even if the ungodly observed it, a large 'if' – would not close off the options of a crude third-world proliferator like Saddam (who is incidentally a signatory of the NPT). Can [Brian] Wicker [the Catholic philosopher and disarmament campaigner], [or] [Patricia] Lewis [the director of the Verification Research and Training Centre (VERTIC) in London] suggest any specific country in respect of which it can plausibly be claimed, in the past quarter of a century or the near future, that the absence of a CTBT has led to the acquisition of nuclear weapons capability? The world's general anti-proliferation strategy rests on a varied mix of policies and pressures; the case that a CTBT would in practice play a decisive part in the mix is hard to see.

… All this is no doubt debatable. But in my view the bishops ought to husband the exertion of their influence in politically-controversial matters for situations where the right course is clear and of major importance. This is far from such a case; and I fear, frankly, that for them (or for a group who will be supposed, given Bishop Kelly's signature, to carry something of their authority) to sign up to the 'Wicker' line here would tend actually to weaken their influence, since it would be widely seen as reflecting (if you will forgive the shorthand) a shallow acceptance of the routine views of the bien-pensant Left.[39] 〞

Proliferation challenges and crisis stability

Although Quinlan was highly sceptical about multilateral arms control and keen to keep the 'bien-pensant Left' in check, his letters from the period show that he believed the Cold War security apparatus was far from ideal. In the early 1980s, partly through his involvement in the Pembroke Group, he began thinking through how the global security system could be improved, and in particular, how nuclear deterrence and bilateral arms control could be refined to strengthen crisis stability during a period of rapid change in US–Soviet relations. He engaged regularly on this subject with Hugh Beach, Leonard Cheshire and John Howe: members of the defence establishment who were also deeply concerned about the subject of international stability and who at the time shared Quinlan's belief in deterrence. There were important differences in their perspectives, however: Beach, Cheshire and Howe were more troubled than Quinlan by the prospect of nuclear-weapons proliferation. They identified proliferation threats beyond the East–West context, the inequalities at the heart of the nuclear non-proliferation regime, and the problem of building security on a system of nuclear threats, as problems in the strategic framework and as flaws in Quinlan's otherwise persuasive arguments.

An exchange of letters between Quinlan and Cheshire provides some insight into Quinlan's relatively optimistic views on nuclear proliferation in the early 1980s. Cheshire had asked him to comment on a study he was undertaking on the future of nuclear deterrence, in which he planned to explore some of the negative proliferation consequences of reliance on nuclear armouries, and propose an alternative nuclear future in which the UN played a more central role in nuclear governance.[40] Quinlan responded to Cheshire's ideas in a letter dated 5 January 1983:[41]

❝ As you know, I would be reluctant to appear to accept proliferation as inevitable or matter-of-course. I do not of course regard it as entailing automatic catastrophe; nor do I harbour starry-eyed notions that it can be avoided for the rest of human history. I would however want to lead into it by acknowledging that it will make the world less safe; that policy ought therefore to do all that is possible to prevent, confine or delay it; and that policy to that end has not done badly so far, and can continue to play a useful role.

I much welcome the general theme that in the long run we must try and establish some kind of international regime, through the UN or otherwise, to limit the risks. I think nevertheless one must recognise that we are as yet a long way from the point where the UN could perform credibly, reliably and promptly in matters as difficult and critical as these – vetoes, lobbying, favour currying and mistrust are still deeply ingrained. By comparison the Falklands was easy; yet the UN achieved little there.

I suggest that you should acknowledge that most (if not all – I am not quite sure) of the nuclear powers have already given, at the 1978 UN Special Session on

Disarmament, security assurances about the use of nuclear weapons. The precise form and wording varied; but the general thrust was a promise never to use nuclear weapons against a non-nuclear state, unless it was operating in a nuclear alliance. **"**

Cheshire responded in a letter dated 25 January 1983:[42]

" Regarding the probability of proliferation, I presume that the only point of difference between us is that of time scale. I myself tend to take a rather pessimistic view on this, working from the premise that as soon as any one country acquires a capability, or is presumed to have acquired it, others will feel bound to hurry up their own arrangements. David Owen, for instance, from whom I have also received some comments, takes an almost less optimistic view, and is very specific in the reasons he gives for it. However I clearly should have placed more emphasis on the role that non-proliferation and other measures are playing in slowing the process down.

Clearly the UN is a very long way from being able to act in the [manner] I was suggesting. Nonetheless I don't see the Falklands analogy as applying to this problem in the same way as you. With the Falklands we have a dispute between member states, but with nuclear use against a non-nuclear state an act of aggression against the entire international community. Whereas the UN will always be at a disadvantage in the former, I would have thought it might well react completely differently with respect to the latter. The *Sunday Telegraph* have invited me to do an article for their Opinion series, and I enclose what I have just written.[43] Would you be good enough to give me a comment, however brief or hurried?

> I think my mistake in the draft memo I sent you was in trying to present a 'packaged' solution. What I do think is that it would help the debate all round to start focusing some of the attention away from the European scene to the approaching problem of proliferation. **"**

While Quinlan did not share Cheshire's faith in the UN's ability to govern international relations or his proliferation pessimism, he did begin thinking ahead about how greater international cooperation could be promoted in the context of changing East–West relations, as his letter to Hugh Beach of 12 September 1984 reveals:[44]

> **"** You will, I know, be wearily familiar with most of my opinions in this area. Briefly, however, I start from the conviction that nuclear weapons have brought about the reductio ad absurdum of warfare between major developed powers; that this is a very stable condition, unless we are all quite remarkably stupid; and that so long as mankind remains sinful and its political systems diversely imperfect, it is crying for the moon to suppose that we can devise any world security system in which nuclear weapons are unimportant.
>
> Against that background, I am interested in trying to think ahead not just in terms of a decade or so but fifty or a hundred years, to consider what, within a realistic range of assumptions, might be the best attainable characteristics of a long-term global security system – still catering for and indeed in a sense reliant on nuclear weapons, still having to manage a world with at least two antagonistic political systems, but (as I would seek) costing a lot less than now; more consciously built for crisis stability; posing perhaps rather less agonising

moral dilemmas for participants; less apt to generate political frictions (domestic and external) in the process of its maintenance; more takable-for-granted and more boring, so that we can all devote more resources and more attention to other things like the more real and agonising issues we shorthand as North–South.

Some of the matters which seem to me to arise are whether we fuss too much about formal arms control – or, if not, whether we can really do no better than the current tired arms-control agenda, which is still substantially that resulting from an intellectual effort of twenty or thirty years ago; whether (ad hominem, I admit) a major souping-up of conventional defences is really the right avenue to be looking down; whether there are useful things we could usefully be doing in the East/West political field to improve relationships – purely for example, if we cannot dissolve things about which East and West are currently sure to disagree, could we divert a bit more joint attention to useful things, in the Third World or elsewhere, about which they aren't bound to do so? **"**

Similar questions were preoccupying the military historian, Michael Howard, with whom Quinlan also corresponded. The two did not see eye-to-eye on everything, but they were both sceptical over the benefits of what Quinlan referred to as the 'tired' arms-control agenda, and both believed a stronger system of crisis stability was needed. Quinlan had been intrigued by a speech Howard had given on the subject at the Council for Arms Control in May 1986 (entitled 'Is Arms Control Really Necessary?') and sent it to John Howe for comment (Howe was an arms-control enthusiast, who at the time was private secretary to Defence Secretary George Younger). Howe replied to

Quinlan with the following analysis of Howard's arms-control scepticism:[45]

> **"** I agree that the pressure for arms control is fuelled by illusions – and one could no doubt add others to [Howard's] list … for example, the idea that arms-control talks are some kind of easy fix for East–West tension. It is also true that because we allow ourselves to entertain illusions about arms control, we are sometimes led into false positions, such as our hanging our objection to a CTBT solely on the verification peg when in reality it has the much more solid basis that Michael Howard correctly describes. Our line on nuclear testing is not, I believe ultimately consistent with our reliance, in anything other than an ideal world, on nuclear weapons for our security. The zero option for INF is another example, many would argue.
>
> Nevertheless, I find Michael Howard's approach too sceptical. Arms control may pander to our illusions but it also has a more solid contribution to make. Michael Howard describes security as a state of mind. Surely it is more than this; it is a condition in which we not only *feel* safe but *are* safe. Arms control has a contribution to make to the being as well as to the feeling.
>
> I have some doubts, in this connection, about how far the well-known Howard concept of 'reassurance' takes us. Sometimes, it seems to me, he writes as though reassurance is a feeling the public must be encouraged to have if they are to support nuclear weapons policies; sometimes he uses it in the sense of the state of mind of one power in relation to another power's intentions. Sometimes he seems to regard it as a condition of security and arms-control policies; sometimes as a consequence.

I think it is a bit too simple to label arms control as being about reassurance in any of these senses in contrast to defence policy which is about deterrence. The concept of stability is a more traditional and in some ways a rather more fruitful one. There are surely very respectable and non-illusory reasons for arms control, in terms of arms race stability (by which I do not mean a Luddite antipathy to technological development), and crisis stability. Clearly stability of both these kinds has to do with the frame of mind of potential antagonists, but it is not (or ought not to be) a frame of mind based on an illusion; it is based on the way in which the balance of forces is perceived.

There are, of course, plenty of people around who say that the quest for stability, through arms control, is doomed to failure. Certainly arms control is not a means of duping the other side into changes in its force structure which go against its interests. But I do not think it follows from this that arms control has no influence on force structure and therefore on stability. You can argue that arms control has simply codified the way in which the superpowers have wanted to behave anyway. I think this is too cynical. I believe that the ABM Treaty and even SALT have affected the development of the superpowers' armouries. It is inconceivable to me that they would have behaved as they have done if each had not considered, until quite recently, that competition in defensive systems was effectively ruled out. **🙶**

Quinlan's view of the role of arms control fell somewhere between that of Howard and that of Howe. Although he was critical of the Reagan administration's approach to arms control and disarmament, which he regarded as unrealistic and potentially destabilising, he did nevertheless believe arms control could and should, if pursued sensibly, play two crucial roles in a future global security system. Firstly, on a psychological level, he felt it should provide reassurance to domestic and international constituencies that arms racing dynamics are being held in check. Secondly, on a practical level, it should contribute to controlling and minimising defence costs (although not at the expense of deterrence credibility). He set out his ideas on how nuclear deterrence and arms control should be mutually reinforcing in a note to Beach dated 13 November 1985. The note summarises the arguments that later underpinned Quinlan's essay on 'Just Deterrence' and which formed the bedrock of his thinking on the role of arms control when he returned to the MoD as PUS:[46]

> **" There are no adequate grounds, either general or particular, for regarding the idea that the long historical rise in the destructiveness of war can be dependably reversed as probable enough to be a basis for practical policy. The sensible course is not to strive (utterly against the odds) to undo that destructiveness, but to harness its reality – to sustain in place the most efficient system we can devise for the continued prevention of war.
>
> In that perspective, we need mutual deterrence – that is, a war prevention system – which should be: a) as stable as possible. The present system is highly stable but not incapable of improvement – especially in terms of evident reassurance to ordinary publics, not just to experts; b) as inexpensive as possible. The present system is very costly, and stability could certainly be sustained far less expensively; c) as 'non-frictional' as possible – that is, with minimum avoidable political trouble, suspicion and confrontation. Here too there is

plainly room for improvement. Given the basic logic of the system, the first two of these objectives (the third may be debatable) are clearly ones which both sides should share, as a matter not of goodwill or sentiment but of hard-headed self-interest across the ideological divide. East and West may have widely different notions of what they entail in specific terms, but disagreement is not an inherent necessity.

Arms control and disarmament can contribute greatly (though it need not and perhaps cannot be the sole contributor) to all three objectives. The West's policy for it should be consistently developed – and presented both to Western peoples and to Eastern interlocutors – in that framework. (In principle, moreover, the framework should be applied to the whole spectrum of military capability, not just the nuclear element. Britain may indeed have a specific interest in some broadening; it is arguably a curiosity of present arms-control activity that none of it, save MBFR, offers much likelihood of easing Britain's national defence costs.)**"**

The same note went on to criticise what Quinlan regarded as the serious flaws in the Reagan administration's arms-control agenda and how Reagan's vision of the future differed from his own. In a nutshell, whereas Quinlan believed arms control should be used to reinforce nuclear deterrence by making it more stable and cost-effective, Reagan believed in using arms control to pursue technological superiority, strategic dominance and – ultimately – nuclear disarmament. Although Quinlan does not make it explicit in his note to Beach, much of his criticism of the Reagan administration's arms control and disarmament agenda stemmed from the damage it could inflict on UK and NATO interests in Europe, from the impact it could have on the future of *Trident* (given UK dependence on procurement from the US), and from the reality that in a competition for post-nuclear conventional superiority, the UK would be left trailing far behind (thus losing the strategic and political advantages of nuclear-weapon state status):[47]

> **❝** President Reagan's vision [of the future] is evidently very different [to mine]. On the evidence of his attachment to an ambitious form of SDl, and of his references to getting rid of all nuclear weapons (two rather different ideas, incidentally) his concept is to reverse rather than to harness the intolerable destructiveness of war. It is hard to regard the chances of realising such a vision as other than very low, at least within any timescale that can reasonably influence policy now. (No-one can say that invulnerability will be impossible in 2500 AD; but we cannot frame practical policy in such perspectives.)
>
> The trouble with the Reagan vision – if taken at full face value and pursued with sustained resolution – is not just that it is probably unreal. The greater mischief is that the very attempt at it, if taken very far, may well run counter to all the three realistic objectives [set out in the first half of my letter], and so damage what is attainable in the quest for what is not. All this will moreover be widely perceived by Western publics, especially but not only in Europe. In short, the president's rhetoric is pointing up a blind alley, and the penalties of his actually going far into it could be very high.
>
> This does not mean that substantial research into strategic defence systems is unjustified; on the contrary, such research is prudent both as a hedge and for negotiating leverage. Nor will it be productive to assail directly

the general Reagan vision. But it will surely be important that we should, over time, keep to the fore in a measured, sustained and public way the positive themes of policy … which flow from our own vision of the future; and that we should work across a wide front in contributing to the practical development of those themes. **"**

Quinlan developed these ideas further in his essay on 'Just Deterrence', explaining in more detail the dangers of the Reagan approach and the advantages of a Quinlanesque nuclear future, which would be flexible enough to adapt to the changing strategic environment (and crucially, continue to serve British interests). He sent his essay to Howe at the MoD, who shared his opinion of the Reagan agenda and his assessment of its negative implications for Europe and specifically for Britain. But while Quinlan believed his own vision of the future – in which great-power nuclear deterrence was maintained and controlled through a system of mutual confidence-building – offered the best chance of war prevention and stability, Howe identified some serious weaknesses in his strategic framework. Howe's response to Quinlan reveals that these flaws were the same ones Beach, Cheshire and others had long regarded as wide cracks running through the foundations of Cold War debates over deterrence strategy and ethics. Among others, these included: the problem that nuclear proliferation outside the narrow East–West context was not convincingly addressed (Quinlan tended to side-step or leave this issue to the troubled NPT framework to resolve); and the problem that nuclear deterrence is based on extreme threats, which many argue are an absurd basis for building a security framework that would be dependent on forging goodwill, mutual confidence and reassurance. Howe explained his concerns in a letter dated 20 March 1987:[48]

" You are considering the characteristics which morality requires of a security system based on nuclear deterrence; and you define, at one point, deterrence as 'the absolute prevention of war among the great powers'. This definition – and other passages in the essay – prompt[s] the question: how far is this analysis peculiar to, and how far applicable beyond, the East/West security relationship? This question leads on to others, about the morality and about the practical consequences of nuclear proliferation, which, if you were to address in full, would undoubtedly distort the scope of your essay; but I think you do need to say a word about them, if only to acknowledge that the model you describe at the end of a way in which the security relationship between the 'great powers' might, considered as a closed system, develop, might not be the whole story, either practically or morally.

There are a number of threads here. One is: under what circumstances is the possession of nuclear weapons morally legitimate? Is it legitimate only for those states who already possess them – the weapons cannot after all be disinvented? I feel slightly uncomfortable with this simple circularity. Orthodox wisdom would lay down at least two other conditions as well: the strategic framework of which the weapons form part must be a stable one and the parties to it must be rational. But the first of these is again circular – stability is an objective of security policy, not a starting point – and the second would not (in their own view at least) catch the Israelis and maybe no other aspirant nuclear weapons power. These will all be familiar questions to you. They worry me however because I feel intuitively that proliferation is dangerous and immoral and yet I cannot find a fully satisfactory moral basis for drawing the line between the haves and the have nots.

A second thread is a more directly practical one: how should the possession of nuclear weapons by states outside the calm and rational framework postulated at the end of the essay affect the policies of the 'great powers'? I presume the answer is: as regards force structures, not much, at least not until there have been very substantial cuts in the excessive nuclear inventories of the superpowers. But again I think the question is worth a nod, because in the long run the really dangerous strategic instabilities will not be bipolar, between the US and the USSR.

I confess to a doubt about how far one can push the attractive thesis you develop at the end of your essay. I wonder whether the state of complete stability you describe can be based on deterrence alone? It is partly perhaps a conceptual blockage on my part: doubt about how far deterrence (meaning roughly frightening off) is compatible with reassurance. But it does seem to me that the model you develop would have to rest not only on deterrence but also an element of goodwill on both sides, a goodwill that is prior to and not derived from a common perception of the security predicament. I am not convinced that the ideal condition you postulate, in which the security relationship is relegated to the sub-political level and adjusted as necessary by technicians, would be sufficient to maintain deterrence in the world as we find it. I believe that in that world the search for strategic stability is only one of the objectives of the superpowers, whose relationship is characterised otherwise by rivalry and competition in the pursuit of divergent ideals and objectives and by a willingness to use trickery in the pursuit of those objectives and that competition.

This picture may be a caricature, but for the sake of my thesis it has to be true only partially and only of one of the parties. My point is that your model will only work if both of the superpowers are motivated only by a quest for strategic stability. I doubt whether that is the case. You might argue that if they were completely rational, then recognition of the horrors of nuclear war would make strategic stability an overwhelming imperative irrespective of the divergent political aims of the two systems and that the rest of your model would follow. But again I wonder. If the avoidance of nuclear war is such an overriding imperative, then does not the threat of nuclear retaliation lose its potency? The Russians (say) might calculate that they could safely achieve limited political or even military objectives by conventional means, the threat of conventional means, or the threat of nuclear means, if they were confident that the US aversion to risk was sufficiently strong. This is the sense in which I feel that our concepts of deterrence and of stability can pull in opposite directions – the stronger the perception of stability, the less potent the deterrence. One or other of the superpowers might feel that it was worth taking a small risk in terms of stability for the sake of some other divergent objective. The more the management of international security becomes a matter of routine, and the more the shared objective of stability is, as it were, taken for granted, the greater the danger that one side might seek to take advantage of the other side's inertia and risk-avoidance.

The foregoing relates to crisis stability. I am not confident that arms race stability can be achieved, either, without some degree of political entente that goes beyond the harsh logic of deterrence. Americans of the

Perle school see the US/Soviet relationship as a competitive one, and moreover of a zero-sum character; what the Russians lose the US win. The SDI (for all that the vision of a complete defence of populations, in which Perle certainly does not believe, is flawed) will confer a tremendous competitive advantage on the US by playing to its strong technological suit. In a world in which the Soviets are not to be trusted an inch the US must rely on its strength. It is not easy to assail this distorted view by an appeal to logic alone; it is based upon a certain ideology and a certain image of the way the Russians behave. Perle would, I believe, regard the quest for stability by the fine-tuning of force structures as self-defeating; safety lies in military superiority. **"**

Nuclear disarmament

Whereas Quinlan was cautious about arms control and non-proliferation initiatives throughout the 1980s, he was strongly opposed to disarmament. His approach to the former involved complex assessments and calculations about the needs of NATO's doctrine of flexible response and the credibility of the UK independent deterrent; he was supportive of proposals that would not undermine either, and wary of proposals that could, unless handled carefully, gain momentum that could potentially weaken UK and Western European defence. But nuclear disarmament was a different story altogether: not only did he oppose unilateralism as dangerous and irrational under any conceivable circumstances, he also considered multilateral disarmament to be an unrealistic pipedream that could destroy strategic stability and trigger a new period of major warfare between the great powers. As far as he was concerned for most of his career, nuclear weapons could not be disinvented and thus it was the responsibility of defence officials to ensure that they were retained to serve in war-prevention and war-termination roles. It was only at the end of his life that he began to question these beliefs and to argue that a policy of indefinite retention was unsustainable. This final section of the book explores how and why this transformation occurred.

The collapse of bipartisan nuclear consensus: a brief history

From 1964 onwards, the Labour Party became deeply divided over the issue of the UK independent nuclear deterrent and its replacement, which many in the party opposed. These tensions came to a head in 1982, when the left wing of the Labour party succeeded in getting an overwhelming vote in favour of unilateral nuclear disarmament at the party's annual conference: 72% of the conference delegates voted for a policy of abolishing Britain's nuclear deterrent, for repudiating British commitments to station cruise missiles in Britain as well as other nuclear-weapons systems with American crews, and for drastically reducing British defence spending. After the vote, Labour leader Michael Foot declared his strong support for the CND and stated that 'the greatest task that this movement will ever have to undertake is to carry out our policy for securing nuclear disarmament in this country and throughout the world'.[49]

The Labour opposition's U-turn on nuclear policy reflected growing scepticism among British intellectual elites (mostly from academia and the church) about the wisdom of nuclear deterrence. A series of events in the 1970s and early 1980s had given their arguments some traction among the general public and in the British media. Crucially, NATO's December 1979 decision to deploy *Pershing* IIs and GLCMs in Europe, and the January 1980 decision by the Thatcher government to procure *Trident*, had coincided with a period of international instability: the Soviet invasion of Afghanistan, the Islamic Revolution in Iran and a general ratcheting up of Cold War tensions.

Added to this, a series of widely publicised American strategic alerts had led to questions over the potential for accidental nuclear war. In February 1980, the BBC documentary television series, *Panorama*, broadcast a programme exploring the state of Britain's civil-defence planning, which triggered widespread fear about the aftermath of a nuclear exchange. These fears were heightened further by the anti-Soviet rhetoric of the newly elected US President, Ronald Reagan, in 1981, and by the release of deeply disturbing films such as *The Day After* (1983), *Threads* (a 1984 television docudrama), and the film version of British cartoonist Raymond Briggs' book, *When the Wind Blows* (1986) – all stories featuring ordinary people caught up in apocalyptic nuclear wars.[50]

Public fear of nuclear attack led to a resurgence of the CND: official membership of the organisation jumped from 3,000 to 15,000 in 1981–2, and to 50,000 by 1983. In October 1981 and June 1982, an estimated 250,000 people marched through London in support of unilateral nuclear disarmament – at the time, the largest mass demonstrations ever to have taken place in the UK. Emotions were running so high that in 1982, the Ministry of Defence was forced to cancel a planned civil-defence exercise due to a decision by numerous Labour councils to declare their areas 'nuclear-free zones' and to refuse to cooperate with central government.

The actions of the Labour councils were evidence of growing dissent, which generated concerns about the potential for escalating social unrest. On one side, growing numbers of the British public doubted the ability of 'the establishment' to prevent a full-scale nuclear war, and some (in common with peace campaigners in Germany) were convinced that it was NATO defence planners, just as much as those of the Warsaw Pact, who were putting their lives at risk.[51] On the other side, members of the establishment were worried about the radicalisation of the nuclear debate, and were concerned that influential members of the anti-nuclear elite were falling victim to a clever Soviet propaganda campaign, the goal of which was to weaken NATO.[52] As the next general election approached, a February 1983 poll revealed that defence policy had topped public services as a dominant election concern – a dramatic change from all similar polls conducted since the Second World War, which had indicated that defence was rarely a major election issue. The Thatcher government's response to these public concerns was to expose the weaknesses in the arguments being made by the unilateralists – a strategy that Quinlan played a key role in, both in his private capacity and via numerous semi-official activities in which his pro-deterrence arguments were put to official use on a non-attributed basis.[53]

Quinlan and the dormant seeds of disarmament

Quinlan believed many disarmament advocates were well-meaning but poorly informed about the implications of nuclear disarmament; they were only willing to accept what he considered to be the exaggerated risks posed by nuclear weapons rather than the full picture of their costs and benefits, while at the same time unwilling to grasp the dangers of unilateral disarmament. It was a skewed picture, dominated by 'woolly thinking' and naivety. Quinlan was committed to correcting these arguments, and much of his correspondence was devoted to this goal.

Extracts from a letter from Quinlan to Bob Beresford dated 20 May 1981, which he wrote in response to a pro-disarmament report by Roger Ruston, give an early insight into Quinlan's effort to inject some logic and balance into the disarmament discourse of the early 1980s:[54]

> **❝** I confess that I should regard the report as more balanced if it reflected a fuller acceptance that the subject is beset

with difficulties on every side – the sort of recognition to be found for example in a recent article by Sydney Bailey (who will be well known to you as a Quaker – thus a pacifist – who has brought a penetrating mind to bear on these issues for many years) – 'today there is no policy about the threat or use of nuclear weapons which does not pose appalling moral and practical dilemmas' – and the context makes quite clear that this includes, in his view, policies of renunciation. To be candid, the report seems to me to be a little short of intellectual humility, and of charity for those who think differently. Some recognition of genuine difficulty and dilemma might conceivably find a place in the Introduction, which in its present form seems to me often tendentiously or polemically written.

[...] I noted that the report is still very light on the likely practical consequences on unilateral renunciation of nuclear weapons. The Postscript seems to me perfunctory – even evasive – about this. To deal with the issue just by making unspecific references to conducting the renunciation 'as safely as possible' seems to me redolent of the owl's advice to the mouse that was having trouble with the cat. What happens if we can find no way (and the literature scarcely abounds with promising suggestions) that does not look, to reasonable judgement, extremely dangerous? Father Ruston's position requires him to say, I take it, that we must nevertheless do what is right and accept the practical consequences even if they are, or seem likely to be, very grave. If this is so, it would surely be fair to say so very clearly. I accept of course that his own judgement may be that the consequences would not be grave, but that is an opinion which many do not share, and in which he has no special expertise; he may be right, but he must surely cater for the possibility that he is not.

This brings me indirectly, to a further comment. The report takes little account of the general Western judgement that atheistic communism, against which our security arrangements primarily seek to protect us, is an enormous evil, in terms of lost life as well as lost liberty, as is shown by its fruits from Lenin through to Stalin and Mao to Pol Pot ... Father Ruston is of course fully entitled to take a different view of Communism's reality but that is a matter of practical judgement, not ethical principle; and, again, it seems to me that a balanced report would recognise the problems which what is argued would pose for people who honestly form a different practical judgement. Another aspect of much the same thing is a recurrent tendency – or at least this is the impression left with me – to give the Russians the benefit of the doubt more readily than NATO, including particularly the US. This is an attribute which many people are perfectly free to adopt, if they so judge; I wonder however whether it is really the impression wanted here. **"**

Quinlan's concern about the imbalance in the disarmament discourse was shared by all members of the Pembroke Group, and indeed one of their goals was to devise strategies to address this situation: their aim was to come up with compelling pro-deterrence arguments that would help inform the public debate and to highlight the flaws in misguided disarmament advocacy. The correspondence between Quinlan and Cheshire returned to this subject again and again, as the two men shared their concerns over what they regarded as a blinkered utopianism among disarmers, and their failure to fully comprehend the revolutionary, war-preventing role that nuclear weapons served. This topic concerned Cheshire so much that he decided to write a paper on the subject, drafts of which he sent to Quinlan for advice on how to make his arguments as logically watertight and persuasive as possible. Quinlan was more than happy to help. Though sometimes thorough to the point of appearing pedantic in his critiques of others' work, he suggested only a handful of very minor changes to the following section of Cheshire's paper, showing how closely their views aligned on the dangers of unilateral nuclear disarmament:[55]

> **"** Unilateralism, like pacifism is a general term which covers a wide variety of individual views from the absolute stance which demands renunciation of all nuclear weapons by the entire Western Alliance unconditionally and irrespective of the consequences, to that which advocates merely a phased British renunciation while remaining under the American umbrella. Most unilateralists uphold the right of self defence even against a nuclear attacker, but there is an inherent contradiction in this proposition for the following reasons:
>
> (1) Nuclear disarmament would not put an end to nuclear weapons, even if both East and West were to destroy their entire stocks and were to stop using nuclear power, and even if the United Nations were to prohibit all research or manufacture. International society is built upon the inviolable principle of the territorial integrity and political sovereignty of individual states, and verification would be an impossible task. In any case, the family of nations has neither the political unity nor the policing power to enforce the rule of law if broken by a sufficiently determined and well-armed state. Unilateral disarmament would only result in nuclear weapons

becoming the sole property of those nations which did not have the good-will to renounce them. It would be the equivalent of permitting the criminal element in society to acquire an overwhelming superiority of weapons as compared with the police.

This is not to take a pessimistic view of man, just to point to the twin realities of man's capacity to manufacture the weapon to suit his purpose and the ever continuous thread of violence that runs throughout human history and shows no sign of disappearing. The nuclear decision must be taken not just in its contemporary context, but with the whole future of mankind in view, bearing in mind the possibility of a nuclear-armed Hitler. Few generations can have had a greater responsibility than ours.

(2) In the present East–West context, the side that unilaterally abandons its nuclear capability is no longer able to put up an effective defence against an attack from the other … and must therefore dramatically reduce its conventional forces. Having once fallen out of the technological 'race' there would be no possibility of ever redressing the military balance. This would leave the nuclear side in a position of total and impregnable military superiority with no counterbalancing force on the international political scene, and would create a situation unprecedented in the history of man. Pacifism stands as a logical proposition but nuclear unilateralism does not; to do so it must concede renunciation of the power of military defence against a nuclear adversary with all that this would imply in the contemporary context and for the longer term future.

By addressing itself to the nuclear problem specifically, rather than to the more fundamental one of war in general, the proposition [of unilateral disarmament] risks implying that conventional war is acceptable. Yet an East–West conventional war would be a catastrophe of enormous proportions. At all events, to advocate nuclear disarmament, not total disarmament, is to admit the possibility of armed attack and to grant the right of a conventional defence against it, and if, as unilateralism claims, the nuclear deterrent does not deter, far less will a conventional deterrent deter. Thus a third world war becomes more, not less, likely.

Unilateralism quite legitimately presents the likely consequences of the use of nuclear weapons in worst case terms, but fails to confront the consequences of a Soviet take-over of Europe in anything approaching similar terms. In order to make a valid moral judgement this dire prospect needs to be honestly and fully faced.

Some forms of unilateral disarmament take the view that the use of nuclear weapons constitutes so great an evil that they must be renounced even for the purpose of deterrence, whatever the consequences. But this prompts the question: what if renunciation results in a nuclear strike by one country against another whereas retention would in all probability have deterred such use? One cannot demonstrate that this could never happen, or even that it is highly unlikely: on the contrary, as will be proposed later in this paper, a case can be made for showing that it is just what might happen.

If, then, such a catastrophe does happen, is renunciation still held to be the morally correct choice, and if so on what grounds? Or have we, albeit out of the best of motives, unwittingly opened a door to the very crime which we are seeking to avoid? 🙴

Their shared belief in the dangers of unilateral disarmament and the logic of deterrence helps explain Quinlan and Cheshire's wariness of the CND, and their collaborative efforts to debunk what they believed to be strategically irresponsible and intellectually vacuous anti-nuclear myths put about by the campaign. Bruce Kent was a particular target of their criticism – their belief that he tended to dodge the difficult questions on how to maintain stability without nuclear weapons earned him the nickname 'the slippery monsignor' from Quinlan.[56] A series of letters dating from September/October 1985 shows how Quinlan and Cheshire collaborated in a joint effort to counter Kent's pro-disarmament arguments. Cheshire took the lead by engaging Kent in a public debate on nuclear disarmament in *The Tablet*; while Quinlan, unable to put his own name in print for constitutional reasons, played a behind-the-scenes role, providing quiet advice to Cheshire on how to burst Kent's balloon. Quinlan seemed to take great pleasure in this opportunity, revealing a chink of wickedness beneath his usual British establishment reserve.

An early letter in the series, sent from Quinlan to Cheshire and dated 23 September 1985, shows that Cheshire had initiated the public exchange with Kent, and although he had sought Quinlan's advice from the beginning, he initially had to make do without it. Subsequently, however, Quinlan jumped in with gusto, delighted to have the chance to help a friend challenge Kent and, by extension, the CND:[57]

> **“** Please forgive this slow reply to your letter; with Ministerial re-shufflings, I have had a busy fortnight. But I was delighted that – as indeed I had already marked – you wrote to *The Tablet* as you did. I think some of your argument is precisely to the point, and it is excellent that someone with weight has pinned Bruce Kent

down. It is, I think, significant that he has not immediately bounced back with a riposte – he is usually very quick on the draw. He has, it seems to me, been making a lot of play recently with his 'multilateralist' wriggle – and wriggle is all it is.[58] To put the matter another way, he has been pretending (on the basis of a specialised use of the word) that because everyone, of course, would like to see reduced armaments on both sides, not just on one, we are all with him; whereas the reality is that 'multilateralist' and 'unilateralist' are in customary usage well-established short-hand ways of referring to two plainly incompatible views of what Britain or the West should do if/when it turns out that the other side will not play. As it happens, I heard Cardinal Hume in conversation the other day refer to this Kent ploy in terms which show that he understands the point very well – I had the strong impression, though he did not explicitly say so, that he was drawing on your letter – he used almost exactly your way of putting the argument. **"**

Cheshire had written the following letter to *The Tablet*, dated 29 August 1985:[59]

" Sir,

Monsignor Kent (July 13) says that he has never met anyone who urges immediate unilateral disarmament by the West, and that there is no essential difference between multi and unilateralism, on the grounds that the latter is merely one step towards achieving the former. The term unilateralism, he maintains, is the greatest hindrance to clarity of thought in this crucial debate.

If there are some for whom this statement makes for clearer thinking, I have to say that for me it does the opposite. Yet it brings us to the very core of the debate, and therefore deserves to be pursued.

Father Bruce is a committed pacifist, and pacifism denies the state the right of armed defence, even against the likes of Hitler. It is a view based on high moral principles which appeals to many, especially the young, it is the logical, and for the time being the only, alternative to deterrence in the nuclear age, and should be looked at by everyone who seriously seeks a way through the moral dilemma we face. But I see little room for it in the description of unilateralism [in Kent's letter]. If the pacifist were to strive for anything less than total and early disarmament regardless of what the other side does, he would compromise the very essence of his convictions. Once this central issue becomes fudged, we are all the losers, for, pacifist and non-pacifist alike, we all have the same goal in mind – the priceless gift of freedom and peace.

Father Bruce has told us the step he would now like us to take, but we also need to know where the steps he has in mind are intended to lead us? Just supposing we dismantle our independent deterrent, and then find that the Soviet Union does not reciprocate, what comes next? Do we restore the lost defences and re-negotiate from a position of strength, or do we, as pacifism requires, continue disarming until finally, if there is still no similar response, we are totally and unilaterally disarmed?

If the latter, then multilateralism and unilateralism cannot be looked upon as similar, if the former, or some variant of it, then I do not think Father Bruce is any longer a pacifist. **"**

Although Kent did not immediately respond to Cheshire's letter, he did eventually, prompting Quinlan to demolish his arguments in a letter to Cheshire dated 30 September 1985:[60]

> I spoke too soon about the absence of a rejoinder from Bruce Kent! It is just as well that I am professionally debarred from intervening in the correspondence myself, for I should be sorely tempted to an intemperate contribution. Bruce's letter is one more illustration that – for all his commitment and sincerity of basic cause, as I continue to accept – he has become over the years … [an anti-nuclear][61] polemicist. His final paragraph is personally offensive (whereas your own letter was very careful in this regard) and most of the rest is at best verbosely evasive of the specific point you wrote about.
>
> Of course we all accept that one-sided measures (and there are recent Western examples) can play a part in arms control and disarmament; nothing you wrote implied otherwise. To that extent it is indeed possible that unilateralists and multilateralists (in the well-established short-hand which Bruce is trying so hard to disinvent in order to obscure distinctions) could if they chose travel a useful part of the road together; whether the likeliest steps in common are those Bruce proposes is by the way – I believe you yourself have chosen to stay out of the *Polaris/Trident* issue, and Bruce's little burst on this is wholly irrelevant to your letter, a typical politician's handful of dust in the reader's eyes. (The whole piece, indeed, is a vignette of the platform controversialist's art – the Houdini change of subject, the diversionary counter-attack, the more-in-sorrow-than-in-anger jab ad hominem, the false classification (see below), the suggestio falsi beating-your-wife rhetorical question to end on).

There remains, as you pointed out clearly and Bruce continues to dodge, an absolutely basic difference – both conceptual and practical – between those who regard nuclear possession as intrinsically wrong and those who do not. The attempt in his second paragraph to identify the divide as lying simply between those who are complete pacifists and those who reject nuclear possession on a particular view of just-war reasoning is dishonest; he knows quite well that there is a large third group of Christians who believe nuclear possession to be morally defensible. He also knows that in the available indications the Pope, Cardinal Hume and major Western hierarchies lean to this – is their Catholicism to be in doubt? Or do their utterances not really matter? Bruce's reverence for Church sayings, itself not without irony, is evidently selective.

It is interesting to learn that he apparently accepts some interim Western possession of nuclear weapons as being in practice, whatever the underlying moral analysis, tolerable on grounds of realism. That realism, already of four decades' standing, is going to have to last a long time, for there is not the slightest basis for expecting change for decades to come in its main foundations. One wonders what, if that is so, are to be the criteria for the duration of Bruce's tolerance; if it is not indefinite, how will he avoid coming to the 'moral self-indulgence' of calling for unilateral nuclear disarmament? One wonders also why he has been disseminating assiduously to military personnel at nuclear bases a pamphlet powerfully urging upon them a duty to renounce their functions on the ground – a basic and general one, not specific to any particular type of nuclear weapon – that the possession of such weapons is absolutely contrary to international law and morality. (The fact that the argument is developed in a way that no informed non-bigot could regard as honestly objective and balanced is, again, by the way.) 🙰

Just a few days later, Quinlan followed up his letter with another, in which he sketched out a draft response for Cheshire to send to *The Tablet* (in an effort to help Cheshire mount the strongest possible counter-attack):[62]

> 🙰 Our letters crossed, I think. As you will gather, I do not believe that Bruce Kent's letter is confused, but confusing, and meant to be; I regard it – on the basis of much observation of his methods over the years – as a piece of deliberate obfuscation or wriggling. He is both tenacious and practised enough to go on wriggling, and I judge it unlikely therefore that he will allow himself to be pinned down (or let you have the last word); but I entirely support your inclination to undertake another round. That should at least increase the chance that readers of the Tablet will perceive the reality of the matter.
>
> In these circumstances I think I would be disposed to concentrate on the one central theme, and not to pursue his diversionary attempts on, for example, what the UN Report meant, and the rationality or otherwise of strategic nuclear action.
>
> Purely by way of illustration (our writing styles differ, I know) I have tried my hand herewith at the sort of draft I would be minded to use – this may at least serve to suggest ways of presenting the argument. I realise, on re-reading, that (though I have tried to tone down my inclinations!) it probably still carries a shade more

asperity than you may want; that reflects, no doubt, the shortcomings of my character, but also my honest view that in exchanges of this kind Bruce is not in the business of candid truth-seeking dialogue. **"**

Quinlan's draft response to Kent ran as follows:[63]

" Dear Sir,

Monsignor Bruce Kent's latest letter (28 September) ranges diversely. I hope you will allow me to stick to the point I raised with him in your 7 September issue, for I still do not see precisely where he stands.

The issue turns on this fundamental question: has the West a moral duty to divest itself of nuclear weapons irrespective of the actions of others? The unilateralist/ multilateralist short-hand, though perhaps over-simplified, seemed to me to have become established usage for distinguishing between those who say Yes and those who say No; and the fact that the latter can still support particular unilateral measures (such as the West has indeed sometimes taken) should not allow a semantic dispute to divert us from the major distinction, which in my view remains important.

That distinction is not however the one suggested in Monsignor Kent's second paragraph, which offers a classification of Christians between those who are pacifists and 'those who try to take Just War precepts seriously', with both groups accepting that the present situation of deterrence is grossly immoral. There is a large group of Catholics and other Christians whose views this classification dismisses by implication as illicit; and it appears to include (for example) the Pope, Cardinal Hume and the United States, French and West German hierarchies

– Monsignor Kent is not entitled, on any reasonable interpretation of their words, to claim their endorsement of his opinion that the possession of nuclear weapons to prevent war is grossly immoral.

Even within the limited part of the opinion spectrum which he describes, it is not yet clear precisely where Monsignor Kent himself now stands. It is evident from his third paragraph that he does not wish to urge the immediate Western renunciation of nuclear weapons – in other words, that he thinks it necessary and morally acceptable to tolerate some nuclear possession for a period of time. (I am a little surprised at the implication, clearly present in his 13 July 1985 letter, that [the] CND has never withheld this degree of pragmatic tolerance; but that is by the way.) What then needs explanation is the basis of the tolerance, and the criteria for its duration. I assume that Monsignor Kent is not recommending it simply because governments are thought unlikely to listen to a morally correct message; that would be a strange basis for Christian reticence. Given that, the only basis I can see whereby someone of Monsignor Kent's fundamental conviction (that possession is grossly immoral) could extend tolerance beyond the forty years of nuclear-weapon possession there has already been would be some expectation that an international process credibly leading to complete abolition was under way and likely to come to full fruition in a modest further span of time. Frankly, I do not believe this to be realistic (despite the occasional rhetoric of politicians) and I cannot imagine that Monsignor Kent does either. If he does not, I do not understand what he is waiting for, nor why or for how long he dismisses as 'moral self-indulgence' the idea of urging on the West a comprehensive duty, not conditional on the actions of the East, to renounce the weapons. That is where his own moral logic points; and if he cannot accept it, I respectfully suggest that he must review his premises. One way or another, he should disclose the full basis and implications of his reasoning. **"**

Cheshire wrote to thank Quinlan for his draft, but explained that he felt his response to Kent should come from his own thinking. Still, he took Quinlan's advice on board and used it in his subsequent correspondence with Kent, which he copied to Quinlan. He combined Quinlan's sharp logic with his own extraordinary personal experiences of the Second World War, which gave his letters added edge. For example, in one of the last letters in the Cheshire/Kent series, Cheshire ended with the words: 'I know from living experience what a terrible thing it is to have to drop an atomic bomb on another man's city, particularly when you are young'.[64]

The shared horror of major conventional war and mutual belief that nuclear weapons provided the best hope of preventing it was at the core of Quinlan's and Cheshire's disarmament scepticism – both believed a common weakness among anti-nuclear campaigners was their lack of strategic knowledge and vision. Although advocacy groups made worthy and superficially convincing arguments against the morality of nuclear use, they could not muster a major war-preventing alternative to nuclear deterrence, and as a result their case always collapsed on strategic grounds. Quinlan and Cheshire regarded the denial of real-world dynamics among the majority of disarmament activists as self-indulgent at best: those at the sharp end of defence decision-making did not have the luxury of denying strategic realities, they had to make the difficult decisions, and they had to live with their choices.

Although most of their critiques of the disarmers' arguments focused on the East–West context, and specifically on the question of a return of major conventional war in Europe, Quinlan and Cheshire believed an unhealthy demonisation of nuclear weapons and general incomprehension of their war-prevention and war-termination roles extended well beyond Western Europe; it was a strand in contemporary thought that crossed cultures and spanned the world. This comes across in a number of their letters, and is most clearly expressed in their discussion of the disarmament movement in Japan. Cheshire had decided to write a book on defence dilemmas, written from the perspective of his personal experiences during the atomic bombing of Nagasaki. As part of the project, he had agreed to participate in a BBC documentary, which followed his return to Nagasaki in mid-1984. On his return to England, Cheshire wrote to Quinlan to explain that his visit had not gone according to plan: due to his role in the war, the Japanese authorities in Nagasaki had banned him from attending a peace ceremony that was being held to remember the victims of the nuclear attacks. In his letter, Cheshire commented that this awkward situation had saved him from what his daughter (who had attended the ceremony) had told him was 'a very dreary and meaningless occasion'.[65] However, his real reason for writing to Quinlan was not to recount his difficult experience in Nagasaki but to share his impression of how the Japanese had demonised and misunderstood the role of nuclear weapons: '[they] have, as it were, put the two atom bombs into a watertight compartment, completely isolated from the realities of the war … they appear to have no understanding at all of the role they played in bringing the war to such an extremity nor to what would have been necessary to finish the war but for the bombs. They merely look upon them as an unprovoked, unnecessary and criminal act against them.' Quinlan concurred with Cheshire's judgement, writing that his own 'slight contacts with Japanese folk bear out what you say about their incomprehension'.[66]

In Britain, a number of pro-disarmers responded to the criticisms of prominent strategists by launching studies that assessed nuclear issues in the logical, intellectual and unemotional way that Quinlan, Cheshire and other members of the Pembroke Group were demanding. Their goal was to deal directly with the constant refrain from the pro-deterrence advocates, to address the difficult questions of how to achieve a disarmed world, how to maintain international stability on the road to zero, and how to govern a nuclear-weapon-free world. During his time in the civil service, Quinlan was quite dismissive of the fruits of these efforts. On the one hand, he respected the fact that a core group of influential disarmament advocates had the intellectual honesty to tackle questions that so many others had simply swept under the carpet. On the other hand, he was not convinced by their conclusions: they addressed the difficult problems without resolving them, and as a result their studies failed to advance disarmament thinking in a way that was practical and useful for defence planners.

The Alternative Defence Commission was one of the highest profile efforts devoted to studying the strategic implications of nuclear disarmament. It was set up in October 1980 as an independent group of politicians, academics, trade unionists, churchmen and journalists, all of whom were interested in exploring the defence options that would be open to Britain if it unilaterally disarmed and refused to station NATO nuclear forces on its territory.[67] Walter Stein, who was a prominent member of the Commission, used Quinlan's arguments on the logic and morality of nuclear deterrence to frame his opposition to the pro-deterrence case. His proposition was that the UK should lead the way in creating a safer world by unilaterally disarming, and in doing so jump-start a process of phased multilateral disarmament, the ultimate goal of which would be to divest the world of all nuclear and conventional weapons 'under the sign of the UN':[68]

> 66 Michael Quinlan's 'practical realism' simply bypasses the moral problem [of whether it is right to use unjust means in the service of a just cause]. In this sense it is Machiavellian. It simply and essentially bypasses the fact stressed by Roger Ruston and Brian Wicker that – whatever the desired consequences – 'deterrence is a system of hostage-taking on a mass scale'. This point is morally conclusive. There is no way in which nuclear deterrence can function except, ultimately, as a threat against civilian populations.
>
> [...] No one can fail to recognise that the spread of nuclear weapons and the multiplying perils this must bring with it, is now at its height; that unless a total, rapid change can be brought about, under the leadership of the nuclear powers themselves, this momentum will tend towards a total loss of control by all powers of their, and the world's, destinies. It seems amazing that Michael Quinlan's imperturbability does not even mention these facts. They alone totally invalidate his deterrence optimism. And he fails to recognise what a vital role could be played by Britain in this respect, as a nuclear power prepared to abandon its nuclear status. Only the force of such an example can hope to speak to the nuclear aspirations of non-nuclear powers. Would this not be a task within British competence, a task for a creative patriotism?
>
> ... We (Britain, the Church, individuals) can help to signal the need for a proportionate transformation. Is it not time – whatever the difficulties – to move towards phases of nuclear and full disarmament, under the sign

of the United Nations? Should Britain's 'independent deterrent' not rather give way to a unilateral transformation that could signal to other nations that one, at least, of the nuclear powers is indeed ready to respond to its own real, and the world's real, needs: the need for disarmament and feeding the hungry? Minds like the distinguished mind of Michael Quinlan are needed to aid us towards these ends. **"**

As far as Quinlan was concerned, the proposals put forward by Stein and the other members of the Commission were well-meaning but flawed. He sent his critique of the Commission's first report, 'Defence Without the Bomb', to Cheshire in a letter dated 2 January 1985:[69]

" The Report seems in general well-written, honest, intelligent and accurate as to the facts it cites. These characteristics mean that most of the difficulties of alternative defence, in its various forms, can be found acknowledged directly or indirectly somewhere or another in the text. But that is not the same as giving these difficulties adequate prominence and weight in the broad thrust of the book, or in the summings-up and conclusions at the end of the chapters on various options or aspects.

There is a great deal of 'may', 'might' and 'could' about the book's consideration of the future implications of the continuation of current defence policies, or the adoption of alternative ones. This is in itself reasonable enough. But the drift of the argument often seems gradually to assume that the uncertainties claimed in relation to present policies should be taken as turning out unfavourably, whereas those in relation to its own preferences go the other way.

As a look at the membership would lead one to expect, the general 'world-view' running through the book is not that of the main political majorities in the West; in particular, there is a tendency towards equating East and West in moral terms, which most people in the West would reject. This is illustrated by the fact that, in an apparent striving for 'evenhandedness', the book recurrently tries to postulate credible scenarios in which Britain might be forcibly threatened by the US as much as by the Soviet Union.

The book is not directed to an open and unconstrained attempt to identify the most effective way of keeping the world free from East–West war. It starts from the firm premise that the possession of nuclear weapons is unacceptable, and from that position it then asks, in effect, what is the best that might be done without them.

Despite this absolute moral presupposition, the book rarely – and certainly not consistently – addresses itself to the hard case: that of a non-nuclear West facing a nuclear East. Its discussion of particular options for Britain (it is a very Britain-centred study) is set overwhelmingly in a context where the ring continues to be held generally by a nuclear US continuing to counterbalance the Soviet Union; in effect, therefore, it still relies on US nuclear strength. There is another key respect in which the book fails to test its moral preferences against the truly hard case. It directs itself essentially to the realities of today, as perceived by the authors – the Soviet Union much as it seems now (and, even at that, perceived rather more kindly than many serious commentators would think reliably wise). It does not tackle with any firmness the problem that nuclear knowledge is with us for the rest of human history, and that our precepts must be ready to stand the test of, for example, another Hitler.

The book does not face up consistently, if at all, to the basic fact that nuclear weapons are utterly decisive against other weapons. It tries to persuade itself that, for one reason or another, a nuclear-armed USSR might elect not to use its full power if it got into conflict with a non-nuclear adversary. To postulate this – especially in a situation of one-sided Eastern possession, which the book ought in logic to face up to – is to postulate that the Soviet Union, having got itself into serious war with (for example) Western Europe, might deliberately forgo victory. This seems, at the mildest, an undepend-able hypothesis. The whole nature of major war is that one seeks to do to one's adversary whatever he will find hardest to cope with or counter. There could hardly be a clearer or more concrete illustration of this than at Hiroshima or Nagasaki in 1945, when US use of atomic weapons was plainly and instantly recognised by the Japanese Government, for all its warlike characteristics and even amid the passions of war. The book contains no adequate tackling of this vivid instance. **"**

Quinlan was also critical of the work of the Common Security Programme – another high-profile effort to address the real-world challenges of nuclear disarmament. This initiative was led by international relations scholar Stan Windass, who took up where the Alternative Defence Commission left off when it wound up in 1987.[70] Windass used the concept of 'common security' as the intellectual underpinning for his work on nuclear disarmament, an idea introduced into public debate by the Report of the Palme Commission of 1980–82.[71] In common with the Alternative Defence Commission, Windass was concerned with shifting the discourse about nuclear disarmament away from utopian visions of peace towards the more concrete realities of security, but to do so in a way that recognised the dynamics of interdependence rather than ethnocentric national self-interest. His main goal was to provide an alternative to what he regarded as the increasingly counter-productive maintenance of extended nuclear deterrence as the backbone of security policy for Western Europe. He believed that through technological advances in conventional weaponry, precision-guided munitions could be used to design non-provocative strategies that could replace nuclear deterrence – an idea that earned him significant allies among political elites in the Labour Party, and attracted the interests of diplomats, peace campaigners, academics and even nuclear strategists.[72]

Quinlan and the British defence establishment, however, did not share this enthusiasm for Windass's efforts, as is clear from the following exchange of letters. The first letter, dated 1 September 1987, was sent by Quinlan to Moray Stewart at the MoD, while Quinlan was serving out his last few weeks at the Department of Employment:[73]

> ❝ Many thanks for sending me the Windass papers – returned herewith. I find them rather depressing. At a certain level of very broad generality the approach is worthy enough, and to that extent I can see why so many figures of substance have lent their names to it – at much the same level I would broadly agree, as you can perhaps deduce from [my article on deterrence] ... But it is regrettable that support of this quality should have been mobilised behind a particular executant of such evidently second-rate banality – the more he gets into the specifics (which are what any real life policies

must deal in) the plainer it becomes that he lacks any consistent clarity or depth of analytical grasp. There are many aspects of reality where he does not reach beyond verbal superficiality; and there is little evidence that he has the will or the comprehension to tackle hard choices or powerful lobbies (like the maritime one). At best, I suspect an outcome of all-things-to-all-men fuzziness. **"**

Subsequent letters on Windass and the Common Security Programme were written after Quinlan had taken up his position of MoD PUS, including the following request, dated 19 November 1987, that Quinlan sent to David Nicholls (who at the time was MoD policy director):[74]

" Could I seek a steer on Stan Windass? He has written seeking to make early contact, and suggested lunch. I have never met him, but I have seen from time to time material of his, including a recent package on a 'Common Security Programme'. It all seems to me very well-meaningly third-rate, and my instinct would normally be to be as discouraging as civility allows. I am however struck, and a shade puzzled, by the weight of eminent and good quality support (at least in verbal form) which he has apparently managed to enlist. If you had any guidance to offer on whether a) he is substantively meritorious enough, or b) it would be otherwise politic, to warrant attention, I should be grateful to have it.

I am sending a copy of this letter to John Boyd, in case there is an FCO view. **"**

David Nicholls sent the following reply, dated 30 November 1987:[75]

" I was interested to learn, from your letter of 19 November, that Stan Windass has been in touch with you: while we share your evaluation of the Common Security Programme, there is no doubt that not only has Windass had considerable verbal support, but that people from all parts of the political spectrum have been 'putting their money where their mouths' are!

Like you, we're puzzled by all this, and initially were also suspicious. But over time we've come to conclude that the Common Security Programme is at least well meaning and have avoided snubbing Windass. But I seriously doubt whether Windass or his programme is sufficiently meritorious for you to become involved (we advised Clive Whitmore against seeing him in September). "

John Boyd (FCO) responded in a similar vein on 7 December 1987:[76]

" Your letter of 19 November to David Nicholls asked whether we had a view on Stan Windass. We come across him at arms-control seminars. He also calls here from time to time. He is well meaning, beta minus on a good day[77] and as you say well funded.

Windass' Common Security Programme is a curate's egg. Its merit is that it contains work on important areas that have otherwise tended to escape the academics (e.g. confidence building). Jonathan Dean, the former MBFR player is a regular contributor. Windass is also co-director of an NGO called 'Just Defence'. Its prime objective is to highlight the merits of 'non-provocative', i.e. non-nuclear and 'morally just' defence policy. Our enthusiasm on this front is qualified. To sum up, we doubt whether he merits your attention. "

344 | On Nuclear Deterrence

The MoD–FCO exchange about Windass displays a level of insularity among the inner circle of the UK defence elite during the final years of the Cold War. Windass's 1984 paper 'Three Phases of Denuclearisation' (which Quinlan had been sent by Frank Cooper and had filed among his letters) was flawed on many levels, but it had begun to address some of the most intellectually challenging questions associated with nuclear disarmament. In his 1984 paper, Windass had set out a bold, three-stage global disarmament strategy. The first stage would see an end to extended deterrence, via the establishment of nuclear-weapon-free zones, the withdrawal of battlefield- and then all land-based nuclear weapons from Europe, and the introduction by the superpowers of 'no-early-use' doctrines. The second would see strategic reductions down to a minimum deterrent by all the NWS, which would go hand in hand with the development of stringent, universally accepted verification processes and technologies. Once a reliable global verification regime was in place, the third stage of the strategy would be nuclear abolition, which would involve 'the participation of the whole world community' and would be dependent on effective oversight by a United Nations Committee on Disarmament. With its emphasis on caution and maintaining safety and security throughout the disarmament process, it might seem strange that Windass's strategy was so unappealing to Quinlan and the defence establishment. But there are some important points to bear in mind: firstly, few predicted the collapse of the Soviet Union, and so there was little sense of urgency to prepare for a post-Cold War world; secondly, the dominant belief among Quinlan and his colleagues was that nuclear weapons could not be disinvented and thus had to be managed through the maintenance of a credible deterrent (at the time, devising strategies to achieve a nuclear-weapon-free world therefore seemed a pointless pipedream); and third, the UK had invested heavily in *Trident* – a process Quinlan had played an important part in and which he recognised had important opportunity costs in other areas of government. It is therefore hardly surprising that a strategy that involved the UK abandoning *Trident*, either unilaterally or through a multilateral process, seemed 'depressing' and half-baked.

The green shoots of disarmament

Two events had a major impact on Quinlan's disarmament scepticism: the first was the collapse of the Soviet Union; the second was his own retirement from the civil service in 1992. Suddenly free of his official responsibilities and no longer at the sharp end of defence decision-making, Quinlan was able to delve more deeply into many of the challenging questions that he had had to snatch time to address as a public servant. It was not long before he realised that, during his time at the MoD, he had become stuck in what he described as 'obvious-adversary patterns of thinking' – an intellectual rut that he had carved out for himself during his time spent debating, analysing and shaping Cold War deterrence strategy.[78] But a combination of altered threat perceptions and time on the outside began to change that. It was not that Quinlan lost his deterrence optimism; far from it – his belief in the fundamental logic and morality of nuclear deterrence stayed with him until the end. What changed was Quinlan's assessment of the costs and benefits of nuclear weapons, and his long-held conviction that nuclear disarmament would be categorically illogical unless there was a complete transformation of the international system. He never lost his disarmament scepticism completely, but he did shift position from that of dismissive realist to middle ground 'agnostic', still uncertain whether nuclear abolition was feasible but convinced that it deserved serious attention and rigorous study.

Much of Quinlan's post-Cold War thinking on disarmament can be gleaned from his public contribution to the debate over whether the UK should commission a replacement for *Trident*. As far as he was concerned, it would not be possible to come up with a firm answer either way until accurate information about the costs of replacement were available in the public domain. On balance, he was leaning towards renewal, but he was concerned about the costs, both financial and political, and there was a strong undercurrent of doubt running through many of his pronouncements on the subject. An August 2006 interview between Stephen Sackur and Quinlan on the BBC's political discussion programme 'Hard Talk' reveals many of these doubts, which intensified over time.[79] The following is a transcript of the first half of the interview, which focused specifically on the *Trident* decision (the second half, which is not transcribed here, focused on the issue of how to respond to Iran's nuclear defiance):

> **SACKUR:** Do you believe the British government should commission a replacement for *Trident*?
>
> QUINLAN: I'm not going to give an absolutely flat answer to that. I'm not among the absolutely yes or absolutely no's. I want to know what are the options, what's the preferred option, what does it cost? My general inclination I think is just about in favour of staying in the business. But I wouldn't put it more strongly than that – so far.
>
> SACKUR: I find that extraordinary. I mean, after all, you spent your entire professional life thinking about these things, representing the British government and working for the government and staunchly defending the notion that Britain's independent nuclear deterrent was vital for Britain's national interest.

QUINLAN: But that was in the Cold War, when we were facing an adversary at close quarters – within Europe – a massive superpower of hostile ideology, uncertain dependability and a certain attitude to us. That's not the case anymore. We're facing certainly a more untidy world – in many ways, a nastier world – but there isn't a cogent case of quite the clarity that there was then. I think there are still arguments worth considering, but I don't think they are of infinite value and importance.

SACKUR: Isn't the most basic argument that if Britain is to 'punch above its weight' in the international arena, make sense of its position as a permanent member of the UN Security Council and a strategic partner of the United States, it needs to be a nuclear-capable power?

QUINLAN: I don't think it's as definite as that.

SACKUR: Didn't you yourself say that when you were in the Ministry of Defence?

QUINLAN: I never used the words 'punch above our weight' – that's not a phrase I like. I certainly recognise that there is a case that Britain wants to act confidently around the world and we are one of only a few big countries – and we are still a big country; we shouldn't talk ourselves down – that are willing to take on hard responsibilities in awkward places, as we see now. This gives us a certain confidence, but I don't think it's an absolute requirement that we should have (a nuclear capability) – after all, we said in other contexts that we don't reckon to take on big things unless we're alongside the Americans.

SACKUR: But isn't the other truth that you haven't alluded to that there is more nuclear fissile material out there in the world than we've ever seen before; and there are more unpredictable states and other actors who either have or want to get nuclear weapons and in that context it would seem crazy having had nuclear weapons to throw them away?

QUINLAN: Well, certainly the decision to go on with something is a different decision from starting it from scratch. I think there's more of a case (for nuclear retention) if we're in the situation that we are now to stay in it than there would be starting with a clean sheet of paper. Nevertheless, I don't myself find the arguments quite as absolute as they seemed to me back in the 1980s when I was involved in the decision to acquire *Trident* in the first place.

SACKUR: Do you believe the government has properly handled the debate which is now ongoing about whether to replace the *Trident* missiles?

QUINLAN: Well, the government I think has hardly started in the debate.

SACKUR: Isn't that the point in a way, that there's hardly been a proper debate?

QUINLAN: Indeed. But we haven't had a decision either, so I don't think one can say that the government has missed the boat.

SACKUR: But the government has made a decision, and if it's a decision that reflects the will of the people, the debate should have started, shouldn't it?

QUINLAN: You could argue that both ways. When we acquired *Trident* in 1980 there was only a limited amount of public debate. But the government of the day gave a very full explanation of why it had chosen the course it had chosen and I remember undergoing an extensive and quite fierce cross-examination from the House of Commons Defence Committee. On the whole, the pattern of how governments operate on questions of big defence decisions is to decide what to do and then defend it. I think there is a case – and the government has implied it by terminology that it accepts this – that it is having this debate before the decision is 'finalised'.

SACKUR: But isn't it actually a case of precisely as you put it, of making a decision and then defending it, because we had Gordon Brown who most people who follow British politics expect to be the Prime Minister to succeed Tony Blair, Gordon Brown on the 21st of June talked of 'retaining our independent nuclear deterrent' and that can only make sense if he is prepared to pay the money to replace *Trident*. The decision has effectively been taken.

QUINLAN: We don't know exactly what decision. Certainly Mr. Blair had already indicated and Gordon Brown already has it on record that we ought to stay in the business, but still a big decision to be taken is: how? What size of force, at what cost, and what speed of replacement? That debate I think is still an important one and that's still to be embarked upon. People are already discussing it. I've written on it myself. But the government hasn't yet put in the public domain the facts [that we need] if we're going to have a public debate before the [final] decision.

SACKUR: Well, you're being quite honest, aren't you! You've written a lot about this. You've thought about it over the years. You know as well as I do that [*Trident* renewal] could cost up to £20 – even £25 – billion, depending on what kind of replacement system they go for.

QUINLAN: Well, we don't know the figures…

SACKUR: Where would you draw the line? Where would it become not worth it? Where would it simply just not be worth having our own independent nuclear deterrent? How high would the price have to go?

QUINLAN: I wouldn't be prepared to give a neat cut-off figure where we fall off a cliff. The pace at which we have to spend the money is also an important dynamic. To have to spend 10 billion pounds in two years is different from spending £10bn over 10 years … but certainly if someone came to me and said 'I'm terribly sorry old boy, but you're going to have to spend 50 billion quid, I would be inclined, given this is to be an insurance against very improbable possibilities, to say that's probably too much. If you say, however, that it's £10–15bn, then I'm up for it, I think.

SACKUR: Really? So it all comes down to a calculation of pounds and pence?

QUINLAN: No. It's a judgement about insurance – it's money that if we spend on this, we don't spend on something else in the defence budget or elsewhere.

SACKUR: I come back to the point about an unpredictable world. Looking ahead, we don't know what the threats are going to be in 30 years time. All sorts of things could be in action, many of them quite unpleasant. Let me quote to you a colleague of yours in the business, who I'm sure you know – Lee Willett of the Royal United Services Institute who's done a lot of work on this. His message is that in the end, while others have nuclear weapons and seek to acquire them, we know the only thing that will deter a nuclear weapon is a nuclear weapon. That's his rationale for saying that whatever it costs, we've got to [replace *Trident*].

QUINLAN: I think that's over-simple. Put in that blunt way, that's the same argument [that you could use to justify] everyone having nuclear weapons. Why shouldn't the Germans, the Italians, the Japanese? It's a question of how much security you buy and how much risk you're prepared to take. The fact is that you can imagine scenarios for any kind of scale of military capability you can think of in which we just might want to have nuclear weapons in case they come in handy. With limited resources, even if you doubled the defence budget, I could still write you a scenario in which you need more of this, that or the other, and that's true of nuclear weapons too. Inevitably, one has to make judgements about how much insurance to take and how much risk to accept. There's no escaping that.

SACKUR: One thing that you haven't yet mentioned, but which I believe you actually think is important to this debate, is a simple human failing of vanity; pride. Because you told the House of Commons Defence Committee not so long ago – earlier this year – that 'to leave the French as the only nuclear power in Europe would twitch a lot of very fundamental historical nerves in this country'. Well that's a very odd reason [to replace *Trident*] isn't it?!

QUINLAN: Well, that was an observation about national psychology…

SACKUR: But again, I turn to your long experience in the Ministry of Defence – as the key player in the long-running debate about Britain and its independent deterrent, and you're basically saying that part of the problem is that we're determined to keep up with the French!

QUINLAN: Well, you could put it the other way around – that they're determined to keep up with us…

SACKUR: Either way, it doesn't make much sense.

QUINLAN: Yes. I don't myself think that's a main driver. As I said, it would twitch a nerve and there would be people who would say: 'we can't have the French having it and not us!' I don't take that view but I do believe that there's something in the point that there ought to be some nuclear capability in Europe if Europe is to be any kind of a player and not simply dependent on the US calling the shots. And if we are to have it in Europe, there are difficulties I think about leaving it to the French as the only possessor, what with their idiosyncratic views that we see from time to time on foreign policy issues. To that extent, I'll go a certain distance with the argument, but I'm not suggesting that I think it's a logically respectable argument to say that we've got to have [a nuclear deterrent] because the French have one.

SACKUR: But you're basically saying that you don't regard the French as reliable…

QUINLAN: Their view of their interests and their view of European interests isn't always the same as ours. We saw that over Iraq…

SACKUR: Simple question – can you imagine Britain using its nuclear-weapons capability separate from the United States?

QUINLAN: I think it's very unlikely, but very unlikely is not the same as impossible, and the important thing is not whether we think we're likely to use it – it's whether a possible adversary reckons he can assume that we won't. And I think it's just possible to imagine certain circumstances in which we find ourselves confronting some new possessor who thinks the Americans won't stay with us when the chips are down – but even then [if we retain *Trident*, the adversary will still] have to make a calculation: 'can we assume that the Brits will chicken out [from using their own nuclear weapons] on the day?' The argument essentially for our staying in the business is that it gives us a margin of insurance against [a new possessor]. 🢂🢂

Quinlan's views on the *Trident* replacement issue were inevitably coloured by his years at the sharp end of British defence policy planning – he couldn't quite convince himself that it would be sensible to relinquish a system that the UK had invested in so heavily over the years, although his doubts about the strategic logic of nuclear retention were growing. He was also somewhat on the fence where the global issue of nuclear retention versus nuclear abolition was concerned. The answers were far from obvious: based on the information available, it was not yet possible to reach a definitive answer as to whether global nuclear abolition was desirable or feasible, but it was certainly clear that the costs of nuclear retention were growing. Perhaps the best exposition of Quinlan's thinking on the global abolition debate can be found in an article entitled 'Abolishing Nuclear Armouries: Policy or Pipedream', which was published in the IISS journal, *Survival*, in winter 2007–08.[80] The following extracts show how far his ideas had changed since the days when he dismissed nuclear abolition as a dangerous fantasy:

> **“** There has been a wide divergence – it has scarcely deserved to be called a debate – between two polarised extremes. One pole, which might be called that of the righteous abolitionists, pointed to the commitment [to disarm] and demanded that countries possessing [nuclear] weapons should get on, more or less forthwith, with disposing of them. The other pole, which might be termed that of the dismissive realists, asserted that complete abolition is fanciful dreaming, and that the world must expect to have to concentrate on managing their existence for the rest of human history – or at least, to put the matter slightly less crudely, that successful abolition must imply an international environment so

vastly different from today's that it is idle to spend time now on talking about it.

Both of these viewpoints are surely wrong. The righteous abolitionists tend to talk of giving up nuclear weapons as though it were a sort of international equivalent to giving up smoking – the kind of thing that any sensible strong-minded country ought to be able to do without long-drawn-out shilly-shallying. But this ignores the fact that countries do not acquire or retain a nuclear armoury, with all its costs and other drawbacks, as a matter of idle whim …

The dismissive realists are wrong because, whether or not it may now be believed that the recognition of a long-term goal of abolition implied in the 1968 Nuclear Non-Proliferation Treaty and subsequent declarations at its review conferences was unwise or unreal, it was a goal clearly accepted. It has often been re-affirmed and invoked; and it continues to be relied upon as a load-bearing component in the set of bargains that constitutes the global non-proliferation deal …**"**

Later in the article he returned to the gulf between righteous abolitionists and righteous realists, arguing that the theme of abolishing nuclear weapons is 'one on which there is broad and serious analytical work to be done', whichever side of the debate people came down on. He placed himself between the two camps, describing himself as: 'in the middle' and 'inclined to believe … that the goal has to be taken seriously but will entail a long, difficult and as-yet-uncertain road'.

There are numerous reasons for Quinlan's changing attitude to disarmament. Above all, he was concerned about the political costs of 'nuclear apartheid' – i.e. the inequalities at the heart of the nuclear non-proliferation regime that divided the world into 'haves' and 'haves nots'. Although he still believed that, on balance, many of the arguments used by the nuclear-weapon states to justify their status were legitimate, he was aware that they were beginning to ring hollow in the ears of states that had given up their right to nuclear possession. There was a danger that, unless Britain and the other nuclear possessors began to take their disarmament commitments seriously, the regime that had kept proliferation in check for so many years could collapse. As long as the nuclear 'haves' continued to act as though eventual disarmament was dependent on 'the abolition of all evil in the world', that danger was very real. This, more than any other factor, led him to reassess his own approach to disarmament, move out of the dismissive realist camp, and appreciate the need for a 'cool and careful examination' of what a disarmed world would look like, and what would be needed to create and sustain it.

But there were other contributing factors too. Even though he felt the risk of nuclear-weapons use was extremely low, he believed that the rise of global terrorism and the spread of nuclear energy would generate proliferation pressures that would increase this risk, including by potentially putting nuclear-weapons capabilities in 'unstable hands'. This was a significant departure from Quinlan's Cold War thinking, which was underpinned by the rational-actor assumption and the belief that nuclear deterrence had very wide margins of stability. It was not that nuclear proliferation would necessarily be calamitous for international peace and security in the post-Cold War world (Quinlan continued to believe that nuclear possessors would be risk-averse) but that proliferation increased the chances of accidents and the probability of nuclear use. He dismissed sensationalist claims that nuclear use was 'inevitable' at some point – it was just more likely than it had been under US–Soviet bipolarity. Indeed, his research on nuclear deterrence in South Asia had led him to argue that it was possible for stable deterrence to operate outside the East–West context: dangers existed in the India–Pakistan nuclear standoff, but if both countries developed the appropriate instruments and procedures, these dangers could be managed.[81] Likewise, in the case of Iran, nuclear breakout would be unlikely to generate unmanageable nuclear risks, but it would be damaging to the nuclear-proliferation regime and in any case it was important to try to prevent any increase in the probability of nuclear use, however slight.[82] Thus, overall, proliferation became a more significant factor in his assessments of the costs and benefits of nuclear retention versus nuclear disarmament: the longer the nuclear-weapons states retained their nuclear arsenals, and the more new possessor states emerged, the greater the probability of nuclear use, and the stronger the arguments for exploring whether and how it might be possible to reverse the process.

The difficult question was how to reverse the process in a way that would make the world safer and more secure, rather than creating even more risks – a question that preoccupied Quinlan in his last years. As he saw it, there were three major political challenges that stood above the rest: how to deal with long-running and seemingly intractable regional conflicts, such as the Arab–Israeli dispute; how to manage great power relations (especially between China, Russia and the United States) so that they became more cooperative; and how to develop an effective conflict-prevention system that would take major conventional war permanently off the table.[83] It was the third of these challenges that Quinlan considered to be both intellectually and practically the hardest part of the disarmament enterprise. But there were also huge technical challenges, including the development of reliable technologies and processes to verify and monitor disarmament, and doctrinal and technological studies on whether/how conventional weapons could be used to achieve defence tasks currently assigned to nuclear weapons. Quinlan felt that these questions, which struck deep into the heart of the disarmament debate, had been overlooked or intentionally swept under the carpet by many disarmament advocates over the years (a situation which, as his letters have shown, he found frustrating and even irritating during his career in the service). But with the Cold War over, new threats emerging and old ones receding, it was a problem that urgently needed to be addressed. It was time to try to fix the holes in the arguments of the 'righteous abolitionists' through intellectually rigorous, and politically and technically informed disarmament analysis that confronted the difficult questions head on.

Quinlan's challenge to the scholarly community has since inspired a body of focused research on disarmament challenges. It was immediately taken up by the IISS, which, driven by his clear and forceful exposition of disarmament dilemmas, launched a research study on what a commitment to a world free of nuclear weapons would mean in practice. In June 2007, then Secretary of State for Foreign and Commonwealth Affairs Margaret Beckett announced British government support for the project – especially for the focus on the technical aspects of transparency and verification – and the initiative was launched in earnest, leading to workshops in the UK (at the IISS) and in the US (at the Carnegie Endowment for International Peace), and to a series of publications that have begun to examine the practicalities of global nuclear abolition.[84] In his role as IISS consulting senior fellow, Quinlan played a significant mentoring role in these activities in the final year of this life, corresponding with George Perkovich (co-author, along with James Acton, of the *Adelphi* that set out the IISS disarmament project's preliminary conclusions, entitled *Abolishing Nuclear Weapons*). The following e-mail exchange, which Quinlan printed out and filed among his letters (the only e-mails he saved in this way) shows his close involvement in the project, as he provided comments on the *Adelphi* and feedback on ideas that grew from it. The e-mails also reveal that Quinlan was busy with his own writing, having just signed a book contract with Oxford University Press:[85]

> **❝** [E-mail sent 30 May 2008]:[86]
>
> Dear George,
>
> A further 'overview' look at the [*Adelphi*] draft leaves me still much more than content – it is a high-quality product, and I am sure it will be seen as of real importance in the developing conversation about abolition. I am sure that your decision to bring the main political survey forward, to precede the technical chapters, has been right.
>
> I set out below a few further petty comments that occurred to me as I re-read the first thirty pages. One point of fact at the foot of p. 11 caught my eye. Is it really the case that the Bush administration, in its general stepping back from the Thirteen Steps of 2000, specifically repudiated the acceptance of eventual abolition as the long-term goal? I hadn't understood this. I would be a touch wary of regarding [a well known disarmament advocate] as a conclusive witness on such a point – much though I like her, she is very parti pris (prise?) in these matters.
>
> Good luck, and warmest thanks for all you have done. **❞**

The e-mail ended with a list of numbered comments on the draft – of course with numbered pages and paragraphs – that show Quinlan's thorough and disciplined approach to critiquing drafts stayed with him.

Less than a week later, Perkovich followed up with another e-mail to Quinlan, seeking his opinion of an idea he was pondering to help reduce the operational status of nuclear weapons (an important step in creating crisis stability and in fostering the conditions that would be more conducive to nuclear reductions).

> **❝** [E-mail sent 5 June 2008][87]
>
> Dear Michael,
>
> Now that the Adelphi Paper is off and I'm a bit more relaxed, I wanted to pursue with you a thought I've had about Israel's formulation of not being the first to introduce nuclear weapons ...
>
> That is, the formulation has prompted me to extrapolate an idea of which I'd welcome your critique: what if each nuclear-armed state committed that, in an international security crisis, it would not to be the first to threaten to use nuclear weapons or to [wording inexact] change the operational status of nuclear weapon systems in ways that indicate preparation for use?
>
> If an adversary violated either element of such a pledge, then one would be released to make whatever preparations etc., one needed, because one would be 'retaliating', not bringing nuclear weapons into play first.
>
> These would be political commitments, obviously, but they could contribute to the important goal of devaluing nuclear weapons, putting them into the background of international politics, reducing temptations to use them to posture manliness for domestic/international political reasons, etc. The norm could help in international crises by enabling other states and cool heads within a given nuclear-armed state to urge leaders not to escalate rheto-

ric, etc. Save nuclear gestures until you really mean to use them ...

What do you think? **"**

Quinlan's response shows how, more than 15 years after retirement, he was still focusing on the practicalities of arms control and disarmament. Crisis stability and confidence-building mechanisms had to be built upon more than words; an idea that seemed sound in principle would not necessarily work in practice:

" [E-mail sent 10 June 2008]:[88]

Dear George,

Sorry to be slow off the mark. I have been pondering this interesting and challenging idea.

Reluctantly, I have to say that I end up unpersuaded. I take separately the two components – no first threatening, no first increase in readiness.

I am instinctively wary of pledges that would relate simply to the use of words – hard to define, too easy to slide round, and perhaps at the same time too vulnerable to abrasive (and indeed tension-heightening) argument about what might (or might not) just be careless talk, e.g. to a journalist by a junior minister or the like. (Would something like the US warning in the 1990–91 Gulf conflict to Iraq not to use BW [biological weapons] or CW [chemical weapons] – 'a disproportionate response' – fall foul of the undertaking? That phrase was clearly intended to cast a nuclear shadow, and we know from a senior defector afterwards that the Iraqis so understood it, yet the word 'nuclear' was not used.) What would be the sanction, and how would reality be changed? The threat – and the concomitant deterrent value – of nuclear weapons surely lies in their existence, not in what is said about them, as the example of Israel illustrates. I recognise entirely that leaders would be wise to use language carefully and moderately) but I doubt whether it would be either feasible or helpful to convert that counsel of prudence into anything like a clear-cut rule or advance promise.

'No first increase in readiness' raises different considerations, though problems of specification, sanction and dependability again arise. Quite aside from definitional difficulties (cancelling crew leave? Quietly ensuring that nuclear-capable aircraft are fully fuelled and not away from operating base on unrelated missions?) there is also, so it seems to me, an awkward practical problem. It may well be impossible to distinguish objectively between steps that are part of preparation for attack and steps that are prudent measures of insurance against perceived dangers of pre-emption in time of increased politico-military tension – dispersing delivery systems, putting personnel on short notice, moving warheads or other items out of central storage depots. I attach a brief passage from the South Asia chapter of my projected book (which, by the way, Oxford University Press have just accepted for publication, probably early next year).

In both respects, I believe, the situation of Pakistan is a useful litmus test. There would be concerns in Islamabad broadly analogous to those which (in my view legitimately) lead Pakistan to reject NFU [no-first-use] undertakings. In a crisis like the 2001–02 one, say, Pakistan might well want by its words and actions – again perhaps not unreasonably – to warn conventionally-superior India of nuclear risk (and perhaps reassure its own people about nuclear deterrence).

I am firmly of the view that nuclear-armed countries have a special responsibility always to weigh their words and their actions very carefully (and also that the long-established ones in particular ought to abandon any remaining hair-trigger arrangements). But I fear I don't think – rather as about the NFU idea itself – that attempts to codify the guarantee internationally would either be found negotiable in peace-time or do any real good in crisis or conflict.

But my mind is by no means closed, if you think I have missed points or overstated others.[89] 🟏🟏

Since the publication of the *Adelphi* and the Carnegie volume that grew out of it, serious scholarly studies of disarmament dynamics have multiplied around the world: some of them inspired by Quinlan's own publications; others by the Quinlan-inspired IISS/Carnegie publications.[90] Much of this body of work acknowledges him and his work as a source of influence.

In one of his long letters to Walter Stein, Quinlan explained that his chief goal during the Cold War was to develop a better understanding of nuclear deterrence among defence thinkers and the public at large. Throughout his career in the civil service, he believed that the interesting and important questions centred on how to make deterrence work, and not on whether nuclear weapons, 'which in any case could not be disinvented', were morally licit.[1] He was inevitably drawn into the debates about the latter, but behind everything he wrote was the core assumption that nuclear weapons provided the surest means of preventing major war between the great powers. They presented serious moral dilemmas, but they offered reassurance against a repeat of the horrors of the Second World War, which were still so vivid in his mind. Even though he became known for his controversial belief that nuclear weapons could legitimately serve in a war-termination role against the Soviet Union, it was the question of how to avoid war rather than how to fight it that lay at the heart of his deterrence thinking. War of any kind, whether conventional or nuclear, was monstrous, and he saw it as his responsibility to prevent it. His contemporaries and successors in the MoD shared the same conviction, and they looked to him, with his superior grasp of nuclear strategy and his sophisticated communication skills, to hone British and NATO nuclear policy in the pursuit of peace.

Quinlan's critics did not doubt the sincerity of his commitment to war-prevention and crisis stability; what they challenged was his belief that nuclear weapons could and should serve that purpose. Many took an absolutist position on the immorality of WMD, but others saw weaknesses in his deterrence logic. Some of the most interesting letters in his files were from correspondents who fell into the second category. Perhaps the strongest example of these is the letter from Alastair Mackie (former *Vulcan* squadron commander and vice president of CND), written just as the Cold War was coming to an end and change was in the air. In one simple phrase, Mackie put his finger on the weakest point in Quinlan's logic – a weakness that had always existed, but which took on greater significance as the global order began to shift to a more complex international environment. Despite Quinlan's mastery of nuclear strategy, during his civil-service career, he failed to look 'below and beyond deterrence theory'.[2] He was not tuned-in to the broader dynamics of the nuclear non-proliferation regime, to the long-term implications of the divisions between the nuclear haves and the have-nots, which some of his correspondents believed would challenge future international peace and stability. It was not until his retirement that Quinlan began to acknowledge the full implications of these inequalities, leaving him open to the same charge that he sometimes levelled at others – that is, he became Ptolemaic in his thinking, continuing to think about nuclear weapons within a framework of analysis that was rapidly becoming outdated. Later, he recognised this and acknowledged that too much of his intellectual capital had been invested in the metaphysics of bipolar deterrence. To understand this preoccupation, one needs to understand his deep horror of the Soviet Union and what he considered to be the brutalities of atheistic totalitarianism.[3]

This leads to a final point about Quinlan, which concerns his motivations for devoting so much of his time to his private correspondence on nuclear deterrence. One of Quinlan's friends remarked that what amazed him most about Quinlan was his naive determination to engage in reasoned argument with people whom he had absolutely no hope of convincing, and who, in turn, had no hope of convincing him. He put this down to Quinlan's essential civility, which forced him into an exchange of views that most people in his position would have regarded as a futile exercise and a waste of their time. Quinlan's correspondence has revealed a different view of his motivation, one driven not by civility but by a belief in the power of persuasion and confidence in his own ability to shape the nuclear debate. Especially in the early- to mid-1980s, he genuinely believed he could influence the thinking of even his most accomplished and determined critics – it was a question of highlighting the inconsistencies and weaknesses in their arguments and of encouraging them to face up to the full implications of their anti-nuclear stance. His early success, in the late 1970s and early 1980s, of using sophisticated reasoning to persuade the well known pacifist, Sydney Bailey, that nuclear possession and use could in some circumstances be licit, spurred him to believe that given enough time and effort, other influential deterrence critics could also be swayed. That faith in his own skills and convictions inspired his patient and determined counter-offensive, and kept it going until he began to question and reassess some of his own assumptions.

NATO

NATO is an intergovernmental organisation, an alliance of independent sovereign states, which came together in the interests of joint security and the defence of common values. To facilitate consultation, each member state is represented by a permanent delegation and a staff of civilian and military advisers, who are based at NATO's political headquarters in Brussels. There are no voting procedures in NATO; decisions are reached on the basis of consensus or common consent, involving a continuous process of consultation among member-state representatives. Where differences between members cannot be reconciled, individual member countries are free to pursue their preferred course of action.

The most important decision-making body within NATO is the North Atlantic Council, which is responsible for all NATO policy and operational decisions. It meets at different levels, usually at least once a week with the ambassadors of each country, at least twice a year with foreign or defence ministers, and occasionally with heads of state or government.

The Defence Planning Committee deals with most defence matters and subjects related to collective defence planning. It provides guidance to NATO's military authorities, usually meeting weekly at ambassadorial level and twice-annually at the level of defence ministers. Defence ministers also meet regularly in the Nuclear Planning Group, which keeps the Alliance's nuclear policy under review and discusses a broad range of specific policy issues associated with nuclear forces and wider concerns such as nuclear arms control and proliferation.[1]

NATO's military structure is overseen by the Military Committee, which is the highest military authority in the Alliance but remains under the political authority of the North Atlantic Council. The Military Committee provides guidance to the NATO Strategic Commanders: the Supreme Allied Commander Europe (SACEUR), based in Mons, Belgium, and the Supreme Allied Commander Transformation (SACT), based in Norfolk, Virginia.

NATO nuclear burden-sharing

Sub-strategic (or tactical) US nuclear weapons have been stationed in Europe since the 1950s, when they were deployed to offset Warsaw Pact superiority in conventional forces. In the 1960s, proposals to develop a multilateral NATO nuclear force were floated, but these foundered on the issue of command and control. In the absence of a multilateral force, Alliance members continued to rely on US nuclear deployments in Europe for their nuclear deterrence needs, using the Nuclear Planning Group as a forum for consultation over NATO nuclear policy. These arrangements, known as 'nuclear burden-sharing', remain in place today. NATO strategy has been to publicly state that US nuclear weapons are deployed in Europe, but to 'neither confirm nor deny' the presence or absence of nuclear weapons at any NATO installation or in a specific country. In the event of war, some of these weapons would be transferred to allied forces and delivered by allied aircraft, and could possibly be used in a war-termination strategy in response to conventional attack (NATO nuclear strategy has never ruled out first use).

During the Cold War, US nuclear commitment to Western Europe was driven by intense insecurity: the belief among US decision-makers that a Soviet-dominated Western Europe would present a major military, economic and societal threat to the United States, forcing it to reconfigure its economy, limit its political freedoms and become a garrison state. As a result, Washington was hyper-sensitive to shifts in the balance of power that favoured the Soviet Union, for fear that such a shift would drive the US' Western European allies to opt for neutralism or to seek alternative security alliances with Moscow. For the same reason, the US was sensitive to the way its commitment to its NATO allies was perceived – US leaders constantly sought to reassure their European counterparts that American security guarantees were credible.[2]

As the Cold War progressed, NATO officials were worried that Soviet technological breakthroughs could undermine extended deterrence. Their response was to adopt a doctrine of flexible response and to disperse thousands of US tactical nuclear weapons across Europe, including *Pershing* II missiles in Germany. However, while these steps helped allay NATO insecurities to some extent, the nuclearisation of Europe aggravated public fears of nuclear war in some NATO countries, with the result that Alliance nuclear policy became a highly sensitive and politically charged subject in the late 1970s and the 1980s.

Since the collapse of the USSR, divisions have been growing over the question of whether the continued deployment of US nuclear weapons in Western Europe can be justified on strategic or political grounds and whether it is time for a major overhaul of NATO nuclear doctrine.[3] Some members of the Alliance believe that the presence of US tactical nuclear warheads in Europe is an essential part of NATO's nuclear identity and thus oppose their removal; they would support reductions only as part of a reciprocal process of reductions involving Russia and are wary of boosting non-nuclear means for defence because they fear it could weaken nuclear deterrence. Other members of the Alliance favour the removal of all remaining US tactical nuclear weapons from Europe on the basis that they serve no strategic purpose and their removal would demonstrate NATO commitment to the goal of a world free of nuclear weapons. Although current US policy favours the retention of US tactical nuclear weapons in Europe (according to the 'five principles' outlined by US Secretary of State Hillary Clinton in April 2010),[4] some NATO allies have taken matters into their own hands. In 2001, for example, Greece opted to replace its nuclear-capable fighter jet with a model that cannot carry B61s, forcing the US to withdraw its weapons there.[5] Similarly, in the near future, Germany may retire its *Tornado* fighter jet, opting instead for the *Eurofighter*, which cannot carry B61s.[6]

NATO nuclear deployments

During the Cold War, the US deployed nuclear weapons around the world from Western Europe to South Korea, the Philippines, and the Western Pacific. At the height of hostilities, nearly 13,000 US nuclear weapons were deployed outside the United States, of which the majority (nearly 8,000) were deployed in NATO countries. The weapons were intended to serve a dual purpose: first, to demonstrate the US commitment to the security of its alliance partners around the world, and second, to signal to adversaries that military action against a US ally ran the risk of nuclear escalation.

In the late 1980s and early 1990s, the US withdrew thousands of nuclear weapons deployed at overseas bases, leaving only 'residual' deployments in NATO countries, numbering in the low hundreds rather than the thousands. These deployments have declined further since 2000 – with some estimates suggesting the number of US tactical nuclear weapons in Europe more than halved in the period 2001–10.[7]

© IISS

Status of US nuclear weapons in Europe, 2010[10]

Turkey
- 🔘 Incerlik
- ✈ US aircraft
- 💣 50

Germany
- 🔘 Buchel
- ✈ German *Tornados*
- 💣 10–20

Netherlands
- 🔘 Volkel
- ✈ Dutch F-16s
- 💣 10–20

Belgium
- 🔘 Kleine Brogel
- ✈ Belgian F-16s
- 💣 10–20

Italy
- 🔘 Aviano
- ✈ US F-16s
- 💣 50

Italy
- 🔘 Ghedi Torre
- ✈ Italian *Tornados*
- 💣 20–40

United States*
- 🔘 Seymour-Johnson
- ✈ US F-15Es
- 💣 Unknown

United States*
- 🔘 Kirtland
- ✈ n.a.
- 💣 Unknown

🔘 **Air base** ✈ **Delivery** 💣 **Est. weapons**

*US augmentation force for nuclear operations in Europe

It is difficult to gauge the exact numbers and locations of NATO nuclear forces, or the arrangements for their use. Throughout the Cold War, the US government treated this information as highly secret (because NATO nuclear strategy depended on maintaining a level of Soviet uncertainty regarding nuclear deployments and targets). According to the US National Security Archive, even the US Congress has had difficulty acquiring the facts and figures of US overseas nuclear deployments, despite the openness in US nuclear policy planning (relative to the much higher levels of secrecy in the UK). After the Cold War ended, some historic documents were declassified, but many of these have since been redacted on the basis that they could compromise war plans still in effect or harm US diplomatic relations with NATO countries, such as Turkey.[8]

Research studies, published in 2005–11 by Hans M. Kristensen of the Natural Resources Defense Council, concluded the US currently deploys somewhere between 150 and 200 nuclear weapons in Europe, which are stored at air bases in Belgium, Germany, Italy, the Netherlands and Turkey.[9] US nuclear weapons have been removed from some countries in Europe (including the UK in 2006 and Greece in 2001), but these countries maintain airbases with nuclear vaults in caretaker status, and nuclear weapons could be redeployed there if it was considered necessary.

The remaining US weapons that are stationed in Europe are all gravity bombs. The forward-deployed weapons are thought to include all three versions of the B61 bomb (B61-3, B61-4, and B61-10) – the first two types were built between 1979 and 1989, while the third is a converted *Pershing* II warhead. According to Kristensen, all three have four selective yields down to 0.3 kilotons (the lowest known yield of any US nuclear weapon), while their maximum yields vary from 45 kilotons (B61-4) to as much as 170kt (B61-3).

Trident

Trident[1] is the UK's sole nuclear-weapons system. Developed in the 1980s to replace *Polaris*, it was introduced into service in December 1994. It has three key components: platform, missile and warhead. The platform is the *Vanguard*-class submarine (SSBN), of which the UK has four: HMS *Vanguard* (introduced into service in 1994); HMS *Victorious* (1995); HMS *Vigilant* (1998); and HMS *Vengeance* (2001). These submarines, which have a projected life of about 30 years, are powered by Rolls Royce PWR2 nuclear reactors, and each has 16 missile tubes that house the missiles. The latter are known as *Trident* II submarine-launched ballistic missiles (SLBMs). They are three-stage solid-fuel inertially guided rockets with a range of between 6,500 and 12,000km (depending on the payload) and they are accurate to within a few metres. Each *Trident* II missile is capable of carrying 12 warheads, and each has a MIRV (a multiple independently-targetable re-entry vehicle) capability, which enables each missile to engage multiple targets simultaneously. The missiles were designed and manufactured by the US by Lockheed Martin; those that are not deployed are stored at the US Strategic Weapons facility at King's Bay, Georgia.

The nuclear warheads that are fitted to the tip of the *Trident* II missile were designed and manufactured at the UK Atomic Weapons Establishment (AWE) at Aldermaston, Berkshire. They are closely related to the American W76 warhead, which is a thermonuclear warhead with a yield of around 100 kilotons.

UK nuclear infrastructure

The *Vanguard*-class submarines are based at Faslane in Strathclyde, Scotland, which is also home to the UK's conventionally armed submarines. The warheads that are deployed on the SSBN submarines are stored and fitted to the *Trident* II missiles at the Royal Naval Armaments Depot at Coulport, near Faslane. The submarines are built at a shipyard owned by BAE Systems at Barrow-in-Furness, Cumbria, and at a refit and support site (owned by the UK and US-owned consortium) at Devonport, Plymouth. Nuclear warhead design takes place at AWE, which is a government-owned contractor-operated facility. Like the Devonport site, it is managed by a UK–US consortium. The role of the scientists and engineers at AWE is to build, maintain and certify the existing nuclear-weapons stockpile and ensure good stewardship of nuclear-weapons knowledge. Overall, this onshore manufacturing infrastructure and skills base involves significant fixed costs that have to be incurred if the key capabilities are to be retained. One of the main drivers of nuclear retention (as opposed to unilateral nuclear disarmament by the UK) is the awareness at the elite level in the civil service that once lost, these capabilities are likely to be very difficult and expensive to recreate. Some of the key technical skills involved in warhead design, for example, rely on tacit knowledge, which takes time to acquire and cannot easily be relearned.

A history of the UK's strategic nuclear arsenal

The UK first deployed an operational nuclear-weapons capability in 1953, following its first nuclear test the previous year. The first generation deterrent comprised the 10kt *Blue Danube* free-fall bomb, which was deployed on Royal Air Force (RAF) V bombers (the UK's first thermonuclear weapons entered service in 1961). In the 1950s, the US and UK were involved in a joint programme to develop the *Skybolt* air-launched nuclear missile, but the project was cancelled by the Kennedy administration in 1962. Later that same year, the UK reached an agreement with the US to procure *Trident*'s predecessor – the *Polaris* submarine-launched missile system, which entered service in the late 1960s. US–UK nuclear cooperation was facilitated by the Mutual Agreement for Co-operation on the Uses of Atomic Energy for Mutual Defence Purposes, concluded in 1958, which allowed the UK to draw on US warhead designs (which it then manufactured independently at AWE).

By the 1980s, the UK's strategic nuclear deterrent had three main components: strategic, sub-strategic and tactical. *Polaris* served in the strategic role for use against multiple targets in the adversary's homeland. The system comprised four *Resolution*-class SSBN submarines, which were designed and built in the UK, and 16 *Polaris* missiles, which were purchased from the US. Dependence on the US led the UK to attempt to develop a new, indigenously designed and manufactured payload bus for the *Polaris*, known as *Chevaline*, which would be better able to penetrate Soviet defences. But the system, which was developed at great expense, was overtaken in 1980, when the UK negotiated with Carter and then Reagan to acquire the more sophisticated *Trident* missiles to replace *Polaris*. The 1980s were then spent developing the components of the *Trident* system. The sub-strategic and tactical components of the UK deterrent was fulfilled by the WE177 free-fall bomb, which served against individual targets on enemy territory. US tactical warheads were also deployed on heavy artillery and short-range *Lance* missiles under a US–UK dual-key arrangement.

Following the collapse of the Soviet Union in 1991, the UK began a major programme of disarmament, cutting its nuclear deterrent right back to a single platform (the SSBN) in the space of seven years. The objective was to retain the UK independent nuclear capability but at a minimum level to allow it to be both credible and provide value for money in the post-Cold War strategic environment. The dual-key US tactical nuclear warheads that were mounted on short-range *Lance* missiles and heavy artillery plus the RAF sub-strategic WE177 free-fall nuclear bombs were all taken out of service, leaving *Trident*, which replaced *Polaris* in 1994, as the UK's only system. The *Trident* system was also subject to reductions: the stockpile of warheads was reduced by 20%, and the number of operationally available warheads fell from around 400 during the 1980s to under 300. This cost-cutting exercise continued with the 1998 Strategic Defence Review (SDR), which cut the number of operational warheads further to 200; reduced the number of warheads carried on each *Trident* submarine from 96 to 48; and limited the *Trident* II missile (which is capable of carrying up to 12 warheads) to no more than three warheads per missile.

Current UK nuclear posture

The UK maintains a nuclear posture that is known as a continuous-at-sea deterrent (CASD), which means that one of its four *Vanguard*-class submarines is on patrol at any given time. The purpose of CASD, as stated in the 1998 SDR, is to avoid misunderstanding or escalation if a *Trident* submarine were to sail during a period of crisis. The SDR also stated that the *Trident* II missiles on the submarines are not targeted and are normally at several days 'notice to fire', although the alert status can be changed at any time in response to a crisis, and re-targeting the missiles is not a lengthy process. In addition to *Trident's* principal strategic role, the SDR also identified a sub-strategic (but not tactical) role – that is, an option to deploy *Trident* missiles in a limited strike that would (arguably) not necessarily lead to a full scale nuclear exchange and would serve as a warning or demonstration of resolve rather than a full-scale attack. It is believed that *Trident* missiles intended for this sub-strategic role carry only a single warhead, potentially with a reduced yield. All of the UK's nuclear forces are formally committed to NATO, and although they have been de-targeted, the assumption is that they would cover NATO designated targets. However, the UK retains the right and the capacity to fire its *Trident* II missiles independently at targets designated by the UK government, and thus its deterrent is termed 'operationally independent' despite its primary NATO role and the UK's dependence on the US for nuclear procurement.

The 2006 White Paper, which emerged from a review of the UK nuclear deterrent, maintained the nuclear posture set out in the 1998 SDR, as did the three-page section on the UK deterrent that was included in the more recent 2010 SDSR. The focus has been, and will probably continue to be, on retaining the UK nuclear capability as an insurance policy against potential future threats, and to ensure that any 'value for money' reductions do not undermine the credibility of the deterrent. Nuclear retention appears to be a foregone conclusion for the foreseeable future, despite debate over the wisdom of retaining *Trident* in the current international strategic context. The accepted goal (among senior civil servants and British political elites) of maintaining the credibility of the deterrent at the lowest possible cost to the British taxpayer, means future decisions on *Trident* are likely to hinge on submarine design issues (can the successor to the *Vanguard* submarines be designed in such a way that the UK can scale back from four to three submarines without undermining the credibility of the deterrent?) and on cost-sharing (what types of nuclear cooperation arrangements can be made with France to maintain the UK nuclear deterrent and to reduce the cost of replacing *Trident*?). In these discussions, operational independence is likely to remain sacrosanct for two reasons: the UK establishment continues to justify the UK deterrent on the grounds that it provides a crucial 'second centre of decision' (whereby, if adversaries calculate that the US or France will not risk a nuclear attack in order to deter an attack on the UK or its allies, the UK has the option to fire its *Trident* II missiles independently); and despite the efforts of key nuclear thinkers who disapprove of the argument that the UK should retain an independent nuclear capability for international prestige purposes, the political reality is that prestige factors have always been an important driver of UK nuclear decision-making. The nuclear deterrent represents what Alastair Mackie, vice-president of CND, has called a 'stick-on hairy chest'.[2]

NOTES

Introduction

1 Journalist John Barry tells a wonderful story of how he first met Quinlan: 'My first recollection is going to meet him in his monastic office in the Treasury, to which, if I recall, he'd been exiled only shortly before. I remarked on the dreary surroundings. He said he found them bracing: "I walk down these corridors and I say to myself: In these very corridors people have been making a mess of economic policy for almost 200 years." How could one not warm to him?' Author e-mail exchange with John Barry (journalist for The *Times* and *Newsweek* and Quinlan correspondent), 26 June 2011.

2 Letter from Quinlan to John Blelloch, 27 October 1982.

3 Letter from John Roper to Quinlan, 10 January 1983.

4 For example, in a letter to Richard Perle, US assistant secretary of defense, on 1 September 1987, Quinlan wrote: 'It looks by now overwhelmingly likely, if not yet absolutely certain, that I shall not again have the chance to work as an official in the defence field. But I shall sustain a vivid interest in it; and I much hope that that may from time to time cause our paths to cross.'

5 Lawrence Freedman, 'The Intellectual Legacy of Michael Quinlan', paper presented at the Michael Quinlan Memorial Seminar, Fondation pour la Recherche Strategique (FRS), Paris, France, 21 September 2010.

6 Obviously, these senior officials do not act in isolation. Their judgements are based on important input from scientists, engineers and industrialists, who provide expertise on the technological and cost implications of various policy options. In the past, senior civil servants have been accused of withholding important information from ministers, and of 'bouncing' them into nuclear procurement decisions. See David Owen, *Nuclear Papers* (Liverpool: Liverpool University Press, 2009).

7 Richard Crossman, *The Diaries of a Cabinet Minister*, vol. 1 (London: Jonathan Cape, 1975), p. 31. Quoted in Christopher J. Bowie and Alan Platt, 'British Nuclear Policymaking', Project Air Force Report prepared for the United States Air Force, RAND, January 1984, pp. 23–4.

8 Owen, *Nuclear Papers*, p. 5. Owen acknowledges that secrecy is a legitimate part of defence decision-making, but in his book he raises questions over the nature and extent of that secrecy and the role of senior officials in determining who has access to what information.

9 France does not participate in the NATO NPG because it wants its nuclear deterrent to remain independent of the Alliance. Although it returned to NATO's integrated military structure in April 2009 (having left it in 1966) this does not include NPG participation.

10 Jeffrey A. Larsen, 'The Future of Non-Strategic Nuclear Weapons and Implications for NATO: Drifting Toward the Foreseeable Future', Report prepared in accordance with the requirements of the 2005–6 NATO Manfred Worner Fellowship for the NATO Public Diplomacy Division, 31 October 2006, Unclassified, pp. 23–5.

11 Letter from Richard Perle to Quinlan, 1 July 1987.

12 Freedman, 'The Intellectual Legacy of Michael Quinlan'.

13 Michael Howard, 'Foreword', in Michael Quinlan, *Thinking About Nuclear Weapons*, The Royal United Services Institute Whitehall Paper 41 (1997), http://www.rusi.org/downloads/assets/WHP41_QUINLAN.pdf.

14 Richard Mottram talks admiringly of Quinlan's unequalled ability to rattle through tasks at great speed and with a light touch. When leading the UK delegation to the NATO HLG, Quinlan enjoyed the heavy workload and handled it with ease. Quinlan's efficiency and enthusiasm for his work continued after his retirement – Richard Mottram notes that as Ditchley director 'a Quinlan exposition of even the most mundane administrative matter could be a quirky delight for participants'. Interview with Richard Mottram, IISS, Arundel House, 18 June 2010; Richard Mottram, 'Obituary: Sir Michael Quinlan', *The Guardian*, 2 March 2009.

15 In his Thanksgiving Mass, Father Michael Holman explained Quinlan's belief that 'it is essential for the Christian to get involved with society and its problems, to make them his own, and to use ... our reason and intelligence to improve the state of things, the state of things as they were, not as they might have been, respecting the choices people in our democratic society have made'.

16 Letter from Quinlan to Sydney Bailey, 26 October 1979.

17 The most significant incident involved Clive Ponting, who, as a senior civil servant in the MoD in July 1984, leaked two documents concerning the sinking of Argentine navy warship *General Belgrano* in the 1982 Falklands War. The documents Ponting handed over revealed that the *Belgrano* had been sighted a day earlier than officially reported, was heading away from the Royal Navy, and was outside the exclusion zone when it was attacked and sunk. Ponting later admitted releasing the information and was charged under section 2 of the Official Secrets Act of 1911, but was later acquitted thanks to the 'public interest' defence. The revised Official Secrets Act of 1989 removed the public interest defence, significantly tightening the legislation.

18 Robert Armstrong, 'The Duties and Responsibilities of Civil Servants in Relation to Ministers', UK Home Civil

Service, DEP NS 1391 25/5/85 and DC Deb 26/2/85 c. 128-30. Quoted in *The Civil Service Code*, SN/PC/3924 20/2/2006.

19 Even in periods when nuclear policy is not an issue of major public debate, secrecy pervades many aspects of the British nuclear policymaking process, to the extent that the media is constrained in its freedom to report on nuclear issues. The Official Secrets Act is reinforced by a system of Defence Advisory (DA) Notices, which are addressed to editors asking them not to discuss specified areas of defence policy. Five of these are still in force today, including (as of 2008) DA-Notice 01, covering military operations, plans and capabilities and DA-Notice 02, covering nuclear and non-nuclear weapons and equipment. These notices are issued by the Defence, Press and Broadcasting Committee, which is composed of the most senior civil servants concerned with defence matters and specified journalists. The committee chair is always the current permanent (under) secretary of the Ministry of Defence. The other four civil service officials that sit on the committee are the 2nd permanent secretary of the Ministry of Defence, the Cabinet Office permanent secretary, the permanent secretary of the Home Office, and the deputy secretary from the Foreign and Commonwealth Office. Ironically (given his frustration over the constraints on his own freedom to publish) Quinlan would have chaired this secretive committee himself in the late 1980s – a time when his files show that he engaged much less in public and private debate on nuclear issues. For further information on UK media and nuclear policy in the 1980s, see Christopher J. Bowie and Alan Platt, *British Nuclear Policymaking* (Santa Monica, CA: RAND, 1984), pp. 70–74.

20 Letter from Quinlan to Douglas MacLean and Henry Shue, 4 September 1985.

21 Letter from Quinlan to Richard Harries, 21 June 1985.

22 The Westland affair was a political controversy during Margaret Thatcher's premiership involving the British helicopter manufacturer Westland. The cabinet was divided over whether a European or American buyout of the financially stricken company should be favoured, with Michael Heseltine advocating the former, and Thatcher the latter. These divisions (which reflected deeper disagreements over whether the UK's future lay in closer defence integration in Europe or continued reliance on the United States) split the cabinet, leading to Heseltine's resignation in 1986.

23 *Theological Studies* is published by the three Jesuit Schools of Theology in the US. At the time, the journal was edited by Walter Burghardt from his office at Georgetown University.

24 Letter from Quinlan to Blelloch, 27 October 1982.

25 Letter from Beatrice Heuser to Quinlan, 24 April 1993.

26 He was described in this way at the Michael Quinlan Memorial Seminar, Fondation pour la Recherche Stratégique (FRS), Paris, France, 21 Sep 2010.

27 Freedman, 'The Intellectual Legacy of Michael Quinlan'.

28 Rebecca Johnson, for example, compares belief in nuclear deterrence to religious faith. She draws parallels between pro-nuclear and voodoo

beliefs, arguing that: 'to those not steeped in the nuclear belief system and internal logic, the games, theories and rituals of nuclear deterrence appear no less irrational [than the voodoo belief system]'. Rebecca Johnson, 'Turning Back from Doomsday', in Robert Green, *Security Without Nuclear Deterrence* (Astron Media: Christchurch, New Zealand, 2010), pp. 25–6.

29 In one of his letters (discussed later in this book), Quinlan made a very revealing comment about the threat posed by 'atheistic communism, against which our security arrangements primarily seek to protect us'. He described it as 'an enormous evil, in terms of lost life as well as lost liberty, as is shown by its fruits from Lenin through to Stalin and Mao to Pol Pot'. Quinlan's horror of atheistic totalitarianism remained strong throughout his life, and can help explain why he felt nuclear weapons were morally licit despite their appalling destructive power, and why he was slow to adapt his thinking about nuclear weapons towards the end of the Cold War. Letter from Quinlan to Bob Beresford, 20 May 1981.

30 Lawrence Freedman, 'The Intellectual Legacy of Michael Quinlan', paper presented at the Michael Quinlan Memorial Seminar, Fondation pour la Recherche Stratégique (FRS), Paris, France, 21 Sep 2010.

31 Letter from Andrew Edwards to Quinlan, 20 June 1988.

Part One

1 Letter from Quinlan to Albert Wohlstetter, 24 November 1987.

2 This speech was later published. See Michael Quinlan, 'Nuclear Weapons and the Abolition of War', *International Affairs*, vol. 67, no. 2, 1991, pp. 293–301.

3 Defence Open Government Document 80/23, July 1980.

4 Letter from Walter Slocombe to Quinlan, 24 September 1981.

5 Walter Slocombe, speech to the Conference of the American Society of International Law, April 1982.

6 Scilla Elworthy, interview with Quinlan, January 1988. Elworthy's interview was part of an Oxford Research Group study on the nuclear beliefs of different groups of decision-makers. It was later published and led to a follow-on study on the same topic. See S. Elworthy, H. Miall and J. Hamwee, 'The Assumptions of Nuclear Weapons Decision-Makers', in L. Barnett and I. Lee (eds), *The Nuclear Mentality* (London: Pluto Press, 1989), pp. 69–89, and S. Elworthy, *British Nuclear Weapons Policy: Why it has not changed with the end of the Cold War*, Ph.D. Thesis, Department of Peace Studies, University of Bradford, September 1992 (especially chapter 7: 'The Unchanging Assumptions of British Defence Decision-Makers').

7 Elworthy, interview with Quinlan, January 1988.

8 *Ibid.*

9 John Keegan, speech to the Oxford University Strategic Studies Group, All Souls College, 27 January 1981.

10 This is most likely a reference to Quinlan, who was DUS(P) at the time, or to Quinlan's boss, Frank Cooper, who was MoD PUS.

11 Paul Bracken, *The Command and Control of Nuclear Forces* (New Haven, CT: Yale University Press, 1983).

12 Letter from Quinlan to Connell, 18 April 1984.

13 Presidential Directive 59 (PD 59) was adopted by the Carter administration in July 1980 to refine and codify the doctrine of flexible response (sometimes referred to as 'countervailing strategy'), which was introduced into US nuclear planning in the 1960s.

14 Letter from Uwe Nerlich to Quinlan, 26 February 1985.

15 Letter from Quinlan to Nerlich, 6 March 1985.

16 Extract from Quinlan's RCDS speech of 26 October 1982. Quinlan enclosed the text of the speech in a letter to Albert Wohlstetter, dated 16 February 1988.

17 Elworthy, interview with Quinlan, January 1988.

18 *Ibid*.

19 Letter from Quinlan to John Roper, 5 January 1983.

20 Elworthy, interview with Quinlan, January 1988.

21 Letter from Lynn Davis to Quinlan, 29 February 1984.

22 Letter from Quinlan to Davis, 12 March 1984.

23 Letter from Quinlan to Andrew Edwards, 7 January 1983.

24 Lawrence Freedman, 'The "No-First-Use" Debate and the Theory of Thresholds', included in a letter from Freedman to Quinlan, 16 November 1982.

25 Letter from Birdwood to Quinlan, 23 March 1984.

26 Speech by Birdwood to the House of Lords, 21 March 1984.

27 Lord Jenkins of Putney initiated the debate to 'call attention to the approach of the nuclear holocaust'. In his speech to the House of Lords, Jenkins argued that a nuclear holocaust was drawing near and that it would 'extinguish humanity' unless urgent action was taken to avoid it. He therefore called on the government to call a meeting of all parties so that 'the most experienced minds may get together to discuss the dilemma', combine their wisdom and 'distil policies and proposals which may yet lead us out of this valley of the shadow of death'. Birdwood took the floor immediately after Jenkins. Speech by Jenkins to the House of Lords, 21 March 1984.

28 Although much of Birdwood's speech echoes Quinlan's thinking on nuclear deterrence, Quinlan would have taken issue with his views on the immorality of nuclear weapons.

29 Green Papers are consultation documents produced by the British government. They contain proposals that are still in a formative stage and that are subject to debate by the nation. Often, Green Papers are released when a government department is considering introducing a new law, to allow people inside and outside parliament to debate the subject and offer feedback on proposals. White Papers, in contrast, are statements of government policy. These are put before parliament to invite discussion before a policy is formally presented as a legislative bill.

30 Letter from Quinlan to Roper, 5 January 1983.

31 Letter from Arthur Hockaday to Quinlan, 4 January 1983.

32 Pope John Paul II's thinking on nuclear deterrence shifted a few years later, as he began to view the morality of nuclear deterrence with greater scepticism. In 1988 he grudgingly accepted nuclear deterrence in the short-term but urged its replacement as a political strategy. See Thomas C. Fox, 'Catholics Debate Papal Nuclear Shift', *Bulletin of the Atomic Scientists*, vol. 5, no. 4, May 1988, pp. 30–32.

33 Letter from Hockaday to Quinlan, 4 January 1983.

34 The Council on Christian Approaches to Defence and Disarmament (CCADD) is a Christian forum for expert debate on defence and security issues. It is still active in the UK today.

35 Letter from Quinlan to Jon Connell, 13 February 1986.

36 Ptolemy was the Alexandrian astronomer who proposed a geocentric system of astronomy that was undisputed until it was overturned by Copernicus (in the Ptolemaic system of planetary motion the earth is fixed as the center of the universe with the sun and moon and planets revolving around it). The term Ptolemaic is therefore used to describe someone who fails to adapt their thinking to new scientific knowledge. In this context, those who fail to understand the transformational impact of nuclear weapons on warfare and strategy are Ptolemaics, and those who accept the revolutionary impact of nuclear deterrence are Copernicans.

37 Letter from Andrew Edwards to Quinlan, 20 June 1988.

38 This is a mathematical term. An asymptote is a straight line that is the limiting value of a curve, which is considered a tangent at infinity.

39 Letter from Michael Kaiser to Quinlan, 7 June 1984.

40 Elworthy, interview with Quinlan, January 1988.

41 Quinlan, 'Nuclear Weapons and the Abolition of War', pp. 293–301.

42 For a scholarly article on these dilemmas, which Heuser was working on at the time, see Beatrice Heuser, 'Containing Uncertainty: Options for British Nuclear Strategy', *Review of International Studies*, vol. 19, 1993, pp. 245–67.

43 Letter from Heuser to Quinlan, 3 October 1992.

44 The London Declaration began the transformation of NATO from a Cold War Western alliance to one that incorporated former Warsaw Pact countries from Central and Eastern Europe. It comprised a series of proposals aimed at fostering cooperation between NATO and these countries through a wide range of political and military activities. *Declaration on a Transformed North Atlantic Alliance issued by the Heads of State and Government participating in the Meeting of the North Atlantic Council ('The London Declaration')*, North Atlantic Treaty Organisation, 6 July 1990, http://www.nato.int/cps/en/natolive/officialtexts_23693.htm.

45 The ASLP (*Air-Sol Longue Portée* or Air-to-Ground Long Range Missile), was jointly planned in late 1990–93 by France and Britain for development by the French company Aerospatiale. The UK withdrew from the project in 1993 on the basis that the missile was too costly and strategically unsuitable.

46 Letter from Quinlan to Heuser, 7 October 1992.

47 Letter from Quinlan to Leonard Cheshire, dated 17 March 1982. The letter invited Cheshire to join the Pembroke Group and included a series of annexes setting out the group's rationale and goals. This quote is taken from Annex C, titled 'Christian Ethical Issues in Deterrence: Background Note'.

48 *Ibid.*

49 The Pembroke Group met two or three times a year throughout the 1980s and into the early 1990s, when a decision was taken to disband it due to what many of its members considered to be 'the diminished salience of the nuclear debate' following the end of the Cold War. A number of Pembroke Group members, including Quinlan, continued their involvement in debates on just deterrence through CCADD, which also features prominently in Quinlan's letters and remains active in the UK today. Hugh Beach volunteered to take on the administrative tasks of the Pembroke Group (such as organising meetings and circulating papers) at St George's House, Windsor Castle.

50 Letter from Quinlan to Sydney Bailey, 26 October 1979.

51 Letter from Quinlan to Bailey, 23 August 1982.

52 Letter from Brian Wicker to Quinlan, 21 July 1992.

53 See Quinlan's letters to Frank Winters, 17 March 1982 and Walter Stein, 31 May 1984. Both letters are discussed below. Note that Hugh Beach, Leonard Cheshire, David Fischer, Arthur Hockaday and others were also concerned about the moral paradox at the heart of nuclear deterrence, although they had different ideas about how/whether/when this paradox

could be overcome and how to handle it in the meantime.

54 Letter from Sydney Bailey to Quinlan, 14 November 1979.

55 Letter from Quinlan to Mark Fillingham, 12 November 1985.

56 The use of any kind of weapon against a specified target can have a 'double effect': one that is intended (the destruction of the target itself) and one that is unintended (the destruction of people, facilities and land near the target). Some moral philosophers argue that the unintended deaths can be morally justified in certain circumstances; others dispute this. The debate over double effect is especially heated in relation to nuclear weapons, due to their indiscriminate destructive power. One of the most powerful cases against the moral acceptability of unintended deaths was made by Elizabeth Anscombe, a moral philosopher whose work deeply influenced many of the intellectuals who challenged UK nuclear policy during the Cold War. See Elizabeth Anscombe, 'War and Murder', in Walter Stein (ed.), *Nuclear Weapons and Christian Conscience* (London: Merlin Press, 1961).

57 Letter from Quinlan to Bailey, 9 February 1981.

58 Letter from Quinlan to Bailey, 5 May 1981.

59 Letter from Bailey to Quinlan, 13 May 1981.

60 Letter from Quinlan to Bailey, 18 October 1982.

61 Letter from Quinlan to Hockaday, 19 February 1981.

62 Letter from Hockaday to Bailey, 14 May 1981.

63 Letter from Hockaday to Quinlan, 27 April 1982.

64 Letter from Quinlan to Hockaday, 24 May 1982.

65 Letter from Stein to Quinlan, 23 August 1984.

66 Letter from Walter Stein to Quinlan, 15 April 1984.

67 Letter from Quinlan to Stein, 31 May 1984.

68 The phrase 'bitch-goddess of historical necessity' was first used by Donald MacKenzie MacKinnon (1913–94), a Scottish philosopher and theologian who held the Norris-Hulse Professorship of Divinity at the University of Cambridge from 1960–78. His early works included the volume *Christian Faith and Communist Faith: A Series of Studies by Members of the Anglican Communion* (London: Macmillan, 1953).

69 Letter from Stein to Quinlan, 24 April 1984.

70 Letter from Brian Midgley to Quinlan, 1 August 1980.

71 Letter from Quinlan to Midgley, 29 September 1980.

72 Letter from Midgley to Quinlan, 7 November 1980.

73 Letter from Brian Wicker to Quinlan, 16 June 1987.

74 Letter from Quinlan to Wicker, 3 August 1987.

75 A memo written by Quinlan on 18 December 1978 in response to an internal paper by David Owen (who was foreign secretary at the time) argued that, to be credible, the UK independent deterrent should have the capability to kill up to 10 million Soviets (Owen had argued that one million would suffice). The memo (and a number of other fascinating declassified documents from the period) were found in the National Archives in London by Brian Burnell, a former nuclear-weapons design engineer who now researches British nuclear history. The declassified documents (and Quinlan's role) became the subject of British media attention in December 2010. See Rob Edwards, 'Secret Files from the 70s Reveal Trident Strike Needed "to kill 10m Russians"', *Guardian*, 26 December 2010, http://www.guardian.co.uk/uk/2010/dec/26/secret-files-70s-trident-russians. I am grateful to Brian Burnell for all the fascinating documents he sent me in the course of this project.

76 These arguments were broadly in line with the official US Catholic Church statement on the morality of nuclear deterrence, which was articulated by Cardinal Krol in September 1979. His statement made a distinction between the act of using (or threatening to use) the 'strategic nuclear deterrent', which was condemned, and the act of possessing the deterrent, which it tolerated, while urging reciprocal reductions through bilateral US–Soviet disarmament. However, unlike the US Bishops, Krol did not elaborate on the issue of limited nuclear use, leaving that question open to interpretation (perhaps deliberately).

77 Nuclear use that is limited to demonstrative strikes alone makes no sense for the obvious reason that it is an empty threat (the state that carried out the strike would not be prepared to follow it up with a strike against a higher value target).

78 Francis X. Winters, 'The Bow or the Cloud: American Bishops Challenge their Church', *America*, vol. 29, 18–25 July 1981.

79 Letter from Quinlan to Frank Winters, 17 March 1982.

80 Winters, 'A Moral Argument in Defense of the Choice not to Dismantle the

US Strategic Arsenal', memorandum submitted to the US Bishops Ad Hoc Committee, 25 March 1982.

81 Letter from Quinlan to Winters, 13 April 1982.

82 The Second Vatican Council, known as Vatican II, was an ecumenical council that met between 1962 and 1965 to discuss how the church would relate to the modern world.

83 The judgements refer to Winters' discussion in his article 'A Moral Argument in Defense of the Choice not to Dismantle the US Strategic Arsenal' of a view popular at the time among some US arms controllers (but not shared by Winters): that the US must commit itself to a policy of non-use in Europe. Winters rejected this position, arguing that even if NATO nations gave up the threat and intention to use nuclear weapons, the doctrine of deterrence would still be immoral (due to the presence of nuclear weapons that *could* be used).

84 The Mansfield amendment of 1971 proposed a major, unilateral withdrawal of US armed forces from Europe (half of the 300,000 US troops who were stationed there).

85 Letter from Winters to Quinlan, 30 April 1982.

86 Winters had been shocked by the US bishops' interim draft of June 1982, which advocated nuclear use in response to nuclear attack by the Warsaw Pact. He wrote a private memo to the committee arguing that the limited-use position was incompatible with the statements of Cardinal Krol, and published an article in which he urged that senior American commanders who were Catholic should be counselled that the execution of the nuclear threat was clearly immoral.

Winters, 'Catholic Debate and Division on Deterrence,' *America,* issue 147, September 1982, pp. 127–31.

87 Letter from Winters to Quinlan, 2 August 1983.

88 Faculty members at Georgetown University were divided over the merits of the Pastoral Letter – some shared Quinlan's critical view. William O'Brien, for example, wrote to Quinlan to say he thought the letter 'completely impractical and badly lacking with respect to recognition of the just cause and the threats thereto'. If US and European decision-makers adopted a similar stance, he was concerned they could be tempted to abandon nuclear deterrence and Atlantic collective defence. In response, Quinlan reassured O'Brien that the unilateralist position was weak and that 'the zealots' had already 'lost the argument'. Letter from William O'Brien (Department of Government, Georgetown University) to Quinlan, 13 June 1983; Letter from Quinlan to O'Brien, 21 June 1983.

89 Albert Wohlstetter, 'Bishops, Statesmen, and Other Strategists on the Bombing of Innocents', *Commentary,* vol. 75, no. 6, June 1983, pp. 15–35.

90 Letter from Albert Wohlstetter to Quinlan, 26 January 1984.

91 See Francis X. Winters, 'After Tension, Détente: A Continuing Chronicle of European Episcopal Views on Nuclear Deterrence', *Theological Studies,* vol. 45, June 1984, pp. 343–51.

92 In his 1981 pamphlet 'The Morality of Nuclear Weapons', Ruston assessed the US bishops' interim position on nuclear possession and concluded that it was deeply flawed. He argued that: 'There is no way in which the present possession of nuclear weapons, intended for whatever purpose, can be

justified in Catholic morality' and that 'no individual may morally co-operate in their possession'. He based his case on the argument that the intention to do something immoral in certain circumstances is in itself immoral – thus, if the UK had to choose between nuclear use and surrender to the adversary, the latter would be the morally licit course of action. This was refuted by Quinlan, who argued that surrendering to an atheistic totalitarian regime would be an immoral act.

93 James O'Brien, 'Draft Statement by the Bishops' Conference of England and Wales on Nuclear Weapons', sent by Bob Beresford to Quinlan, 21 April 1982.

94 Letter from Quinlan to Kenneth Francis, 8 June 1983. Quinlan thought Ruston's moral arguments against nuclear deterrence were powerful and had the potential to sway the Church hierarchy and public opinion. This is reflected in his determined efforts to ensure that the Church did not associate itself with Ruston's pamphlet. In his letter to Bob Beresford, dated 5 June 1981, he argued: 'I do believe the [Church] Commission [for International Justice and Peace] would be well advised to put, very explicitly, a good deal of distance between itself and the content of anything closely resembling the present text [of Ruston's pamphlet]'.

95 Letter from Quinlan to James O'Brien, 23 June 1982.

96 Letter from Quinlan to Beresford, 20 September 1982.

97 For example, in a letter to John Hunt, Cabinet Secretary, he described his efforts to counter Ruston's anti-nuclear arguments in the Commission on Justice and Peace and raised the issue of whether he should also attempt to steer Basil Hume away from the anti-nuclear camp. Letter from Quinlan to Hunt, 20 August 1982.

98 Letter from Basil Hume to Quinlan, 24 August 1982.

99 Letter from Quinlan to Hume, 1 September 1982.

100 *Ibid.*

101 Letter from Hume to Quinlan, 24 August 1982.

102 Letter from Quinlan to Hume, 1 September 1982.

103 Letter from David Goodall to Quinlan, 21 January 1983.

104 *Ibid.*

105 Letter from Goodall to John Wilkins, 15 July 1983 (copied to Quinlan).

106 Letter from Quinlan to Wilkins, 18 July 1983.

107 While Quinlan's participation in public debates on deterrence ethics was frowned upon by some ministers (and in particular by Defence Secretary, Michael Heseltine), numerous letters in his files reveal strong support for his efforts from his counterparts in the MoD, FCO and Cabinet Office. This support dates back to 1981, when Quinlan began energetically countering Ruston's anti-nuclear arguments in his private correspondence. A letter from Arthur Hockaday (who at the time was second permanent undersecretary of state at the MoD) provides an early example of this support. The letter, written on behalf of the PUS, gives Quinlan an official nod of approval to respond to Ruston in a rejoinder in *The Tablet,* as long as he did not trigger and long and emotional exchange, and as long as he 'avoid any suggestion either that what you are now writing is ministerially approved or that there is a difference between what you say with ministerial approval and what

you say on a personal basis'. Letter from Arthur Hockaday to Quinlan, 7 August 1981.

[108] Brian Wicker, 'True Hope and False Gods', paper presented at the CCADD International Conference, 19–23 September 2008, Washington DC.

[109] Letter from Quinlan to Wicker, 30 September 2008.

[110] The footnote in question stated that 'some of this pressure was doubtless subjective, simply coming from the fact that the bishops were also loyal citizens of their state. But in other areas, as with the US Bishops' pastoral letter 'The Challenge of Peace', it also came from spokesmen for the government who were invited to give their views to the drafting committee of bishops.'

[111] Letter from Wicker to Quinlan (undated, but most likely sent in October 2008).

[112] Letter from Quinlan to Winters, 17 March 1982.

[113] Letter from Quinlan to Beresford, 20 August 1982.

Part Two

[1] The terms LRTNF, TNF (theatre nuclear forces) and INF (intermediate-range nuclear forces) tend to be used interchangeably in the literature. They all refer to nuclear weapons for use in sub-strategic roles (as opposed to tactical nuclear weapons, which are developed for battlefield use). For information on the changing NATO nuclear force mix, see Appendix 1.

[2] Michael Quinlan, 'NATO Nuclear Deterrence Concepts', shortened version of his speech to the Royal College of Defence Studies, 26 October 1982 (rewritten in 1987).

[3] The following history is partly based on the analysis of official Cold War documents published in William Burr (ed.), *Thirtieth Anniversary of NATO's Dual Track Decision: The Road to the Euromissiles Crisis and the End of the Cold War*, National Security Archive, George Washington University, 10 December 2009, http://www.gwu.edu/~nsarchiv/nukevault/ebb301/index.htm. Where there are gaps in the official sources, I have used secondary sources to supplement the information. Additional useful sources include J. Michael Legge, 'Theatre Nuclear Weapons and the NATO Strategy of Flexible Response,' RAND Occasional Paper, April 1983; *The Modernisation of NATO's Long Range Theatre Nuclear Forces*, Report for the Committee on Foreign Affairs, US House of Representatives, Library of Congress, December 1980; and D.C. Elliot, *Decision at Brussels: The Politics of Nuclear Forces*, The California Seminar, August 1981.

[4] Declassified State Department cable 261791 to US Embassy, Bonn, 'Bilateral with the FRG on TNF Issues', 16 October 1978, Secret.

[5] State Department cable 258185 to US Embassy, London, 'TNF Bilateral with UK', 11 October 1978, Secret.

[6] Briefing Book for Director of Central Intelligence Stanfield Turner, 'SCC Meeting 12 April 1979 White House Situation Room', Top Secret, Excised

copy. Source: CIA Research Tool (CREST), National Archives Library, College Park, MD.

7   State Department cable 247871 to all NATO capitals, 'HLG: US Draft Report', 21 September 1979, Secret, Excised copy.

8   For a more detailed discussion of the rationale for the 1979 NATO LRTNF decision, see Legge, 'Theatre Nuclear Weapons and the NATO Strategy of Flexible Response,' pp. 36–7. Legge was a UK MoD official and Quinlan acolyte. He spent a sabbatical year at RAND in 1982 writing up a report on the NPG, HLG and NATO strategy. In his report, Legge drew a distinction between US and European thinking on NATO LRTNF deployment: where US negotiators viewed NATO TNF modernisation as a direct political and military response to the Soviet modernisation programme (without necessarily matching the Soviet effort system for system), the Europeans (led by the UK and Quinlan in particular) saw it as a way to maintain 'a complete spectrum of deterrent options so that the Warsaw Pact should not be able to escalate a conflict to a level where the Alliance would have no credible response.' Legge, p. 36.

9   State Department cable 247871 to all NATO capitals, 'HLG: US Draft Report', 21 September 1979, Secret, Excised copy.

10   State Department cable 258185 to US Embassy, London, 'TNF Bilateral with UK', 11 October 1978, Secret.

11   US Mission to NATO cable 10805 to State Department, 'Nov 20 NAC on Arms Control Issues', 24 November 1978, Secret, excised copy.

12   US Mission to NATO cable 07693 to State Department, 'TNF: Permreps 6

November Discussion of Integrated Decision Document – Detailed Report', 7 November 1979, Secret, excised copy.

13   US Mission to NATO cable 08322 to State Department, 'TNF Modernisation – Detailed Report of Discussions on IDD at 28 November Session of Reinforced Permreps', 29 November 1979, Secret.

14   Quoted in Gerhard Wettig, 'The Last Soviet Offensive in the Cold War: Emergence and Development of the Campaign Against NATO Euromissiles, 1979–1983', Cold War History, vol. 9, no. 1, February 2009, pp. 90 and 92.

15   Roger Hilsman, From Nuclear Military Strategy to a World without War (Westport, CT: Praeger, 1999), p. 90.

16   Quoted in Vojtech Mastny, 'How Able was "Able Archer"?' Journal of Cold War Studies, vol. 11, no. 1, Winter 2009, p. 117.

17   Ibid., p. 118.

18   For more information on the Able Archer incident, and an assessment of the different interpretations of what happened, see Benjamin B. Fischer, A Cold War Conundrum: The 1983 War Scare (Washington DC: CIA, 1997). His response to the recent release of relevant official documents related to the incident can be found in an updated monograph of the same name, published in March 2007 and available on the CIA website at: https://www.cia.gov/library/center-for-the-study-of-intelligence/csi-publications/books-and-monographs/a-cold-war-conundrum/source.htm.

19   For example, see Mastny, 'How Able was "Able Archer"?'

20   Fischer, A Cold War Conundrum (2007 version): 'The "Iron Lady" and the "Great Communicator"'.

21 Quinlan was dismissive of the *Able Archer* incident, as he was of the Cuban Missile Crisis (because he believed in the wide margins of deterrence stability). See Quinlan, *Thinking About Nuclear Weapons: Principles, Problems, Prospects* (Oxford: Oxford University Press, 2009).

22 Letter from Quinlan to Brendon Soane, 12 July 1982.

23 Letter from Quinlan to Andrew Edwards, 7 January 1983.

24 Letter from Hockaday to Quinlan, 4 January 1983.

25 The Multilateral Force (MLF) was a 1960s US proposal to produce a nuclear-armed fleet of submarines and warships, manned by international NATO crews. The proposal was developed in response to the complaints of Western European countries unhappy that the nuclear defence of Europe was dependent on US nuclear capabilities and resolve. The MLF was intended to give the Western European NATO members a more active role in NATO's nuclear deterrent. The proposal failed due to internal NATO differences over basing and financing.

26 In fact, as Quinlan himself claimed at the time (and as official documents released in the US in recent years have substantiated) the initial impetus for NATO TNF deployment came not from the US government but from Western European governments, and it was UK officials who persuaded their US counterparts of the logic of the case.

27 At the time, John Barry had been conducting research for a book on NATO nuclear policy (which was to include the LRTNF decision of 1979). The book was never completed, but Barry did feed some of his research into newspaper articles and TV programmes. He has no recollection of the material he sent Quinlan (and he is not sure whether this particular draft was published), but he recalls that he often sought Quinlan's feedback on his drafts as well as amplification of information that he suspected his other contacts were withholding. He explained that 'once he took one seriously, Michael was very willing to be helpful'. Email exchange with John Barry, 26 June 2011.

28 This refers to a period in 1977–8, when the Carter administration dropped US plans to deploy enhanced radiation weapons (often referred to as 'neutron bombs') in Europe. Neutron bombs were low-blast/high-radiation yield weapons developed to negate the conventional superiority of the Warsaw Pact (their function was to incapacitate and kill Soviet tank crews without inflicting the massive collateral damage of a nuclear strike). The plans were strongly criticised by the Soviet Union and by domestic constituencies in Western Europe, for killing people while leaving infrastructure intact. In response to criticism, Carter cancelled the programme – a step that was derided by commentators who believed it would undermine the US allies' confidence in the credibility of the NATO alliance.

29 Letter from Quinlan to Tom Burns, 28 July 1981.

30 Letter from Dan Martin to Quinlan, 29 February 1984.

31 Letter from Quinlan to Martin, 5 March 1984.

32 Letter from Martin to Quinlan, 26 April 1984.

[33] Letter from Quinlan to Michael Bowen, 3 April 1984.

[34] Letter from Quinlan to John Hunt, 20 March 1984.

[35] Robert C. Aldridge, *First Strike! The Pentagon's Strategy for Nuclear War* (Boston, MA: South End Press, 1983).

[36] Letter from Quinlan to Martin, 15 April 1987.

[37] Letter from Robert Aldridge to Quinlan, 30 April 1987.

[38] In the context of nuclear confrontation, fratricide refers to the phenomenon of incoming nuclear weapons being destroyed by the fireball of other nuclear weapons previously detonated in the same locality.

[39] Letter from Quinlan to Aldridge, 11 May 1987.

[40] Letter from Aldridge to Quinlan, 19 May 1987.

[41] Letter from Quinlan to Martin, 16 July 1987.

[42] Fred C. Ikle, 'Reagan's New Idea – What About it? The Vision vs. the Nightmare', *Washington Post*, 27 March 1983.

[43] Letter from Quinlan to David McGiffert, 24 March 1983.

[44] In the early 1980s, Perry served on the Packard Commission, which was set up by the Reagan administration to investigate US military procurement and defence expenditure.

[45] At the time, Brown (who had served as US secretary of defense in the Carter administration) was a visiting professor at the John Hopkins School of Advanced International Studies.

[46] William J. Perry, 'An Expensive Technological Risk', and Harold Brown, 'It May Be Plausible – And it May be Ineffective', *Washington Post*, 27 March 1983.

[47] Letter from Quinlan to Hockaday, 16 July 1985.

[48] These comments were enclosed in Quinlan's letter to Hockaday of 16 July 1985.

[49] Letter from Quinlan to Richard Perle, 20 August 1984.

[50] Letter from Quinlan to Moray Stewart, 2 January 1985.

[51] Letter from John Reichart (USAF Defense Plans Division) to Stewart, 13 February 1985.

[52] Letter from Stewart to Quinlan, 14 February 1985.

[53] For further information, see MoD document *The Future Character of Conflict*, which was published in February 2010 in preparation for the Strategic Defence and Security Review, and in the 2006 White Paper, which was published after a review of nuclear policy conducted under the Labour government. The February 2010 document concluded that 'it cannot be assumed that the West will retain sufficient military advantage over rising powers in all circumstances, which may embolden actors where previously they had been deterred'. The continued possession of the UK's independent deterrent was therefore argued to be essential to protect Britain's vital interests in a world likely to see increasing conflict over resources. The conclusion of the 2006 White Paper was that *Trident* should be replaced to maintain continuous-at-sea-deterrence (CASD) because: 1) the fundamental principles relevant to nuclear deterrence have not changed since the end of the Cold War and are unlikely to change in future; 2) it is not possible accurately to predict the global security environment over the next 20–50 years; and 3) *Trident* provides the cheapest credible nuclear deterrent for the UK. The rationale for

maintaining an independent nuclear deterrent rather than relying on the US or France is summarised in a single, crucial paragraph in the 2006 White Paper: 'An independent centre of nuclear decision-making enhances the overall deterrent effect of allied nuclear forces. Potential adversaries could gamble that the US or France might not put themselves at risk of a nuclear attack in order to deter an attack on the UK or our allies. Our retention of an independent centre of nuclear decision-making makes clear to any adversary that the costs of an attack on UK vital interests will outweigh any benefits. Separately controlled but mutually supporting nuclear forces therefore create an enhanced overall deterrent effect.' *The Future of the United Kingdom's Nuclear Deterrent*, White Paper, December 2006 (CM6994); *The Future Character of Conflict*, DSDA Operations Centre, February 2010; *Securing Britain in an Age of Uncertainty: The Strategic Defence and Security Review*, October 2010 (CM7948).

54 Some of this history of the UK *Trident* decision is based on the analysis provided in Lawrence Freedman, *Britain and Nuclear Weapons* (London: Palgrave Macmillan, 1981) and the chronicle of events set out in Peter Hennessy (ed.), *Cabinets and the Bomb* (British Academy Occasional Papers no. 11, Oxford University Press, November 2007). With Frank Cooper's permission (Cooper was MoD PUS at the time), Quinlan assisted Freedman's research on British nuclear policy, providing feedback on his drafts. Freedman's book is thus a very reliable source of information on official British nuclear thinking at that time.

55 It is not clear whether the files originally contained correspondence from this period. As explained in the introduction, material that was considered too sensitive was removed before the start of this project, and is being archived separately under restricted access arrangements. Unfortunately, I have not had access to that material, and I have no idea what was removed.

56 Mottram was secretary to the groups that worked on the Duff–Mason report. He explains that the work was overseen by Quinlan and no one else, and that the report played an important part in the decision to opt for *Trident*. Interview with Richard Mottram, Arundel House, London, 18 June 2010.

57 In the official cost estimates, the cruise-missile system was assessed to be more expensive in like for like deterrent terms, but Owen disputed this assessment.

58 Hansard, House of Commons Debates, Fifth Series, Volume 977, 21 January–1 February 1980.

59 Defense Open Government Document (DOGD) 80/23, July 1980.

60 In published official documents, Quinlan stated that the UK had faith and confidence in the depth and resolve underlying the US commitment to defend Western Europe from Soviet aggression 'by whatever means are necessary, without exception'. But he added that because deterrence was a matter of perception, the Soviet leadership might calculate that as a conflict developed, US resolve to intervene in Western Europe might waver. The existence of the UK independent deterrent was considered 'an important insurance against any

such misconception', particularly given that France's nuclear policy barred the French government from making a clear commitment to NATO deterrence and no other European country possessed an independent deterrent.

61 Margaret Thatcher, *The Downing Street Years* (London: Harper Collins, 1993), p. 247. Quoted in Kristan Stoddart, 'British Government Optioneering Studies on Alternative Nuclear Force Postures', discussion paper presented at the workshop titled *Stepping Down the Nuclear Ladder: Options for UK Nuclear Weapons Policy*, Department of Peace Studies, University of Bradford, 17–18 September, 2009.

62 *Ibid.*, p. 4.

63 'Strategic Successor Systems', Chiefs of Staff Committee Meeting Speaking Note, 10 June 1980, DEFE 25/325.

64 Stoddart, 'British Government Optioneering Studies', pp. 5–6.

65 *The Times*, 29 March 1982.

66 The term 'Gaullism' has its roots in General de Gaulle's decision to create a French national nuclear deterrent to symbolise France's independence from the Anglo-Saxons. For a discussion of the origins of France's nuclear-weapons programme, see Wilfred L. Kohl, 'The French Nuclear Deterrent', *Proceedings of the Academy of Political Science*, vol. 29, no. 2, November 1968, pp. 80–94.

67 Letter from Quinlan to Keith Middlemas, 24 April 1985.

68 Letter from Quinlan to Hockaday, 11 January 1983.

69 These declassified documents (and Quinlan's role) became the subject of British media attention in December 2010. See Rob Edwards, 'Secret Files from the 70s Reveal *Trident* Strike Needed "to Kill 10m Russians"', *Guardian*, 26 December 2010.

70 See Part I, note 75.

71 See Michael Quinlan's discussion of David Owen's 1978 paper on British deterrence requirements, in which Quinlan refuted Owen's claim that a UK capability to inflict damage that led to 'a million Soviet dead' would be 'more than adequate' to deter Soviet aggression. Quinlan dismissed this, arguing that the Soviets had a higher 'threshold of horror' and it was 'at best highly questionable' whether a deterrent based on the capability to kill one million Soviets would 'give a British government the confidence to act resolutely in a dangerous situation'. DEFE25-433e21_02, 18 December 1978 (classification personal and top secret).

72 Edwards, 'Secret Files from the 70s'. I am grateful to Brian Burnell for forwarding copies of the original documents.

73 This phrase first appeared in the *1980 Open Government Document on Trident* (OGD 80/23), which Quinlan wrote following the review of British nuclear policy that took place in the lead-up to the *Trident* decision.

74 A top secret map dating from 1978 reveals UK nuclear targets around Moscow – a series of Soviet command and control bunker complexes around the Moscow ring road. MoD, *Future of the UK Nuclear Deterrent*, Annex A. Paper titled 'Unacceptable Damage'. DEFE 25/335.

75 Lawrence Freedman, 'British Nuclear Targeting', *Defense Analysis*, vol. 1, no. 2, 1985, pp. 81–99.

76 According to Mottram, who knew Cooper and Quinlan well and succeeded them as MoD PUS, Cooper took a much more common sense

approach to defence issues than Quinlan. Unlike Quinlan, Cooper doubted the value of communicating British nuclear doctrine to the public, and did not share his enthusiasm for nuance or complex deterrence theory. This is reflected in his correspondence with Quinlan.

77 Letter from Brian Midgley to Quinlan, 7 November 1980.

78 It is clear that Quinlan took Midgley's comments to heart. In a letter to Beresford, he made the following comment: 'I recognise that there is a difficulty – reflected in some degree in my private correspondence with Brian Midgley, which you have seen – for the ordinary concerned (but not 'in the know') Christian adhering to this general theory if Governments do not say whether their [targeting strategy is likely to lead to disproportionate civilian deaths], or if what they say is not enough for him to judge for himself whether it is so or not. (Paragraph 12 of the *Trident* memorandum is relevant.)' Letter from Quinlan to Beresford, 24 October 1980.

79 Michael Quinlan, 'The Morality of Nuclear Deterrence', *Farm Street Talk*, 14 February 2008.

80 Freedman, 'British Nuclear Targeting', pp. 81–99.

81 Letter from Quinlan to Richard Harries, 6 February 1986.

82 Letter from Midgley to Quinlan, 7 November 1980.

83 Letter from Neville Mott to Quinlan (originally undated; received by Quinlan on 15 March 1986).

84 Letter from Quinlan to Mott, 2 June 1986.

85 Letter from Hockaday to Quinlan, 4 January 1983.

86 At the time, Barry (who was conducting research for a book on NATO and UK nuclear policy) had access to very senior sources. In addition to David Owen and Quinlan, his sources included Fred Mulley (defence secretary), Paul Lever (MoD), Frank Cooper (MoD PUS) and numerous heavy hitters in Germany and the US. He was also granted access to contacts at AWE, after Thatcher took an interest in his work. Barry's research is thus a reliable source of information on nuclear decision-making in NATO and the UK, which helps explain why he was one of only a handful of journalists who were taken seriously by Quinlan.

87 Letter from Barry to Quinlan (undated; sent some time in October 1980).

88 Owen exposed the pressure and tactics used by senior civil servants (and especially John Hunt) in his recent book, *Nuclear Papers*, in which he discussed declassified documents dealing with British nuclear targeting and procurement in the late 1970s. In an e-mail to me, he described the situation as 'one of the most serious examples of officials deciding what politicians need to know, on an issue which is pre-eminently a political, not a military decision'. When I asked him whether the 'top-down' nature of nuclear decision-making was still a problem in the UK, he replied that the problem was not the top-down nature of decision-making as such, but rather the exclusion of the top (the political leaders) by the middle (senior civil servants). He was particularly concerned about the way the Blair government made the decision to go ahead with the replacement of *Trident* in 2006 – in particular: 'the extraordinary fact that the Chiefs of Staff had such a brief discussion of the issue', which he believes is

evidence that 'the nature of nuclear decision making within Whitehall is still seriously defective'. David Owen, *Nuclear Papers* (Liverpool: Liverpool University Press, 2009), pp. 6–9; author e-mail exchange with David Owen, 22–29 June 2011.

89 Official documents, which have recently been declassified, back up many of Owen's concerns about the culture of secrecy among senior civil servants involved in nuclear decision-making in the UK. Owen revisited this issue in an interview with the *Guardian* in December 2010, in which he argued that Quinlan was part of an MoD elite that repeatedly hid information from ministers about Britain's nuclear weapons. It is clear that Owen and Quinlan never saw eye-to-eye on nuclear issues. Owen acknowledges Quinlan's intellectual skill and his superior theoretical grasp of nuclear strategy, but he argues that he was 'not well connected to how politicians think about [nuclear-weapons] decisions, which they, not he, have to contemplate making'. Edwards, 'Secret Files from the 70s'; author e-mail exchange with David Owen, 22–29 June 2011.

90 Owen eventually supported the *Chevaline* upgrade of *Polaris*, but only if it was justified on the basis of so much money having already been spent and not on the grounds of the Moscow Criterion.

91 This could come across as a strong allegation against Callaghan, but in fact Owen later qualified this point, arguing that Callaghan 'stretched the elastic' of ministerial responsibility, but 'not unreasonably'.

92 Peter Hodgson (1928–2008) was an extraordinary individual. He was a nuclear physicist, Catholic moral

philosopher, defence expert, active political campaigner (for the Social Democrats and Liberals), and author of numerous books on popular science.

93 Letter from Hodgson to Quinlan, 19 October 1986.

94 *Ibid.*

95 'Britain United: The Time Has Come', Liberal–SDP Alliance Manifesto, 1987, http://www.politicsresources.net/area/uk/man/lib87.htm.

96 Letter from Quinlan to Blelloch, 30 March 1987.

97 Letter from Alastair Mackie to Quinlan, 30 November 1988.

98 Letter from Elizabeth Llewellyn-Smith to Quinlan, 17 August 1987.

99 Beatrice Heuser, 'Containing uncertainty: options for British nuclear strategy', *Review of International Studies*, vol. 19, 1993, pp. 245–67.

100 Letter from Quinlan to John Keegan, 11 October 1993.

101 The official title of the 'unusual Air Ministry committee' that Quinlan was referring to was the Air Ministry Strategic Scientific Policy Committee – a group of scientists first brought together in 1958–59 by the Chief of Air Staff to study the credibility of the British independent nuclear deterrent. Issues the committee studied included the requirements and problems of limited war and the vulnerability of the British deterrent to attack by Soviet missiles. The committee was initially chaired by Zuckerman, and the first Secretary to the Committee (D.C. Humphreys) was succeeded by Quinlan. Correspondence relating to the work of the group (most of it dating to 1959) is filed in the Zuckerman archive at the University of East Anglia (reference GB 1187 SZ/AMSSP).

102 This is a reference to Henry Tizard (1885–1959), the British chemist, inventor and chairman of the Aeronautical Research Committee, which developed radar technology. Tizard was the instigator of the British Technical and Scientific Mission (known as the Tizard Mission), which visited the United States in 1940 in an effort to procure US technology to help with the British war effort.

103 Solly Zuckerman, William Hawthorne, James Lighthill and William Cook were all members of the Air Ministry Strategic Scientific Policy Committee. When Zuckerman left on his appointment as chief scientific adviser to the MoD, Zuckerman attempted to recruit Andrew Huxley to the group.

104 Margaret Aldred, 'Britain's MoD Links with the Academic Community', *Army Quarterly & Defence Journal*, vol. 123, no. 3, July 1993, pp. 261–9.

105 Letter from Keegan to Quinlan, 29 September 1993.

106 Letter from Quinlan to Keegan, 11 October 1993.

107 Letter from Quinlan to Nick Witney, 4 November 1992.

108 This is a reference to a meeting of defence ministers from NATO countries, which was hosted by France's defence minister, Pierre Joxe, on 30 September 1992.

109 Letter from Quinlan to Patrick Turner, 18 June 2006.

110 *Resolution*-class submarines carried the UK's *Polaris* missiles from the late

1960s to 1994. (They were replaced by the *Vanguard*-class submarines, which are armed with *Trident* missiles). See Appendix 2 for further information.

111 Robin Cook (1946–2005) was a British Labour Party politician. He was foreign secretary in the Cabinet of Prime Minister Tony Blair from 1997–2001, and leader of the House of Commons from 2001–03 (he resigned in 2003 in protest against the invasion of Iraq). Cook was an outspoken critic of British and NATO nuclear strategy. In 1980 he was appointed to an NGO committee that was set up to campaign for European nuclear disarmament (the committee was established by the Bertrand Russell Peace Foundation following the NATO LRTNF decision).

112 *The Future of the United Kingdom's Nuclear Deterrent*, p. 7.

113 Continuous-at-sea-deterrence refers to the British strategy of keeping at least one nuclear-armed submarine on patrol at any time in order to deter a 'bolt from the blue'. This policy, which has demanding operational requirements, has been in place since the introduction of *Polaris* in 1968.

114 *Securing Britain in an Age of Uncertainty*, p. 39.

115 Kitty Donaldson and Helene Fouquet, 'Britain and France to Share Nuclear-test Facilities, Carriers', *Bloomberg*, 2 November 2010, http://www.bloomberg.com/news/2010-11-02/u-k-france-to-share-nuclear-test-facilities-carriers-in-defense-treaty.html.

Part Three

1   The arms-control distinction between theatre and strategic nuclear weapons worked in the UK's favour in this respect: when the US and the Soviet Union discussed cuts in their strategic nuclear-weapons systems during the SALT process in the 1970s, the British nuclear arsenal was defined as a theatre force; but during the 1980s, when the superpowers negotiated the INF agreement in theatre systems, the British deterrent was recast as strategic. Successive British governments were thus able to publicly declare their faith in multilateral arms-control throughout the period, and at the same time avoid getting caught up in reductions that would have threatened the UK's minimum deterrent and its already limited nuclear independence.

2   State Department, Bureau of Intelligence and Research, 'Theatre Nuclear Force Negotiations: The Initial Soviet Approach', 10 August 1979, Secret.

3   US Mission to NATO cable 10805 to State Department, 'Nov 20 NAC on Arms Control Issues', 24 November 1978, Secret, excised copy. US Mission to NATO cable 07693 to State Department, 'TNF: Permreps 6 November Discussion of Integrated Decision Document – Detailed Report', 7 November 1979, Secret, excised copy.

4   Letter from Michael Pakenham to Quinlan, 6 February (no year is given, but the content of the letter suggests it was written in the early 1980s).

5   Quinlan's letters reveal that at the time, he had a limited understanding of the nuclear non-proliferation regime and proliferation dynamics beyond the East–West context, which could explain why he was slow to adapt his thinking to new strategic realities as the Cold War ended. As others have noted (including William Walker and Lawrence Freedman), Quinlan's conservatism during the late 1980s and early 1990s was striking.

6   Letter from Quinlan to John Roper, 5 January 1983.

7   Handwritten note, written by Quinlan in 1998 to explain how and why he became involved in drafting Thatcher's June 1982 speech to the UN Special Session on Disarmament.

8   Thatcher believed that the FCO and Joint Intelligence Committee (JIC) had behaved incompetently in the lead-up to the Falklands war, failing to warn ministers of the impending invasion by Argentine forces until it was too late to avert it.

9   In crises leading to limited war, the British Cabinet usually assigns responsibility for decision-making to a small ad hoc committee. The group set up to manage the Falklands War was called the Falklands Committee.

10 Notes enclosed in a letter from Quinlan to John Coles, 15 June 1982.

11 First draft of the text Quinlan wrote for Thatcher's speech to the UN Special Session on Disarmament, sent in a letter from Quinlan to John Coles, 15 June 1982.

12 Quinlan used this term to refer to unilateral disarmament steps.

13 Although the UK gave strong rhetorical support for bilateral talks on eliminating intermediate-range nuclear systems, defence officials (including Quinlan) were wary of the strategic implications of the zero option. For further information, see

part two of this book, especially the discussion of the history of the NATO LRTNF decision.

14 In an interview for the documentary series, *Panorama,* in 1976, Solzhenitsyn declared: 'In what tribulations will these selfish leaders yet involve us! The Communists cannot renounce aggression. It is in progress now: the devilish growth of armaments, guns which begin to fire themselves. These madmen will clearly succeed in plunging both our country and the whole world into war'.

15 Quinlan shared many of Sakharov's beliefs in the immorality of Communism and especially his repellence of its enforced atheism. A postscript to Sakharov's *Memorandum* of March 1971 read: 'The persecution and destruction of religion, which has been carried on with perseverance and cruelty for decades, has resulted in what is undoubtedly one of the most serious infringements of the rights of man in our country'.

16 Quinlan sent the text of the final speech to Sydney Bailey on 30 June 1982, with a note that read: 'You may like to have the enclosed copy of the Prime Minister's final text at the Special Session last week. I shan't venture any commentary or evaluation!'

17 Letter from Gilmore to Quinlan, 25 June 1982.

18 Letter from Quinlan to Freedman, 25 September 1986.

19 This is a reference to Michael Carver (1915–2001), commander in chief Far East of the British Army (1967–69); chief of general staff (1971–72); chief of defence staff (1973–76), and outspoken critic of UK and NATO nuclear policy. Carver wrote a book examining the logic of nuclear disarmament, titled *A Policy for Peace* (London: Faber and Faber, 1983).

20 At the time, the UK officially supported the creation of regional NWFZs outside Europe (in areas where they were deemed to contribute to security) subject to four conditions: 1) that nuclear weapons did not already feature in the security of the region concerned; 2) that a balance of security was maintained; 3) that all states in the region accepted the concept; and 4) that the zone was mainly land-based. These conditions reflected the UK desire to promote regional stability but at the same time to ensure that its own interest (including its nuclear deterrent) were not compromised. These and other details on the UK position on NWFZs were set out in a letter from the Richard Luce (minister of state) to the Manchester Town Clerk, J. Hetherington, on 30 July 1984.

21 Under the freeze proposals, the NWS would have been obliged to hold their nuclear arsenals at 1985 levels, and halt all other aspects of their nuclear weapons programmes.

22 In the late 1970s and early 1980s, the Soviet Union undertook a major nuclear modernisation, while the West carried out little or no modernisation. Between 1972 and 1984, the Soviets introduced three new types of ICBM, four new SLBMs and a new bomber with a potential intercontinental capability. In the same period, the US introduced only one new SLBM and the air-launched cruise missile (ALCM). The MoD calculated at the time that the Soviets had 2,700 strategic systems and the US about 1,900, and that the Soviet strategic forces were not only newer than US systems but also had greater destructive potential.

Most significantly, as a result of the development of the SS-20 missile, the Soviets were believed to possess massive superiority in long-range intermediate nuclear weapons, which could reach Western Europe and were thought to significantly outnumber NATO warheads. Freezing this imbalance was considered a wild proposal, because although NATO did not aim to match Soviet systems weapon for weapon, its nuclear strategy depended on the maintenance of a credible range of deterrents.

23 Letter from Pakenham to Quinlan, 9 April 1985; Letter from P.J. Weston to Pakenham, 21 March 1985.

24 Letter from Quinlan to John Hunt, 15 April 1985.

25 The US bishops had come out in support of Freeze, lending credibility to the campaign and to a rapid increase in its membership in the United States. The campaign organisers believed that if they could get the support of leading church figures in the UK, British public support would also take off. Letter from Carol Freeman, Freeze executive officer, to the archbishop of Southwark, 31 May 1985.

26 Letter from Michael Bowen to Quinlan, 9 July 1985.

27 Letter from Quinlan to Bowen, 13 June 1985.

28 Letter from Quinlan to Beresford, 15 August 1985.

29 The British Atlantic Committee (BAC) was the British arm of an international advocacy network of pro-NATO groups established in the 1950s. In 1994 it merged with Peace through NATO to form the Atlantic Council of the United Kingdom.

30 Letter from John Killick to David Mellor, 22 June 1987.

31 SACEUR is based in Mons, Belgium.

32 Letter from Quinlan to Beresford, 22 April 1987.

33 Letter from Killick to Quinlan, 11 November 1987.

34 This speech was later published. See Quinlan, 'Nuclear Weapons and the Abolition of War', pp. 293–301.

35 The PTBT dates back to 1963, when the UK, the US and the USSR agreed to stop all nuclear tests above ground. From 1977 to 1980, an attempt was made to convert the PTBT into a CTBT, banning all nuclear testing below ground as well, but the US broke off the negotiations. From 1985–87, the Soviets attempted to kick-start negotiations on a CTBT by placing a unilateral moratorium on its own nuclear testing, but this was never reciprocated by the US or the UK.

36 FCO Memo on the PTBTAC, 23 November 1990.

37 Parliamentarians for Global Action (PGA) is a non-profit, non-partisan international network of legislators whose aim is to promote peace. In 1990, PGA representatives lobbied the US, UK and Soviet Union to support a CTBT. Douglas Hogg (minster of state for foreign and commonwealth affairs, 1990–95) received a PGA delegation on 27 November 1990.

38 Letter from John Hunt to Quinlan, 25 July 1991; Draft of a letter from Patrick Kelly, chairman of the Committee for International Peace and Justice, to Douglas Hurd, dated 24 July 1991.

39 The phrase 'bien-pensant Left' usually has negative connotations – it is used to describe Left-wing activists who are regarded by their critics as being self-righteous and hypocritical, or well-meaning but short-sighted or deluded.

40 Letter from Leonard Cheshire to Quinlan, 11 October 1982.

41 Letter from Quinlan to Cheshire, 5 January 1983.

42 Letter from Cheshire to Quinlan, 25 January 1983.

43 In his draft letter to the *Sunday Telegraph*, Cheshire opened with the statement: 'I find it strange that we worry so much about the danger of East–West nuclear war and so little about the far greater dangers resulting from nuclear proliferation'.

44 Letter from Quinlan to Hugh Beach, 12 September 1984.

45 Letter from John Howe to Quinlan, 20 November 1986.

46 Letter from Quinlan to Beach, 13 November 1985.

47 Second part of letter from Quinlan to Beach, 13 November 1985.

48 Letter from Howe to Quinlan, 20 March 1987. Unfortunately, the files do not contain a response from Quinlan to Howe's insightful letter. Howe identified some fundamental logical inconsistencies in Quinlan's thinking about nuclear weapons – inconsistencies that became more obvious as the Cold War receded. It would have been interesting to see how Quinlan would have dealt with Howe's critique.

49 *The Economist*, 2–8 October 1982, p. 61.

50 The Conservative government issued a civil-defence handbook entitled *Protect and Survive* to reassure the jittery British public, but the initiative backfired, heightening fears to the point of panic. According to reports at the time, another step the Thatcher government took to try to counter rising panic was to secretly pay a firm to run a massive advertising campaign to 'fight CND'. But this step also backfired badly when the campaign sponsor was revealed.

51 After a period of intense activity, the anti-nuclear movement died down in the second half of the 1980s. According to Beatrice Heuser, this was 'less because of any government policy of openness than because of progress made in arms reductions (both conventional and nuclear) and to the reduced salience of nuclear issues. Beatrice Heuser, *Nuclear Mentalities? Strategies and Beliefs in Britain, France and the FRG* (Basingstoke: Palgrave Macmillan, 1998), p. 15.

52 Soviet infiltration of the peace movement in Europe and the US became a major preoccupation of Western governments in the early 1980s. In an article in the 14 February 1983 issue of *Time*, a CIA source estimated that the Kremlin was spending up to $4 billion a year on overt and covert propaganda, which included its infiltration of the peace movement. Oleg Kalugin, a retired KGB spy, claims that the Soviet ran 'peace congresses, youth congresses, festivals, women's movements, trade union movements, campaigns against US missiles in Europe … [using] all sorts of forgeries and faked material – targeted at [Western] politicians, the academic community, at [the] public at large'. The aim 'was to weaken [the] military, economic and psychological climate in the West'. 'The KGB: Eyes of the Kremlin', *Time*, 14 February 1983; 'An Interview with Retired KGB Maj. Gen Oleg Kalugin', *CNN Interactive*, January 1998.

53 Heuser, *Nuclear Mentalities*, p. 22.

54 Letter from Quinlan to Beresford, 20 May 1981.

55 Letter from Quinlan to Cheshire, 8 March 1983.

56 Unlike Walter Stein and other nuclear deterrence critics, Kent did not correspond with Quinlan, which partly explains the lack of balance in the way Kent's arguments and role are portrayed in Quinlan's correspondence.

57 Letter from Quinlan to Cheshire, 23 September 1985.

58 Kent had argued that 'no phrase has done more damage to constructive thinking about disarmament in recent years' than that of 'unilateral disarmament'. He argued that every state is capable of taking independent steps as part of the disarmament process, and that independent steps would lead to effective multilateral agreements. He gave the example of the US independent commitment not to conduct atmospheric tests in 1963, which led to the Partial Test Ban Treaty. Letter from Bruce Kent to *The Tablet*, 13 July 1985.

59 Letter from Cheshire to *The Tablet*, 29 August 1985.

60 Letter from Quinlan to Cheshire, 30 September 1985.

61 Here, I have deleted the actual words Quinlan chose to describe Kent (the phrase he used can be found in the original letter, which is archived at King's College, London). The personality clash between Quinlan and Kent may partly explain Quinlan's uncharacteristically intemperate language – the two men were like chalk and cheese; they were an anathema to each other and happy to be seen as such.

62 Letter from Quinlan to Cheshire, 2 October 1985.

63 Draft of a response to Kent, which Quinlan wrote for Cheshire to send to *The Tablet* and enclosed in his letter to Cheshire of 2 October 1985.

64 Letter from Cheshire to Kent (copied to Quinlan), 11 November 1985. The reference to dropping an atomic bomb on another man's city stems from Cheshire's experience in the Second World War, when he was the official British observer of the nuclear attack on Nagasaki.

65 Letter from Cheshire to Quinlan, 18 September 1984.

66 Letter from Quinlan to Cheshire, 2 January 1985.

67 The Alternative Defence Commission was co-sponsored by the Lansbury House Trust Fund and the School of Peace Studies at the University of Bradford. It produced two major reports: *Defence without the Bomb* (London: Taylor and Francis, 1983) and *The Politics of Alternative Defence* (London: Paladin, 1987), and several supplementary papers. The commission was wound up in 1987. The papers are archived at the University of Bradford (details of the collection are available at http://www.brad.ac.uk/library/special/cwlADC.php).

68 Extract from a draft paper by Walter Stein called 'The Nuclear Crisis', sent to Quinlan by Tom Burns in August 1981.

69 Letter from Quinlan to Cheshire, 2 January 1985.

70 Stan Windass was a contemporary of Michael Quinlan, Bruce Kent, and Brian Wicker – they all attended Oxford University at the same time (1948–52). As the following letters reveal, Quinlan and the civil service elite were dismissive of Stan Windass's work in the late 1980s, but after his retirement Quinlan began to address many of the questions Windass had raised.

71 The Palme Commission was launched in 1980 to assess why past disarmament efforts had succeeded or failed and to explore how arms-control and disarmament momentum could be generated during the Cold War. It was chaired by Olaf Palme (former prime minster of Sweden, who was assassinated in 1986), and was represented by members from North and South, East and West. The report of the commission, which was released in 1982, proposed measures for arms control and disarmament that could be pursued at the 1982 UN Special Session on Disarmament. It argued that the threat of war was more serious than it had been for many years, that the nuclear-arms race was accelerating, and that the doctrine of extended deterrence offered a risky and fragile basis for preserving international security. In its place, it proposed a strategy of common security, whereby the United Nations' role in safeguarding security would be strengthened, and the UN body would oversee a process of phased nuclear and conventional disarmament. For further information on the Palme Commission report and its significance, see Joachim Muller (ed.), *Reforming the United Nations: New Initiatives and Past Efforts, Volume 1* (Cambridge, MA: Kluwer Law International, 1997), pp. I/91–I/95.

72 An early exposition of Stan Windass's vision for non-provocative defence can be found in his book, *Avoiding Nuclear War: Common Security as a Strategy for the Defence of the West* (London: Potomac Books, 1985). For a wider discussion of the concept of common security, see Barry Buzan, 'Common Security, Non-Provocative Defence and the Future of Western Europe', *Review of International Studies*, vol. 13, no. 4, October 1987, pp. 265–79.

73 Letter from Quinlan to Moray Stewart, 1 September 1987.

74 Letter from Quinlan to David Nicholls, 19 November 1987.

75 Letter from Nicholls to Quinlan, 30 November 1987.

76 Letter from John Boyd to Quinlan, 7 December 1987.

77 This is a misleading assessment of Windass's abilities (given his first-rate education at Oxford University, where he gained a First Class in English Literature; his subsequent research on defence ethics at Leuven University; and his contribution to the literature on nuclear disarmament).

78 Letter from Quinlan to John Keegan, 11 October 1993.

79 'Hard Talk', BBC, 29 August 2006.

80 Michael Quinlan, 'Abolishing Nuclear Armouries: Policy or Pipedream?' *Survival*, vol. 49, no. 4, Winter 2007–08.

81 Michael Quinlan, 'India-Pakistan Deterrence Revisited', *Survival*, vol. 47, no. 3, Autumn 2005, pp. 103–16.

82 'Hard Talk', BBC, 29 August 2006.

83 Quinlan, 'Abolishing Nuclear Armouries,' p. 11.

84 George Perkovich and James M. Acton, *Abolishing Nuclear Weapons*, Adelphi 396 (Abingdon: Routledge for the IISS, 2008). Other studies that have either spun off from the IISS Adelphi Paper or been directly inspired by Quinlan's publications, include: George Perkovich and James M. Acton (eds), *Abolishing Nuclear Weapons: A Debate* (Washington DC: Carnegie Endowment for International Peace, February 2009).

85 Quinlan had signed a contract with Oxford University Press for his book *Thinking About Nuclear Weapons:*

Principles, Problems, Prospects. The book was published in March 2009, just weeks after he died.

86 Email from Quinlan to George Perkovich, 30 May 2008.

87 Email from Perkovich to Quinlan, 5 June 2008.

88 Email from Quinlan to Perkovich, 10 June 2008.

89 Perkovich regrets that he did not respond to Quinlan's thoughtful response to his proposal. In an e-mail to me, he explained that he would have agreed emphatically with Quinlan's comment that 'the threat – and concomitant deterrent value – of nuclear weapons surely lies in their existence, not what is said about them …' but he would have added that 'this is precisely why greater effort should be made to deepen the norm against making nuclear threats'. He agrees that seeking to be too formal in such commitments would raise the problems Michael identified, but stresses that 'this would not undermine the case for making greater effort through quiet diplomacy to impress upon leaders of nuclear-armed states to eschew rhetoric and actions that call attention to these weapons'. Author e-mail exchange with Perkovich, 27 June 2011.

90 Among many others, these include: Barry M. Blechman and Alexander K. Bollfrass (eds), *Elements of a Nuclear Disarmament Treaty* (Washington, DC: Stimson Center, 22 January, 2010); James M. Action, *Deterrence During Disarmament: Deep Nuclear Reductions and International Security* (Abingdon: Routledge for the IISS, 2011); Scott Sagan, 'The Case for No First Use', *Survival* vol. 51, no. 3, June–July 2009, pp. 163–82; Morton Halperin, Bruno Tertrais, Keith Payne, K. Subrahmanyam and Scott Sagan, 'The Case for No First Use: An Exchange', *Survival* no. 51, no. 5, October–November 2009, pp. 17–46; and Tanya Ogilvie-White and David Santoro (eds), *Slaying the Nuclear Dragon: Disarmament Dynamics in the Twenty-First Century* (Athens, GA: University of Georgia Press, forthcoming 2011/12).

Concluding remarks

1 Letter from Quinlan to Walter Stein, 31 May 1984.

2 Letter from Alastair Mackie to Quinlan, 30 November 1988.

3 Quinlan's horror of atheistic totalitarianism came through in a number of his letters, including his letter to Beresford of 20 May 1981.

Appendix 1

1. France rejoined NATO's integrated military command in 2009, 43 years after Charles de Gaulle withdrew from the structure in protest at US domination. During that time France did not participate in the Nuclear Planning Group.

2. See Stephen I. Schwartz (ed.), *Atomic Audit: The Costs and Consequences of US Nuclear Weapons Since 1940* (Washington DC: Brookings Institution Press, 1998).

3. For more on this debate, see Steven Andreasen, Malcolm Chalmers, and Isabelle Williams, 'NATO and Nuclear Weapons: Is a New Consensus Possible?', Royal United Services Institute (RUSI) Occasional Paper, August 2010.

4. The five principles: 1) as long as nuclear weapons exist, NATO will remain a nuclear alliance; 2) as a nuclear alliance, sharing nuclear risks and responsibilities widely is fundamental; 3) the broad aim is to continue to reduce the role and number of nuclear weapons … Since the Cold War ended, NATO has already dramatically reduced its reliance on nuclear weapons; 4) Allies must broaden deterrence against a range of 21st century threats, including by pursuing territorial missile defence, conducting contingency plans to counter new threats to the Alliance; 5) in any future reductions, our aim should be to seek Russian agreement to increase transparency on non-strategic nuclear weapons in Europe, relocate these weapons away from the territory of NATO members and include non-strategic nuclear weapons in the next round of US-Russian arms control discussions alongside strategic and non-deployed nuclear weapons. Excerpts from the remarks by Secretary of State Hillary Rodham Clinton at the NATO working dinner on nuclear issues and missile defence (Tallinn, 22 April 2010).

5. Eben Harrell, 'What to Do About Europe's Secret Nukes?', *Time*, 4 January 2010.

6. *Ibid.*

7. Andreasen, Chalmers and Williams, 'NATO and Nuclear Weapons', p. 5; Hans M. Kristensen, *U.S. Nuclear Weapons in Europe: A Review of Post-Cold War Policy, Force Levels and War Planning* (New York: Natural Resources Defense Council, 2005), http://www.nukestrat.com/pubs/EuroBombs.pdf, p. 8.

8. William Burr (ed.), 'How Many and Where Were the Nukes?', National Security Archive Electronic Briefing Book No. 197, posted August 18, 2006, updated October 11, 2006, http://www.gwu.edu/~nsarchiv/NSAEBB/NSAEBB197/index.htm, p. 11.

9. Kristensen, *U.S. Nuclear Weapons in Europe,* p. 8; Hans M. Kristensen, 'United States Removes Nuclear Weapons from German Base, Documents Indicate', Federation of Atomic Scientists (FAS) Strategic Security Blog, 9 July 2007, http://www.fas.org/blog/ssp/2007/07/united_states_removes_nuclear.php.

10. Source: Hans M. Kristensen, Federation of Atomic Scientists 2010, http://www.fas.org/programs/ssp/nukes/images/euronukes2010.pdf. Kristensen notes that the national Turkish nuclear strike mission probably ended in 2001. US nuclear weapons were removed from Ramstein airbase in Germany in 2005

and from RAF Lakenheath in the UK in 2006. The weapons were removed to the US, but could be redeployed to Europe to augment European forces.

Appendix 2

[1] Some of the following information is drawn from the House of Commons Defence Committee document, *The Future of the UK's Nuclear Deterrent: The White Paper*, 7 March 2007, HC 225-I, http://www.publications. parliament.uk/pa/cm200607/cmselect/cmdfence/225/225i.pdf, pp. 8–13.

[2] Alastair Mackie, *Some of the People All the Time* (Lewes: Book Guild Publishing, 2006).

Adelphi books are published eight times a year by Routledge Journals, an imprint of Taylor & Francis, 4 Park Square, Milton Park, Abingdon, Oxfordshire OX14 4RN, UK.

A subscription to the institution print edition, ISSN 1944-5571, includes free access for any number of concurrent users across a local area network to the online edition, ISSN 1944-558X

2011 Annual Adelphi Subscription Rates			
Institution	£491	$864 USD	€726
Individual	£230	$391 USD	€312
Online only	£442	$778 USD	€653

Dollar rates apply to subscribers outside Europe. Euro rates apply to all subscribers in Europe except the UK and the Republic of Ireland where the pound sterling price applies. All subscriptions are payable in advance and all rates include postage. Journals are sent by air to the USA, Canada, Mexico, India, Japan and Australasia. Subscriptions are entered on an annual basis, i.e. January to December. Payment may be made by sterling cheque, dollar cheque, international money order, National Giro, or credit card (Amex, Visa, Mastercard).

For more information, visit our website: **http://www.informaworld.com/ adelphipapers.**

For a complete and up-to-date guide to Taylor & Francis journals and books publishing programmes, and details of advertising in our journals, visit our website: **http://www.informaworld.com.**

Ordering information:
USA/Canada: Taylor & Francis Inc., Journals Department, 325 Chestnut Street, 8th Floor, Philadelphia, PA 19106, USA. **UK/Europe/Rest of World:** Routledge Journals, T&F Customer Services, T&F Informa UK Ltd., Sheepen Place, Colchester, Essex, CO3 3LP, UK.

Advertising enquiries to:
USA/Canada: The Advertising Manager, Taylor & Francis Inc., 325 Chestnut Street, 8th Floor, Philadelphia, PA 19106, USA. Tel: +1 (800) 354 1420. Fax: +1 (215) 625 2940.

UK/Europe/Rest of World: The Advertising Manager, Routledge Journals, Taylor & Francis, 4 Park Square, Milton Park, Abingdon, Oxfordshire OX14 4RN, UK. Tel: +44 (0) 20 7017 6000. Fax: +44 (0) 20 7017 6336.

The print edition of this journal is printed on ANSI conforming acid-free paper by Bell & Bain, Glasgow, UK.